*Perrette Sinclair*

# Guidelines
# for Infrastructure
# Development
# through
# Build-Operate-Transfer
# (BOT) Projects

D1381775

**UNITED NATIONS INDUSTRIAL DEVELOPMENT ORGANIZATION**
**Vienna, 1996**

ID/SER.O/22

UNIDO PUBLICATION
Sales No. UNIDO.95.6.E
ISBN 92-1-106304-3

*Graphic/DTP: Claudia Univazo*

# Preface

The build-operate-transfer (BOT) approach has in recent years played a growing role in the implementation of industrial and infrastructure projects such as oil and gas fields, power plants, toll roads and water supply and treatment facilities in both industrialized and developing countries. Owing to the strategic importance of BOT projects for developing countries, UNIDO is increasingly being asked by member countries to provide information, advice and guidance on the elaboration of these projects. In response to this need, it has taken the initiative of preparing these Guidelines for Infrastructure Development through Build-Operate-Transfer (BOT) Projects, which are intended to provide both a general overview of the conceptual, legal and financial issues associated with BOT projects and practical guidance for project development, negotiation and implementation.

The structure and content of the Guidelines follow the usual path of BOT projects, from identification of project opportunities through feasibility studies, formation of a consortium, bidding procedures, contractual and financial packages, to the operation, maintenance and transfer of ownership. The Guidelines also highlight the ways in which BOT projects can promote technology transfer and capacity building. The main goals of UNIDO in preparing the Guidelines are to help developing countries to take advantage of the potential benefits of using a BOT strategy to implement infrastructure projects and make well-reasoned decisions based on their particular objectives and requirements, and to elucidate how projects can be made to attract financing from the private sector.

There is no perfect BOT model for all infrastructure projects, and the host countries themselves have to shape the approach to suit their national requirements. Those countries that have had the most success in implementing BOT projects generally attribute it to creating a win-win situation: the BOT approach allows them to pursue their national interests while at the same time it encourages private sector investment.

The Guidelines should not be regarded as rigid and unchangeable. Infrastructure development is a dynamic process, and the BOT approach has evolved to suit the needs of programmes in individual countries. They should, however, serve as a comprehensive reference work, based on experience worldwide, for officials, managers and practitioners dealing with BOT issues. Fresh experience accrued by Guidelines users and the technical assistance work of UNIDO in the field of BOT will eventually provide the feedback needed to update and expand the Guidelines.

The Guidelines are based on the long-standing experience of UNIDO in matters such as contractual arrangements, procurement, policy and institution building, technology transfer negotiations, capability building, feasibility studies, engineering and environmental protection, as well as on contributions from numerous outside experts and sources. For these Guidelines, UNIDO has tried to continuously update the material, in keeping with the rapid on-going development of the field.

The Guidelines were prepared by the UNIDO Investment and Technology Promotion Division, Technology Service, under the supervision of José de Caldas Lima and coordinated by Ricardo Seidl da Fonseca. Other UNIDO staff providing inputs or detailed comments include Z. Csizer, S. A. Hasnain, B. O. Karlsson, L. Kurowski, J. Navratil and A. A. Yusuf. Three UNIDO consultants, Mark Augenblick, Pang Chung Min, and Ole Steen-Olsen, drafted and reviewed the major portion of the text and three other UNIDO consultants, Ruth Flynn, Geoffrey Norman Haley and Branko Vukmir, also contributed text.

A number of outside experts provided advice, comments and suggestions for improvement. Their names are listed here, along with their affiliations, although their contributions were made on an individual basis and do not necessarily reflect the opinions of their institutions: José D. Vistulo de Abreu, President, Gabinete de Travessia do Tejo em Lisboa; Alexander Auboeck, European Bank for Reconstruction and Development; Rolf Bollinger, European International Contractors; Gianni Carbonaro, European Investment Bank; Pierre Guislain, World Bank; Francis Koh, Singa Infrastructure Management; Ranjit Mathrani, Vanguard Capital; Sayin Yusuf Bozhurt Oezal, Turkish Parliament; Jeff Ruster, Banamex; Robert Tiong, Nanyang Technological University (Singapore); Uri Winterstein, Lloyds Bank and Junaid Zaidi, Pakistan Council for Science and Technology.

# CONTENTS

## Boxes

## Figures

## Tables

# INTRODUCTION TO THE BOT CONCEPT

# ▪ What is BOT?

BOT is the terminology for a model or structure that uses private invest-ment to undertake the infrastructure development that has historically been the preserve of the public sector. "Project finance" is the corner-stone of the BOT approach. It means essentially that lenders look to the project's assets and revenue stream for repayment rather than to other sources of security such as government guarantees or the assets of the project sponsors.

In a BOT project, a private company is given a concession to build and operate a facility that would normally be built and operated by the government. The facility might be a power plant, airport, toll road, tun-nel or water treatment plant. The private company is also responsible for financing and designing the project. At the end of the concession period, the private company returns ownership of the project to the gov-ernment, although this need not always be the case, as will be discussed below. The concession period is determined primarily by the length of time needed for the facility's revenue stream to pay off the company's debt and provide a reasonable rate of return for its effort and risk.

The acronym BOT stands for "build, operate and transfer" or "build, own and transfer" (the terms are used interchangeably). Variants include BOO (build, own and operate, i.e. without any obligation to transfer); BOR (build, operate and renewal of concession); BOOT (build, own, operate and transfer); BLT or BRT (build, rent or lease and transfer); BT (build and transfer immediately, BTO (build, transfer and operate); possibly sub-ject to instalment payments of the purchase price); DBFO (design, build, finance and operate); and DCMF (design, construct, manage and finance); MOT (modernize, own/operate and transfer); ROO (rehabilitate, own and operate); ROT (rehabilitate, own and transfer). For the purpose of these *Guidelines* the acronym BOT will include all these variations.

Some commentators have written that the BOT concept has its histori-cal roots in the concession systems of the nineteenth and early twentieth centuries. Others believe that BOT projects differ so significantly from the old concession approach that their roots are much more recent. The old concessions normally entitled the private sector to the virtually free use – some authors have called it "exploitation" – of the project, with very little participation and control by the host governments.

In contrast, in a properly structured BOT project today, the host gov-ernment decides on the need for the project and its scope, requires that the design, performance and maintenance of the project be tailored to the objectives of the country and selects the private sponsors by means of an appropriate bidding or evaluation process in order to arrive at a price that is fair to both the host government and the sponsors.

Unlike the old concessions, modern BOT arrangements are designed and implemented as public/private partnerships, with private sector finance and efficiency truly serving the public interest.

BOT projects offer significant potential for technology transfer and local capability building and for helping to develop national capital markets, as well as a variety of other benefits, all of which will be covered in the *Guidelines*. A properly negotiated and drafted BOT project agreement limits the private sponsors to a reasonable rate of return and ensures that the project serves the host country's national interests, economic and otherwise.

Most BOT projects are first identified by the host government. Through a published request for proposals the host government asks for bids to have a particular project delivered on a BOT basis. Chapter 6 of the *Guidelines* describes procurement options in detail. It is also possible, however, for a project opportunity to first be identified by a private entrepreneur, who will propose it to the host government. A number of successful BOT projects have been realized in this fashion.

Many developing countries have begun to promote infrastructure projects on a BOT basis. Such projects are financed on a limited recourse basis and built and operated as a private venture under a project agreement with the host government or one of its agencies. At the end of the operation period, the project is transferred to the host government, usually at no cost or only nominal cost. A number of BOT projects have now been successfully completed and put into operation, and many others are on the way.

## ■ Financing techniques and legal instruments

The BOT concept, it is worth noting at the outset, does not involve a new or novel mechanism for obtaining financing for a project or for structuring it. It uses the well-established approach and legal instruments of a technique known as "project finance". As seen by the lenders, a BOT project involves a private sector borrower who seeks financing on either a limited recourse basis or a non-recourse basis. In theory, the lender in a non-recourse financing arrangement will look only to the project's assets and revenue stream for repayment, not to additional sources of security, such as the total assets or balance sheet of the project sponsors. In practice, as will be discussed below, almost all BOT projects are financed on a limited recourse basis, as opposed to a purely non-recourse basis.

Project finance techniques were applied in the United States of America to the development of commercial real estate and were further developed in the 1970s in the North Sea in connection with oil and gas projects. They are being used for numerous private infrastructure projects involving power plants, roads, railways, bridges, telecommunication facilities and water treatment plants.

Infrastructure financing is different, of course, from financing an aircraft or a shopping centre. In equipment or real estate financing, the lender's primary security is the capital value of the asset. Toll roads or power plants, on the other hand, have uncertain capital value and a very limited potential for resale. The lender's primary security, therefore, is the contracts supporting the project and, most importantly, the certainty of the revenue stream set forth in the project agreement.

Different types of infrastructure have different risk profiles. The revenue from a power plant project is relatively secure and predictable. The host government or public utility may enter a well-defined agreement with the project company to purchase the power output of the plant. Compare, however, the source of revenue from a power plant to that from a toll road: since the revenue from a toll road depends on the individual travelling decisions of tens of thousands of potential users, the terms of a project agreement for a toll road are based primarily on travel forecasts by experts. Such forecasts are obviously less certain and the agreement less secure than a well-drafted, long-term power purchase agreement with a creditworthy utility.

Notwithstanding that different projects involve different risks, financial markets have become increasingly sophisticated in devising packages to finance almost any type of reasonably predictable revenue stream.

## ■ Advantages and challenges of the BOT approach

The BOT approach to financing infrastructure projects has many potential advantages (see box 1) and is a viable alternative in most countries to the more traditional approach using sovereign borrowings or budgetary resources. Unlike in a fully privatized approach, the government retains strategic control over the project, which is transferred back to the public sector at the end of the concession period.

The BOT approach is attractive because it taps private sector financing that would otherwise not be available for infrastructure projects. These additional sources of finance allow the host government to accelerate the development of critical projects that would otherwise have to wait for scarce sovereign resources to become available. BOT funding obligations do not appear as direct liabilities in host government accounts, which in some cases may be politically important or help to improve the country's credit rating.

The sponsors' commitment of substantial equity and their need to protect and make a profit on their investment give them a strong incentive to develop, design, construct and operate the project as efficiently as possible. Likewise, the fact that commercial lenders will be committing substantial sums on a limited recourse basis provides additional assurance that the economic viability of the project will have been thoroughly analysed at the outset by knowledgeable financial experts. The mobilization of private sector capital, initiative, know-how and discipline in the development and implementation of infrastructure projects is therefore a very positive feature of the BOT approach.

There are numerous other potential benefits to be derived from the BOT approach to infrastructure financing. They include technology transfer, the training of local personnel and the development of national and regional capital markets and new financing instruments.

Although the returns that equity investors and lenders require are usually higher than the interest and fees a host government would have to pay on sovereign borrowings, there are numerous potential offsetting savings for the host government. Lenders and sponsors will bear a substantially greater risk in exchange for the higher return. More importantly, having the design, procurement, implementation and operation of the BOT project largely in the hands of the private sector should provide economies and efficiencies that will balance out or outweigh the higher financing costs. Where comparable projects (e.g. other power plants) remain in the public sector, a competing private sector project may serve as a useful benchmark against which the host government can measure its public sector performance.

The BOT approach, of course, is not a panacea for the host government. BOT projects are complex from both financial and legal points of view. They require time to develop and negotiate. They require host government involvement and support. They require a suitable political and economic climate, political stability, a defined and stable legal and regulatory environment and a freely convertible currency, as well as other elements that are appropriate for foreign investment generally.

> **Box 1. Potential advantages to the host government of using the BOT approach for infrastructure development**
>
> - Use of private sector financing to provide new sources of capital, which reduces public borrowing and direct spending and which may improve the host government's credit rating.
>
> - Ability to accelerate the development of projects that would otherwise have to wait for, and compete for, scarce sovereign resources.
>
> - Use of private sector capital, initiative and know-how to reduce project construction costs, shorten schedules and improve operating efficiency.
>
> - Allocation to the private sector of project risk and burden that would otherwise have to be borne by the public sector. The private sector is responsible for the operation, maintenance and output of the project for an extended period (normally the government would receive protection only for the normal construction and equipment warranty period).
>
> - The involvement of private sponsors and experienced commercial lenders, which ensures an in-depth review and is an additional sign of project feasibility.
>
> - Technology transfer, the training of local personnel and the development of national capital markets.
>
> - In contrast to full privatization, government retention of strategic control over the project, which is transferred to the public at the end of the contract period.
>
> - The opportunity to establish a private benchmark against which the efficiency of similar public sector projects can be measured and the associated opportunity to enhance public management of infrastructure facilities.

A critical challenge for developing countries is to identify the factors that make projects financeable in the private sector. The *Guidelines* aims at helping governments to identify those factors, specifically as they relate to infrastructure projects.

Since BOT entails the financing of infrastructure projects by the private sector, there is a common misconception that the "public" nature of the project can be largely ignored, and the host government often assumes that it has minimal involvement in BOT projects. It will be seen why this assumption is not well-founded and why governments must lead as well as provide support in most projects.

Fortunately, the experience of the last decade makes clear the basic structure needed to make a BOT project viable. Standard solutions have been worked out for the problems that earlier seemed to present insuperable difficulties. Even if a government agency knows little about BOT, the knowledge exists and is available from private advisors as well as organizations, such as UNIDO, that have expertise and experience.

The advantages and challenges of BOT projects will be discussed in more depth throughout the *Guidelines*.

# ■ Characteristics of a BOT project

BOT projects involve a number of elements, all of which must come together for a successful project. Figure I illustrates a typical BOT project structure and the interrelationships between the various parties. The remaining subsections of chapter 1 discuss the primary characteristics of a BOT project. In chapter 2, the development phases of a typical BOT project are traced. Together, these chapters are designed to give the reader an overview and a context for the more detailed chapters that follow.

## Role of the host government

The BOT approach requires varying degrees of government support depending on the type, size and complexity of project and the host country's economic and regulatory conditions. It is easier for a government to attract private investment for a project in the industrial, oil and gas, or mining sectors. The goods, raw materials or services produced by an industrial project can be sold, usually into established markets, and often abroad or to foreign users for foreign currency. The challenge is greater in the case of infrastructure, where the revenue stream may depend entirely on purchase agreements with the host government, as in the case of a power plant (contract-based revenues), or on the uncertainties of local consumer demand, as in the case of a toll road or urban transit scheme (market-based revenues).

The absence of freely convertible currency adds a further complication. Political and economic uncertainties pose additional obstacles to the BOT approach.

Theoretically, an important attraction of a BOT project is that it will be privately financed, without any financial commitment from the host government, and that government involvement will be minimal because it is a private sector project. In practice, however, host government direction and support – legislative, regulatory, administrative and sometimes even financial – are essential in most developing countries.

First, the extent to which the host country's laws encourage foreign investment must be examined. The government may need to provide various types of support to the project, including special legislation or exemptions in the areas of taxation, labour law, immigration, customs, currency convertibility, profit repatriation and foreign investment protection. Thus, the first subject for government review is the general legal and regulatory framework that guides the BOT project from start to finish.

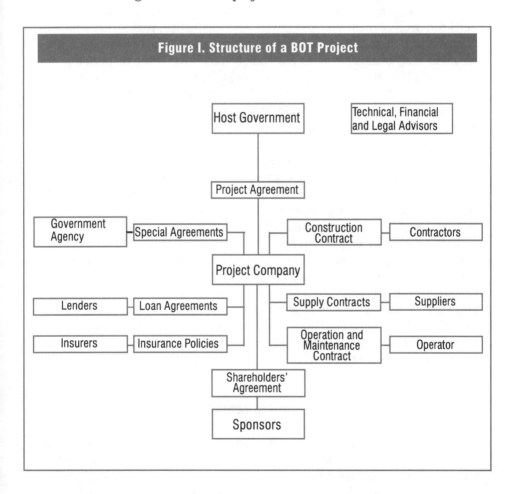

Figure I. Structure of a BOT Project

The host government then has to authorize the project at issue, a process that can require special legislation and governmental approvals. Next, it selects and administers a procurement process. It may also have to conduct a preliminary feasibility study to demonstrate the economic viability of the project to prospective bidders. Most countries have found it essential to draft a clear request for proposals and to adopt a transparent, well-defined bid and selection process. Usually, the government will start the bidding process with a prequalification phase, defining clearly the evaluation criteria for this phase as well as for the main tender phase.

Often the host government remains the ultimate client or purchaser of a BOT project. It must therefore truly want the project and should, from the outset, appoint a focal point or a specific body for the BOT project and give it sufficient authority and political influence to shepherd the project through the various administrative, regulatory and legislative challenges. These challenges may include opposition from government authorities or agencies that would have been responsible for the project if it were not being done on a BOT, privately sponsored basis. Successful approaches have ranged from appointing a high-level, intergovernmental committee to appointing a project manager with clear-cut authority to coordinate all authorization procedures. Challenges may also arise from public opposition to a project where, for example, the environmental or social impacts are questionable.

Once a project sponsor has been selected, the host government or one of its agencies enters into a concession or project agreement with the project company. This agreement will detail the host government's expectations, as well as the rights and obligations of the project company.

It is crucial for a government's financial, technical and legal representatives to have enough experience (or to retain experienced advisors) to protect and enhance the national interest during project development. Private sector sponsors are entitled to a fair return on their investment and risk. Similarly, the host government is entitled to a project that is properly designed, constructed and maintained, on terms and conditions that are fair. Both parties must be flexible and prepared to accommodate their respective interests in a balanced way.

## The project company

The private project company is the concessionaire of the BOT project; its rights and obligations are defined in the concession or project agreement with the host government. A consortium (or consortia) of private sector sponsors (public/private partnerships are also possible) is formed early in the BOT process, before the establishment of the project company, to review the request for proposals, prepare a feasibility study and submit a bid. The selected sponsor or sponsors usually create a special-purpose, limited liability company known as the "project company" or the "joint venture company". The project company will be capitalized with a limited equity contribution from each sponsor.

The project company is the vehicle for borrowing the funds to finance the project above and beyond the equity contributions of the sponsors. It is also the entity that will enter into the necessary contractual ar-rangements with the host government, the construction contractor, the operator (often a specialized operating company), equipment and raw material suppliers, and so on.

A sponsor consortium includes parties that are interested in entering into one or more of the contracts, such as a large international engineer-ing and construction firm, one or more large equipment suppliers, and a firm with expertise in operating and maintaining the particular type of project. These parties are willing to contribute equity to the project in the form of cash, manpower, time and effort and/or to give back of a portion of the fees they would normally earn on their contracts in order to have the opportunity to be the principal contractor, supplier or opera-tor for the project.

The project company may include other equity investors, such as an investment banking firm or merchant bank that acts as financial advi-sor to the project, an international lending institution, or other institu-tional or even public investors. In special cases, equity participation of the host government is possible.

There are potential conflicts of interest between the sponsors as own-ers of the project company and the sponsors as suppliers of goods and services to the project company. However, these conflicts can be miti-gated by the board of the project company, which does not want to see a particular sponsor obtain unduly favourable terms that would operate to the disadvantage of the overall project.

The bid selection process also serves to brake the tendency of a project company to agree to pay inflated prices under contracts with its spon-sors. The presence of equity investors in the project company, who have no interest in any individual contract, or a minority equity participation in the project company by the host government also mitigates these po-tential conflicts of interest.

Finally, the loan underwriting process of the commercial lending insti-tutions provides further assurance that the project economics have been thoroughly analysed, that costs and expenses have been identified and will be controlled, that revenue and profit expectations are reasonable and that financial management of the project will be properly handled.

It is normally advisable to include among the sponsors a strong, well-connected and well-respected private sector participant from the host country. This might be a civil works contractor or an industrial, commercial or financial group. A local partner can help the sponsors understand the local environment, deal with the host government and resolve local issues as they arise. It can provide logistical support during the development stage of the project and play an important role in raising local equity or debt financing if the local economy is sufficiently developed for this purpose. The local partner may also be one of the conduits for the transfer of technology and training from the project sponsors to the local economy.

## The project agreement

The project agreement (called a concession agreement in some countries) is at the heart of all BOT projects. It defines the rights and obligations of the project company and the host government for the development and operation of the project. It gives the project sponsors the right and obligation to finance, construct and operate the project for a specified period. It allocates project risks initially between the private sponsors and the government. The project agreement is at the centre of the web of contractual arrangements which, taken together, define the BOT project.

The obligations and risks of the sponsors are further spelled out in agreements for construction, for operation and maintenance (O&M) and for supply. These agreements with the primary contractor, the operator and various suppliers of equipment, fuel and other goods and services to the project must be harmonized and in accord with the basic economics of the project.

## Project finance

The BOT approach is a special form of project finance for infrastructure development. The rate of return of a BOT project must be sufficient not only to repay the lenders but also to reward the sponsors for committing their equity and know-how and for assuming the risks involved in such projects. The challenge of structuring the project finance is to establish a mix of debt, equity and mezzanine financing that optimizes the use of financial sources as it ensures a sound security base.

The project company raises the necessary debt financing or lending for the project from private sector lenders and from export credit agencies and bilateral and multilateral financial institutions. The lending is sometimes on a non-recourse basis, because the lenders do not have any direct financial recourse to the sponsors who own the project company or to the host government that guarantees the entire debt.

More often, however, BOT project financing is on a limited-recourse basis: recourse is available against the project company and its assets, including real estate, plant and equipment, contractual rights, performance bonds, insurance, government guarantees and other commitments the project company has obtained.

The most important asset, and the one on which the financing is principally based, is normally the project company's contractual right to a revenue stream judged sufficient to pay for the financing. For a power plant, this asset may be in the form of a separate long-term take-or-pay power purchase agreement. For a toll facility, it may be the right, specified in a concession agreement with the host government, to operate the facility for a number of years. The latter asset is partly market-based, because the revenues depend on future traffic and not on a firm revenue-producing contract. There are also cases where other "contractual assets" are the foundation of a project: for example, a contract providing supplies of an essential commodity at below-market prices (of, say, oil to a power station) might be the most important single "asset" for the project. In either case, the lenders must be convinced that the revenue stream will be large enough to ensure timely repayment of the debt.

Equity capital for BOT projects is basically provided by the sponsors, but also by institutional investors, local or international capital markets and specialized funds.

## Financial requirements for a BOT project

The financial viability of a BOT project must be clearly demonstrable to potential equity investors and lenders. Verification is usually required in the form of independent feasibility studies, ground and geological studies, demand studies, demographic projections and so forth.

The project must have a dependable source of revenue that will be sufficient to service principal and interest payments on the project debt over the term of the various loans and to provide a return on equity commensurate with whatever development and long-term project risk the equity investors are being asked to take. In the case of a power plant, the revenue will normally be contract-based: that is, based on a long-term off-take contract with a government power authority. In the case of roads, tunnels and bridges, the revenue will normally be market-based: that is, based on the tolls to be generated, with the traffic risk borne exclusively by the project company.

There is no reason, however, to think of either of these categories as inviolable. In both situations, a mixture of contract-based and market-based revenue is often seen. Thus, power off-take contracts often combine a minimum fixed capacity fee with a variable fee for electricity actually purchased. The capacity fee is paid to the project company merely for having the capacity available. This is a purely contract-based fee. It guarantees the project a certain minimum revenue regardless of the amount of power actually produced. The variable fee, on the other hand, is often market-driven, based on the kilowatt hours of electricity actually purchased to satisfy customer demand. For this part of the fee, the project company would be taking a market risk and would normally expect to reap substantial rewards. Other options can be developed according to the specific country experience, the regulatory framework and the interest of the negotiating parties.

Similarly, revenues for toll roads, bridges and tunnels could be based partly on a government commitment to pay either a minimum capacity fee or additional fees if a minimum level of traffic is not achieved. This approach would take some of the market risk out of a primarily market-based project. Long-term contracts with prospective users (for example, the contracts with the national railroads of France and the United Kingdom of Great Britain and Northern Ireland in the case of the Channel tunnel) would serve a similar function.

Since the lenders will be relying on the project to service their loans, they will insist that the total cost of the project be determined at the outset. Lenders as well as investors must have confidence that the project can actually be built and operated with the funds being committed. BOT projects transfer the construction risk to the project company and are therefore normally designed and constructed on a fixed-cost, turnkey basis. Proven technology is normally required. Experimental or state-of-the-art technology would add to the risks of the project and make limited-recourse financing more difficult to obtain.

The less predictable the total costs, the more the lenders will insist on stand-by commitments from the sponsors or the host government. The riskier the project is perceived to be, the more recourse they will have to have from other parties. In summary, to be able to secure financing, sponsors of BOT projects will need a very clear and detailed description of the concession scope and limits.

## Equity investment

Most BOT projects involve a combination of equity provided by the sponsors and debt provided by commercial banks, international financial institutions and bilateral government lenders. The percentage of equity seems to fall most often between 20 and 30 per cent of the total project cost, although in some projects it has been outside this range.

The returns earned by equity investors in BOT projects are difficult to estimate. The reasonableness of the return obviously depends upon the degree of risk taken by the investor and the additional benefits the project brings to the host government (such as timeliness, efficiencies and new technology). The projected rate of return for the base case assumptions is often set forth in government requests for proposals and in offering memoranda circulated by investment banking firms.

If the project performs at better than base case, the rate of return to the equity investors can improve substantially. This is an area where a host government needs to be particularly vigilant so as not to "pay" too much for the project. On the other hand, incentives can be structured to reward results and performance that exceed the base case, so that the benefit is shared between the project company and the host government, without allowing the equity investors to earn exorbitant windfall profits. In some cases, the length of the concession could vary with return, decreasing if the revenues are greater than had been contemplated in the financial projections of the base case. A successfully structured BOT project that achieves such benefit sharing will produce a win-win result for both the host country and the sponsors.

## Security for lenders

Lenders to a BOT project will insist on a variety of security measures. These measures are collectively referred to as the security package. They go far beyond a simple mortgage or deed of trust covering the project assets. Since the lenders recognize that if the project company defaults, there will be no ready market for a partly built toll road or a power plant that does not work, various devices to protect the lenders are usually found in BOT projects. These are discussed in detail later. To the degree that these security measures ensure that the project remains financially viable and performs as intended, they are also in the overall interest of the host government.

## Risk identification and management

Critical to the success of every BOT project is the identification, allocation and management of project risks. The subject of risk allocation is discussed throughout the *Guidelines* and addressed in detail in chapter 8. Two examples, inflation and currency risk, will suffice to introduce the subject.

Both lenders and equity investors normally insist on some mechanism to protect themselves against inflation risk. This protection may be provided by price escalation clauses in the off-take agreement (in the case of a power project) or by clauses in the project agreement allowing the project company to increase tolls (in a toll road project). Such price escalation clauses are intended to take account of increased costs due to inflation. They may also be drafted with the intent of maintaining the purchasing power of the project's net income and equity in general.

A typical BOT infrastructure project that sells its output into the local economy receives its earnings in local currency. Yet a substantial amount of the financing, both debt and equity, usually comes from a foreign source or sources. Both lenders and equity investors want a firm assurance that they will be able to recoup their original investment, together with interest or dividends, in foreign currency at a reasonable exchange rate. The host government, therefore, must be prepared to provide some mechanism to assure foreign investors and lenders that (a) they will be authorized to convert local currency earnings into foreign currency; (b) there will be enough foreign currency available when the time comes for the host country or its banking system to make the conversion; (c) the exchange rate will not be highly unfavourable; and (d) it will be possible to remit the foreign currency abroad.

## Government guarantees and special agreements

Although host governments do not normally provide a direct government guarantee for loans made to a BOT project company, they may be asked to provide such guarantees, or similar assurances, for some aspects of the project. For instance, if a government-owned corporation has contracted with the project company (as when a government utility enters into a long-term off-take contract or undertakes the long-term supply of fuel or energy to the project), the government itself may be required to guarantee the utility's performance. Similarly, the host government will usually be called upon to give certain guarantees on the availability of foreign exchange and exchange rate fluctuations, either directly to the project company or indirectly to foreign export credit guarantee agencies. Essential preconditions (access roads or transmission lines, for example) or *force majeure* on clauses contemplating financing readjustments in clear circumstances may also require government guarantees. The basic agreement with the project company will normally contain numerous other obligations of the host government or agency involved.

## Role of outside advisers

Host governments, like the other parties, will normally find it useful, depending on their experience, to retain technical, financial and legal advisers who are familiar with project finance structuring and the types of private sector arrangements involved in BOT projects. The project sponsors will themselves have substantial technical expertise and will have experienced investment bankers and international legal counsel on their side. The addition of comparable advisers and counsel to the government team can help the host government structure the initial BOT proposal in the most favourable way, can lend considerable credibility and creativity to the host government's position during the development phase and can help to ensure that the drafting of the complex contractual documents proceeds as efficiently as possible to the execution of definitive agreements.

The complexity of both the procedures and the documentation required to bring a BOT project to financial closing should not be underestimated. Few government offices will have enough staff to do the work within the allotted time and will need temporary support from outside advisors and legal counsel, brought in to implement a particular project. Although the cost of employing such advisers may be considerable, the resulting benefits – bringing the project to a successful completion, allocating risks and responsibility appropriately, and otherwise ensuring that the host government's interests are fully protected – will more than offset it.

## Complexity of the BOT process

The process of developing a BOT project may be complicated, time-consuming and, from the point of view of the sponsors, very expensive. For large projects, several years can elapse before signature of the project agreement or closing of the financing. In that time, the sponsors may spend considerable amounts for feasibility studies, professional fees to advisers and consultants, and other out-of-pocket expenses, to say nothing of the cost of their own management time. It is therefore critical that the host government should do everything possible to ensure an orderly, fair and efficient process, from bid solicitation, selection, contracting and permitting, through to project implementation.

Host governments, in other words, must understand the complexity of the process and be willing to provide the timely support required for success. Fortunately, valuable experience has been gained over the last decade in a number of countries by commercial banks, export credit agencies and multilateral financial institutions. All have come to understand the BOT process better, and standard solutions to recurring problems have been developed.

# PHASES OF A BOT PROJECT

Chapter 2 discusses the phases in a typical BOT project: project identification, government preparation for bidding, sponsor's preparation of a bid, selection, project development, project implementation, operation and transfer. These phases are shown in figure II. Each phase involves a number of contractual documents, which together will form the contract package for the project. A typical contract package is discussed in greater detail in chapter 10.

# ■ Project identification

At the outset, the need for a particular project must be identified and the possibility and advantage of having it carried out on a BOT basis must be recognized. Usually, this is done by the host government and its planning process. The planning authorities estimate demand for electricity, transportation, water and other public services and define priorities. The agency(ies) involved then identify the need for additional power plants over a particular period, or for a road, a bridge, an urban transit system, a port facility or some other infrastructure important to the country's economy. The host government will then focus on the possibility of satisfying that need using one or another form of financing, with one of the possibilities being the BOT approach. Occasionally, an entrepreneur or developer is the first to identify a project and brings the idea to the government.

In either case, a preliminary feasibility study normally has to be carried out. The study will carefully analyse the size, location, technical options, environmental screening and potential revenue stream of the project. Unless the host government already has extensive experience with BOT projects in general and projects of the kind at issue in particular, it will probably want at this point to hire experienced outside consultants to be sure that the project takes into account and protects its interests. Host governments should be aware that technical assistance funds may be available from bilateral and multilateral aid agencies to help defray the cost of studies and consultancy needed in the identification phase.

The lack of consistency in administering BOT projects or their poor management is a familiar complaint of experienced project sponsors. Therefore, at the outset of the process the host government should con-

## Figure II. Phases of a BOT Project

|  |  |
|---|---|
| I. Identification | Identify Project<br>Define Form of Financing<br>Preliminary Feasibility Study<br>Assign Project Manager and Team<br>Government Decision |
| II. Government Preparation for Tendering | Procurement Procedure<br>Prequalification<br>Project Agreement<br>Tender Documents<br>Bid Evaluation Criteria |
| III. Sponsor's Preparation to Bid | Form Consortium/Possibly Project Company<br>Feasibility Study<br>Identification of Potential Partnership<br>Submit Bid Package |
| IV. Selection | Evaluate Bids<br>Clarifications/Adjustments<br>Project Award |
| V. Development | Form Project Company<br>Equity Contributions<br>Loan Agreements<br>Financial Closing<br>Construction Contract<br>Supply Contract<br>Off-take Contract<br>Insurance Contract<br>Operation and Maintenance Agreement |
| VI. Implementation | Construct Facility and Install Equipment<br>Testing<br>Acceptance<br>Technology Transfer and Capability Building<br>Evaluation |
| VII. Operation | O&M during the Concession Period<br>Inspection<br>Training<br>Technology Transfer and Capability Building |
| VIII. Transfer | Transfer Procedure |

sider appointing or contracting a project manager, who will provide the leadership, coordination and institutional memory needed to develop a BOT project. The project manager may be a government employee or an outside expert.

The first step, then, is to identify a project and decide whether to pursue it on a BOT basis. The process of project identification will continue through preparation of a request for proposals and the inviting of bidders to submit design, construction and financing proposals.

# ■ Government preparation for bidding

The next step for the government is to decide the procurement procedure. Alternatives include competitive bidding, sole source procurement or some limited tender system. Most governments will want to prequalify potential investors, whether they adopt purely competitive bidding or some other process. A large number of bidders may not be the government's first priority. Rather, the need to attract serious, quality investors should drive the design of the procurement process. If, as will usually be the case, competitive bidding is used, three, four or five serious competitors may be enough to achieve the host government's objectives.

The request for proposals provides a detailed definition of the project. It normally sets forth criteria that must be met, including size, timing, performance and the nature and range of project revenues. It is also advisable to include the project agreement in the invitation-to-tender documents. This phase is extremely important from the host government's point of view. If the initial project definition is impractical, or if the governments criteria for award are unrealistic or unclear, interested investors will have great difficulty in responding with realistic proposals.

A quality bid package and a transparent, well-defined bid evaluation process are of critical importance for a successful BOT project. Experienced bidders consider the bid package and evaluation process as an important indicator of the project's feasibility and of the host government's commitment to make it a success. The terms of the competition must be clear and consistently applied, or serious competitors will be discouraged from pursuing the process. The issues involved in competitive bidding for BOT projects are discussed in chapter 6.

From the host government's viewpoint, it is the bidding and evaluation process that defines the terms of reference of the project and is largely responsible for the quality of the competition and investors. Experience suggests that choosing the most suitable project consortium is usually the single greatest determinant of the success or failure of BOT projects.

# ▪ Sponsor's preparation of a bid

In response to the request for proposals, a group of interested investors or sponsors normally form a consortium to put together a responsive bid. The consortium members reach a preliminary agreement at this stage on cost sharing, the role each expects to play in the project and the potential project structure. If confidential or proprietary information have to be shared among project participants, which is often the case, the preliminary consortium agreement includes appropriate confidentiality agreements, or the participants will separately enter into such agreements.

The consortium carries out its own more detailed feasibility studies for the project, which are a critical factor in its decision to proceed and in its ability to attract financing. It then seeks tentative loan commitments and preliminary contract prices from potential lenders, equity investors, contractors and suppliers in order to structure its proposal or bid.

The consortium then prepares and submits its bid. The request for proposals should require that the bid contain a credible financing plan, although not necessarily definitive financing commitments. In some instances, the bid should be allowed to suggest amendments or alternative solutions to one or more aspects of the project in order to better achieve the project's overall goal. For instance, the feasibility studies undertaken for the consortium or the consortium's expertise in project design and development may suggest an alternative to some feature of the project as originally outlined in the request for proposals.

# ▪ Selection

In the next phase, the government will evaluate the various bids submitted in response to the request for proposals and select the winner. It is critical that highly qualified technical, financial and legal advisors are available to the government entity evaluating the bids. Bids for any complicated project are never identical and are often very difficult to measure one against another no matter how clear the evaluation criteria may be.

The evaluation of bids for BOT projects will not ordinarily be based on price alone. It is, rather, based on factors such as price, reliability, experience and the degree to which the project as conceived and proposed will lead to other benefits for the host country, such as savings in foreign exchange, promoting technology transfer, and providing employment and training to local employees and contractors.

Having evaluated the submitted bids, the government invites the selected bidder to execute and sign definitive contractual documents.

# ▪ Project development

With the government's acceptance and the signing of the project agreement, the winning consortium is in a position to make definite commitments among themselves to form or structure the project company if it has not already been formed. The equity contributions required for project realization will have to be made. Similarly, the sponsors will now be in a position to approach or go back to potential lenders, as well as to the contractors and suppliers, to obtain more definite commitments on terms and prices.

When all of these agreements have been negotiated by the sponsors and signed, the project will proceed to financial closing. Financial closing is the date on which the lenders and equity investors advance, or begin to advance, the funds for detailed design, construction, purchase of equipment and other steps necessary to conclude the project.

These final steps after the award of the project and the signing of the project agreement are crucial in the development process of any BOT project. Although most of the onus is on the winning consortium, this final phase of project development may require some support from the host government and flexibility on its part.

# ▪ Project implementation

Once the project reaches financial closing, the implementation phase will begin in earnest. Any particular project, of course, may not fall neatly into these distinct phases. Some site assembly or development and even some preliminary construction may take place before financial closing, but the main construction work and the delivery of important pieces of equipment for the project normally take place only afterwards, when the project loan funds become available for disbursement. The construction agreement and process are described in more detail in chapter 12.

The implementation phase ends when the project has passed the specified completion tests and is finally accepted by the project company and in principle by the host government.

# ■ Operation

Next, the project enters the operation phase, which will continue for the period of the concession. During this phase, the project company, either directly or through an operator, operates the project and maintains the facilities in conformity with the criteria set forth in the project agreement and as required by the terms of the various loan agreements and agreements with investors. The revenues or fees received during the operation of the facility allow the project company to recover the investments, serve the debt and make profits. To be sure that operation and maintenance (O&M) are being carried out as required, the lenders, investors and host government have extensive rights to receive reports and carry out inspections of the facilities. The issues associated with O&M are described more fully in Chapter 13.

In both the implementation and operation phases, the host government should seek to derive as much benefit as possible from local capability building and the transfer of technology from the project company and contractors into the local economy. These considerable benefits are described in chapter 5.

# ■ Transfer

The final phase of a BOT project is the transfer of the project to the host government at the end of the concession period. As a rule, the project will have been designed to enable the BOT sponsors to pay off their project debt and to earn the expected return during the concession period so that the transfer to the host government will be for no consideration or only a nominal one. The interest of the host government at the transfer date will be to make sure that the project has been properly maintained and that enough training and technology transfer have taken place for the government to be able to continue to operate the project.

Depending on the type of project and the degree to which it has decided to promote privatization of its infrastructure, the host government may find it advantageous to have the project company or the operator continue to operate and maintain the project under a negotiated extension of the concession or a new operating contract. This result might make sense if, for instance, the government believed operation of the project by a private sector entity provided better and more cost-efficient service than its operation by the government itself. A host government may therefore wish to preserve this option in defining the terms of the project agreement. An alternative could be a new tendering process for a new concession period. The various options and considerations involving project transfer are analysed in chapter 14.

# ECONOMIC FRAMEWORK FOR BOT SCHEMES

**Economic Framework**

**3**

Chapter 3 describes the economic framework for the development of BOT projects. It provides an overview in four areas:

- The role of infrastructure in promoting a country's economic development.

- The potential benefits of private sector involvement in infrastructure.

- Types of private sector involvement.

- The economic benefits and costs of BOT projects.

# ▪ Role of infrastructure in national development

Investment in infrastructure is clearly one of the prerequisites for continued and sustainable economic growth. A developing economy must have adequate services, including transport, electric power, telecommunications, water and sanitation and waste disposal, along with education and health facilities, to successfully meet the challenges of modernizing and diversifying production, expanding trade, coping with population growth, alleviating poverty and improving the environment.

Improved infrastructure provides widespread benefits for the economy. These benefits, as well as their associated costs, have to be identified and estimated.

## The promotion of industrial growth

Infrastructure availability and quality is often the single most important factor influencing domestic and foreign investment, which is critical in promoting industrial growth. An efficient and reliable infrastructure is essential for industries competing in global markets or participating in global production networks. Infrastructure is also a determinant for regional development. A poor or non-existent infrastructure is one main cause of slow industrial growth in the less-developed areas of various countries.

## Reduced costs for consumers and producers

Quality infrastructure allows for increased productivity and lower production costs, as well as the more efficient supply of goods and services to the public. For example, better transport links reduces distribution costs, and investment in technologically efficient power plants reduces energy costs for consumers.

## A multiplier effect on the economy

Direct expenditure on infrastructure fuels demand for firms supplying the contractors, causing ripples throughout the economy, with one effect being the increased use of the labour force and, accordingly, higher income. The multiplier effect depends to a large extent on where the project funds are spent. Civil works, for instance, often have a high local content and involve the use of local raw materials and labour. For developing countries with capacity to produce capital goods and fixtures, infrastructure projects often generate strong backward linkages to the local industry.

## Rise or fall in land values

Most toll roads, airports, ports and rail networks tend to encourage property development in surrounding areas. On the other hand, heavy industries and facilities may have a negative environmental impact, decreasing land value in neighbouring areas.

The government should consider the full economic impact of each infrastructure project before deciding whether the project will be publicly or privately financed.[1]

---

[12] A comprehensive discussion on the role of infrastructure for economic growth in developing countries is presented in the World Bank publication *World Development Report 1994: Infrastructure for Development*.

# ▪ Impact of private sector involvement in infrastructure development

A number of arguments have been made in favour of a major role for the public sector in the provision of infrastructure. First, such projects involve large sums of money and long lead times and hence carry large risks. Secondly, they have widespread social and economic costs and benefits that cannot be captured by user charges. Thirdly, the strategic role of some infrastructure facilities requires direct government involvement in their implementation, operation and control.

However, a number of countervailing considerations are being studied by many governments. Scarcity of public funds and constraints in the access to sovereign loans and foreign technology threaten to delay worthwhile projects. In addition there is concern that some public sector projects have failed to capture the expected benefits because of cost overruns and quality and maintenance problems. Over the past decade, technological changes have lessened the natural monopolistic characteristics of many infrastructure services and allowed State-owned monopolies to be opened up to unbundling, competition and private participation. More countries are turning today to the private sector not only to build the required infrastructure but also to maximize the benefits of investment in infrastructure.

From the standpoint of development strategy, private sector participation in infrastructure implementation and improvement will provide additional finance and may also increase economic efficiency. In the past, many developing countries promoted large investment programmes to establish or strengthen their infrastructure. These investments were made with a view to reducing external costs for enterprises and customers alike. The programmes were conducted by the State or public utility organizations and were largely financed through sovereign loans. However, the heavily subsidized prices at which the output was offered meant that the income from the investments was often insufficient to repay external and internal loans. Adjustment and austerity programmes set up to control the expansion of external and internal debt severely restricted the ability of many governments to invest in new infrastructure or even to adequately maintain existing facilities. Bringing in private sector capital and efficiency is one way to implement and modernize infrastructure, which in turn may lead to economic recovery and growth.

# ▪ Types of private sector involvement

The extent and nature of private sector involvement will depend on the strategic significance of an infrastructure project to the host government and on its attractiveness to private finance. Under concession-type arrangements, the degree to which the private sector is involved in the provision of infrastructure services can vary greatly (see box 2).

Only limited private involvement and commitment are required in contracting out or in a management contract, which could include mechanisms linking the contractor's compensation to the performance of the facility. Private participation increases in a leasing contract, where the private contractor is responsible at its own risk for the performance of the facility and the quality of the service provided, typically against payment of a lease fee.

In a BOT-type scheme, the private concessionaire is also responsible for designing, financing, building (or rehabilitating) and operating the project, which at the end of the concession period is returned to the government. In a BOO scheme, by contrast, the project remains in the private sector.

---

### Box 2. Types of private sector involvement in infrastructure development

- Contracting out or management contracts, where the private sector constructs a facility under a contractual arrangement or manages a facility for an agreed period and fee, without taking on the financing or revenue risk. As a variant of contracting out, the private sector retains some or all of the revenue as its return for operating the facility and thus bears a revenue risk.

- Leasing, where the private sector may design, build and finance the facility and receive lease payments from the public sector for its use.

- BOT-type schemes, where the private sector designs, builds and operates the project for an agreed period and then transfers ownership of the facility to the government.

- BOO scheme, where the facility is not transferred but remains in private hands.

- Privatization, that is, full private sector ownership and control over an infrastructure facility or utility corporation.

---

Finally, privatization (or divestiture) involves the transfer to the private sector of the infrastructure company assets and of the responsibility for financing future expansion and for all investments required to meet the obligations specified in its concession or by the government regulator.

Properly structured BOT projects offer efficiency gains and additional finance approaching those of purely private projects. Unlike outright privatization, they allow the government to retain a greater degree of strategic control over infrastructure development.

Although the BOT approach may not be suitable for all types of infrastructure, it should be considered, broadly, where a number of conditions prevail:

- Privatization is less appropriate because the government wants to retain a greater degree of strategic control over the infrastructure project.

- A significant initial investment in new or improved facilities is required and the government prefers to allocate public funds to other purposes.

- There are opportunities for efficiency gains in the construction and operation of the facility.

- The government wants to establish a benchmark for public sector efforts and thereby help to improve the efficiency of public project implementation and management.

- User charge rates are acceptable to customers.

- The private sector can recoup its investment through user charges.

The types of infrastructure project where BOT contracts have proved most successful are the following:

- Transport schemes, including airports, light rail projects, major intercity and intercountry roads, tunnels and bridges.

- Utility projects, including power, water and telecommunications. If tariffs are set at market levels, it should be possible to rely on user charges and to forgo continuing government subsidy.

There are fewer examples to date of successful BOT contracts in health and education, where the government tends to be the purchaser and therefore bears much of the project risk. There are, moreover, wider social benefits of better health and education that may not be fully captured through user charges. For example, higher educational standards generally stimulate economic growth, but seeking to recover the costs of education entirely through user charges may adversely affect the standards. Innovative schemes that provide for a genuine transfer of risk are, however, emerging in both sectors.

## ■ Economic benefits and costs of BOT projects

BOT projects potentially offer a number of economic benefits:

- Additional sources of finance for infrastructure and, in the case of foreign private sector participation, additional inflow of foreign exchange.

- Government long-term strategic control of infrastructure.

- Efficiency gains and lower operating costs. An independent experienced operator applying well proven and up-to-date technology and having an incentive to manage risks effectively through a well-structured BOT contract is likely to be able to produce output more efficiently and at a lower price to the user. This benefit may enhance the prices of goods and services and increase a country's cost-competitiveness in a wide range of industrial sectors.

- Technology and skills transfer. BOT projects offer host countries the opportunity to obtain up-to-date technology and have their local workforce trained in how to use it. Local capability may be stimulated further by long-term research and development agreements with the private sector sponsor. This benefit may also stimulate technological progress in other sectors of the economy as a result of learning by doing.

- Developing local capital markets. In an appropriate regulatory environment, BOT projects, by virtue of their need for long-term capital, can promote the introduction of new financial instruments (debt and equity) to local financial markets. This will stimulate development of the local capital markets and increase the financial sophistication of local participants, including financial institutions, State-owned utilities, government agencies and private companies.

- Eventual transfer of the assets to local control. The fact that a BOT project will be returned to local ownership and control may enhance the political acceptability of this approach in the first instance. In addition, at the end of the contract period, the government may be able to agree to a new operating and maintenance contract at a lower price than was called for in the original BOT project agreement and for a shorter duration. A shorter concession could also allow the market to be tested. All of this could lead to lower user charges and, if the new operator is a domestic firm, stem outflows of foreign exchange to foreign sponsors.

The economic costs associated with BOT projects include the following:

- Costs due to an imbalance in experience. Governments with little experience in BOT contracts are advised to initiate BOT projects on a manageable scale and seek professional advice to compensate the often greater experience of the private sector.

- User costs imposed for the first time or increased to match market rates. The economic costs of public services, once covered by the State, then become financial costs for the user.

- Overpriced supplies. Potential conflicts of interest on pricing among the project sponsors must be monitored. Care must be taken to ensure that sponsors who supply goods or services to the project do so on a fully competitive basis.

- High financing costs. Financing costs for BOT projects tend to be high, as the legal fees associated with their contractual arrangements are much higher than those for standard commercial contracts. The complexity of the credit also means that lenders need more time than usual to assess a project's merits and will tend to charge higher fees.

Given the importance of infrastructure investment to national development it is essential that the wider economic costs and benefits associated with a BOT scheme are taken into account by governments when designing the economic and legal framework to promote private sector investment in such projects as well as when assessing those projects. The wider costs and benefits outlined above will not be reflected in the financial return to a private sector investor, and corporate objectives may conflict with national objectives and priorities.

Governments will ordinarily wish also to undertake a financial and economic appraisal to determine whether a particular BOT project is worth doing. This appraisal exercise is covered in chapter 7.

# THE GOVERNMENT'S ROLE IN PROVIDING FOR SUCCESSFUL BOT PROJECTS

**Government's Role**

**4**

# ■ Overview

One of the advantages of the BOT concept for a government is that a considerable workload, including responsibility for the financing, designing, construction and operation of the projects, is transferred from the government agencies and ministries traditionally responsible for infrastructure projects to the private sector. This does not, however, imply that the role of the government is limited to supervision and monitoring of the BOT projects. BOT infrastructure projects require that the host government play an active role, in particular in the preconstruction or preinvestment phases of a project.

It is the government that initially approves the use of the BOT concept in connection with the country's infrastructure policy and that then identifies sectors and projects that would be suitable for this approach. It decides the procurement process, manages the procurement proceedings and defines the criteria for the selection of BOT sponsors. The host government or one of its agencies will be directly involved in the agreements that are essential to the arrangement of BOT projects. The most important task will be to draft the project agreement, which spells out in detail the rights and obligations of the project company and the government agency authorized to sign the agreement.

The government normally supports the implementation of the project in a number of ways: these may include providing the project site and access to it, energy supplies, transportation and other logistical support. It will be involved in facilitating licences, permits and approvals, as well as ensuring that they are readily renewable, provided that the sponsors have fulfilled their obligations. The host government normally must ensure that foreign exchange is available with which to repay the loan used to finance the project, the fees of the foreign contractors and the dividends to the foreign project sponsors. The host government (or its agencies) may be the purchaser of the output of the project and may in some cases also be called on to provide financial support to the project, for instance in the form of tax exemptions.

Finally, the government normally has the right to take over the project assets at the end of the concession period or to arrange for some other scheme to operate the project when the original contract period expires.

4

In short, a BOT infrastructure project cannot be realized without substantial commitment and cooperation on the part of the host government. Indeed, the host government's commitment is a critical factor in the assessment of the BOT project's viability by foreign investors and creditors.

By the same token, the government's control of so many of the ingredients of a BOT infrastructure project gives it an opportunity to manage the project in a coordinated and efficient way and thus to ensure that it truly serves the national interest.

# ■ BOT strategy at the country level

Each country must adopt a realistic and consistent BOT strategy based on its particular situation and needs. First and foremost, it must assess realistically its attractiveness to investors.

The range of challenges associated with the development of BOT projects and the need for government support vary from country to country. Since foreign investors and lenders, not surprisingly, tend to favour BOT projects in the more industrialized developing countries, the majority of BOT projects have so far been implemented in countries with relatively high GNP, stable exchange rates and inflation, fairly well defined legal and institutional environments and political stability. Structuring a BOT package in less developed, politically unstable and more indebted countries has proved to be a greater challenge.

This tendency is heightened by the constraints on the availability of finance, underdeveloped domestic capital markets and the shortage of financial resources in many developing countries. In such countries there may also be a shortage of private project sponsors – particularly construction and equipment supply companies – interested in and capable of financing and operating infrastructure projects.

Hence, the real problem facing many governments that have decided to adopt the BOT approach is to design a strategy for government support that will encourage foreign and domestic private investment in the country's infrastructure projects, given the strong international competition for private finance. In doing this, the government must assess the factors that make a developing country attractive to foreign investors and lenders. These factors include political stability, enabling legislation, a credible legal framework that recognizes and enforces contractual obligations, proven political and administrative support for BOT projects and the country's credit rating (which may itself take most of the preceding factors into account).

Many of these factors cannot be changed overnight. If a government decides to adopt a BOT strategy, it may consider taking positive steps to encourage private sector investment and reduce the negative impact of existing impediments. Experience suggests that a proactive government policy to stimulate BOT infrastructure projects can be a decisive factor in the competition for foreign investment in such projects.

There is no general recipe for a proactive government policy, as each policy must be designed for the particular country involved. However, having certain essentials in place will considerably enhance the private sector's interest in BOT infrastructure projects in a developing country:

- An explicit national development policy that clearly commits the host government to promote private sector participation in infrastructure projects.

- A credible legal and regulatory framework to facilitate a BOT strategy.

- A credible administrative framework to expedite the implementation of BOT projects and to support such projects when they encounter the problems inherent in all large projects no matter how they are financed or what country they are in.

- Incentives and various forms of government support to encourage the private sector to participate in BOT projects and a pragmatic approach to risk-reward issues.

- A clear government commitment to conclude BOT deals within a reasonable time.

Each of these essentials is now addressed in more detail. Another essential, an orderly and transparent BOT procurement procedure, is covered in chapter 6.

**Government's Role**

**4**

# ■ The promotion of private sector participation

The host government's commitment to private sector participation in the development of infrastructure services should be clear and unequivocal. To the extent possible, the government should attempt to develop broad political consensus in favour of such a policy. It controls so many of the necessary ingredients for the success of a BOT infrastructure project that no sponsor, investor or lender will participate unless it can count on the firm commitment of the host government for the duration of the project.

Ideally a host government's publicly expressed commitment to private sector participation in infrastructure development should meet three objectives:

- It should convince private sponsors, investors and lenders that the government is firmly committed to BOT infrastructure projects.

- It should disseminate information on private sector involvement in infrastructure services and gain public acceptance for this involvement, which may be particularly sensitive to public opinion if the services were previously provided to the public at below cost or at no cost.

- It should ensure the support of interested groups in the host country, including the public administration and the labour unions, for private sector involvement in what have traditionally been public sector projects and services.

Foreign sponsors of BOT projects and their lenders not only need to know that the host government is committed as a matter of policy to private sector participation in infrastructure development. They must also be satisfied that the host government has a strong rationale for supporting their particular BOT project and is not likely to withdraw that support, delay the project or renounce its obligations.

Thus, each BOT project's economic viability, which to a large extent depends on the country's or locality's need for the project, must be clearly perceived by the government. For instance, the need for better telecommunications or transport systems or for more water or power should be demonstrated in reports and project studies. The government's rationale for adopting the BOT approach, both financial and technical, should be clearly and convincingly defined. A host country's need for the private sector's financial and technical resources to implement and operate a much-needed infrastructure facility can be a strong additional incentive for the government and its agencies to support the BOT project over its projected lifetime.

Finally, each BOT project that is part of a larger infrastructure programme must be ranked as to importance by the government. When governments do not have enough resources to pursue more than just a short list of planned BOT projects, failure to prioritize will lead to delays, which in turn will deter sponsors and lenders.

# ■ The legal framework for a BOT strategy

## The legal framework as a key element in the investors' appraisal of a BOT project

The attractiveness of a BOT project to private investors depends to a large extent on the way the host government addresses fundamental legal issues, such as enforcement of contracts, private ownership, security arrangements, taxes, remittance of foreign exchange and profits, that are critical to the success of all foreign investment in BOT projects. In particular, an inadequate legal framework can undermine the strength and effectiveness of the various types of contracts that constitute the structure of a BOT project. In a broader sense, a supportive legal framework will reduce what is known as the "country risk", a key element in sponsors' and lenders' appraisal of a BOT project in a developing country.

There is no perfect or universal model for a supportive legal and regulatory framework for BOT projects. The legal approach and techniques will vary according to the existing legal system and tradition in a country, its BOT strategy and the specifics of the particular infrastructure sectors. Each country must decide questions such as the following:

- Should special legislation be enacted for BOT projects or existing legislation amended?

- Which terms should be defined by legislation? Which should be left to be negotiated between the parties involved?

- Should government control be enforced by legislation, regulations or administrative guidelines?

Government's Role

4

In some developing countries, namely those where BOT projects are considered part of the government's general economic policy and the existing laws and regulations for that policy are considered adequate, new legislation or regulations may not be needed.

Some of the elements of a legal and regulatory framework for implementing a successful BOT strategy are discussed next.

## The basic legislative authority for awarding BOT projects

A host government must provide the basic legislative and regulatory authority for a given infrastructure project to be built and operated by the private sector. This includes designating the individual ministries, government agencies or local governments authorized to procure and implement BOT projects. It also includes passing regulations that define the responsibilities of government agencies and ministries for the development and implementation of the projects, the issuance of licences and permits, central government approvals and mechanisms for administrative coordination.

Some countries may not need specific legislation for the transfer of public infrastructure to the private sector. For example, in the majority of common law countries, unless there is specific legislation to the contrary, the government and individual government ministers usually have the authority to sell government assets or to transfer them to private operators.

Irrespective of the legal basis for authorizing BOT projects, what matters most to foreign sponsors is the clarity of the authorization. In order to avoid later disputes, foreign sponsors must know for sure who has the authority to award BOT projects and the scope of that authority.

## Enabling public legislation

A wide range of special public legislation and regulatory support may be required to implement and operate a BOT project, depending on the country involved. For example, the host government may have to enact legislation authorizing the acquisition of land for the project, the transfer of public assets to the project and the provision of logistical facilities, work permits or other necessary government inputs. Experience has shown that to avoid delays and frustration it is very important to have such public legislation in place before undertaking a BOT project. Special public legislation may also establish a suitable framework to foster competition in areas previously under the exclusive control of the public sector. Such enabling legislation might, for instance, abolish sectoral State monopolies and State subsidies so as to make non-subsidized private sector participation in the development of infrastructure projects feasible. Since a BOT project involves either private ownership of the land and assets of the project or a leasehold in them, the host government must determine whether the public sector's exclusive ownership of the land and infrastructure assets is to continue or private ownership is to be allowed by enactment of legislation. Likewise, if ownership or lesseeship rights are vested only on nationals of a country, legislative reform will be required to attract foreign sponsors. Again, the domestic laws should be changed before procurement begins.

## Adequate security legislation

The more traditional forms of security arrangements such as land mortgages or security interests in inventory and equipment are not of much interest to the lenders to a BOT infrastructure project. A BOT project may be uniquely valuable to the parties involved but of rather limited value to third parties. Other security devices, discussed below, are usually more important from the lender's perspective.

In some BOT projects, however, the lenders may be willing to rely on project assets (in addition to the project's revenue stream) as security for debt repayment. To the degree that this is so, they may require less security from other sources. The creation and protection of security interests, mortgages and liens in respect to project assets in favour of the lenders and the enforcement of remedies under the security package should therefore be assured by the host country's legal system.

Security arrangements tailored to the BOT nature of a project are normally regulated in the project agreement, the purchase agreement and the credit agreement. Such arrangements may include offshore revenue and retention accounts, performance undertakings from the government of the public agency's obligations under the project agreement, assignment of various contracts to the lenders, the lenders' right to cure any defaults by the project company within a reasonable time and their right to take over the BOT project in the case of default, usually accomplished by provisions in the project agreement and by having the project company's equity owners pledge all of their stock as security for the loans. Legislation, however, may be needed to legally protect these additional kinds of security, which are often critical to the success of BOT projects. For example, enforcement remedies and legislation to prevent other creditors from obtaining conflicting interests must be enacted if they do not already exist in the legislative framework of the country.

Lack of provisions for the protection and enforcement of such security arrangements in a country's legal system has made bankers extremely reluctant to lend to BOT projects. Examples of such customary security arrangements for BOT projects are listed in box 3.

**Government's Role**

**4**

### Box 3. Some standard security arrangements found in BOT projects

- Performance undertaking from host government of its agencies' obligations under the project agreement.

- Offshore revenue and retention bank accounts.

- Approval from the government or the central bank for foreign exchange transactions.

- Assignment of rights over bank accounts to senior lenders.

- Assignment of interests under project contracts such as construction contracts, off-take agreements and O&M agreements to senior lenders.

- Stock pledges.

- Take-or-pay arrangements.

- Security interests, mortgages and liens on project assets.

- Performance and maintenance bonds to secure various obligations of the company.

- Insurance taken out in joint names or assignable to the lenders.

- Notice to lenders of defaults.

- Rights of senior lenders to cure any defaults by the company and the forbearance of the government's rights to terminate the project agreement during the pendency of the cure.

- Rights of senior lenders to enter and take possession of the project facilities in connection with a cure of defaults.

- Rights of senior lenders to appoint replacements for the project company or the O&M company upon a default under the loan documents.

- Support from the government for issuance of approvals and permits to the new project developer or the O&M company if the lenders appoint replacements.

# Legislation to promote foreign investment

Most developing countries have enacted foreign investment codes to encourage and facilitate direct foreign investment. Although the objectives, scope and approach of the foreign investment codes differ greatly, the codes all grant a broad range of incentives and benefits to foreign investors. They need to be made applicable to investment in BOT infrastructure projects, which are simply a different form of foreign investment.

Some issues usually covered in foreign investment codes should be recognized as particularly important to the financial characteristics and long-term nature of BOT projects:

- Right to exchange local currency into foreign currency.

- Foreign exchange convertibility at a reasonable exchange rate.

- Free remittance abroad of foreign currency.

- Full repayment of loans and investment compensation upon any government-mandated transfer of a project before the end of the project period (expropriation, nationalization and acquisition).

- Simplified import licencing and customs procedures.

- The right to bring in foreign nationals needed to construct, operate and maintain projects.

- The right of foreign investors to establish companies in the host country.

- Tax regimes for foreign investment.

Obviously, investment laws that limit foreign investment or that mandate a minimum level of domestic participation in companies or projects require close analysis. The magnitude of a typical BOT infrastructure project will most often require that such laws be adapted or changed before a national BOT programme is implemented.

**Government's Role**

**4**

# A legal framework for the BOT project agreements

The legal authority for the government or its agencies to develop and implement BOT infrastructure projects is not given without any restrictions. Rather, it usually defines more or less explicitly a mandatory legal framework for the BOT arrangements.

The strategies that underlie a legal framework for BOT project agreements vary considerably. Broadly speaking, the legislative approaches can be described as falling in one of three categories: (a) an open agreement approach, providing for a very flexible authority in any given BOT project, (b) a narrow agreement approach, where the legislation itself determines the essential terms of the BOT project agreements and (c) a wide range of approaches between "open" and "narrow".

The majority of countries that have authorized private sector participation in infrastructure projects have applied an open agreement approach. This allows the appointed ministries, government agencies or local governments to tailor all or most of the important terms to be contained in the project agreement. The broad delegation of authority is in principle restricted only by the general legislation of the country and by the objectives of the government's BOT policy. Those objectives are usually expressed in the authorizing legislation.

The open agreement approach provides maximum flexibility. It makes it possible to adjust the BOT framework to the characteristics of the different infrastructure sectors and to the different BOT projects within the sectors. A disadvantage of this approach is that it may take a long time to draft the contracts, which may be overly detailed since there is little overall legislative guidance. If the open agreement approach is used, the national authorities must have experienced administrators and legal advisers to prepare the contract package.

An example of the narrow agreement approach is found in the BOT legislation adopted by the Philippines. There, a rather extensive BOT legal framework, including supporting regulations, has been passed by the national legislative body. This approach is also well known from European concession legislation and from the petroleum sector in the North Sea, where comprehensive legislation protects national interests.

This legislative approach may define the basic contract provisions for the operation and maintenance of the BOT project, the maximum period for private ownership, environmental protection, the training of nationals, repayment terms, limitations on financial support from governments, insurance obligations and so forth. Box 4 lists typical provisions in narrow agreement legislation. Although some important contract terms are left to be tailored to the characteristics of the individual projects, this approach establishes a rather strict and uniform legal framework for BOT projects.

## Box 4. Typical provisions found in narrow agreement legislation

- Key requirements for construction, Operation and maintenance of the project.

- The right to use land, roads and other supporting facilities necessary for the construction and operation of the project.

- Duration of private ownership and operation.

- Transfer of the project, including assignment of shares in the project company.

- Provisions on tariffs, fees, tolls and other charges during the operation of the project.

- Training of nationals.

- Use of national services and goods.

- Transfer of technology.

- A framework or minimum requirement for allocation of risks between the project company and the government.

- Assurance of compliance by the project company.

- Performance incentives.

- Project supervision.

- Coordination of the project with other infrastructure projects.

- Environmental protection measures.

- Contract termination and adjustment.

- Consequences when BOT projects are abandoned before the end of the concession period.

Government's Role

4

The narrow agreement approach allows the legislature and the government to closely control infrastructure development and monitor the realization of the national BOT objectives. It also gives the authorities a stronger hand in negotiating contracts with the private sector and may help to reduce the time and legal costs of finalizing the BOT agreements. On the other hand, the lack of negotiating flexibility makes it difficult to tailor the contract terms to a particular infrastructure sector or to a particular BOT project.

Between the extremes of those two approaches is a wide range of hybrid systems. Typically, they provide some detailed rules and regulations, for instance in foreign investment codes or in detailed guidelines approved by the government, but leave wide discretion to decide terms for a given project. Such hybrid frameworks allow the authorities to respond quickly and effectively to sectoral needs or the needs of a specific project. Their disadvantages may include a lack of predictability and unequal treatment of sponsors.

A fourth type of legal strategy is for the government to set up model or standardized contracts for each BOT infrastructure sector, with a predetermined procedure for approval of tailor-made terms. This approach may streamline the process considerably, reduce legal costs and protect the parties against unbalanced or unexpected terms in the project agreements. This approach is well known from other international contractual arrangements and has been adopted by China and Pakistan.

It is not possible to say which project agreement terms should be left to the negotiating process and which should be determined by legislation, regulation or standardized contracts for each BOT sector. However, it is fair to say that the host country's legal framework for BOT arrangements must be firmly established and ascertainable prior to the tender proceedings.

## General business legislation

Although not directly associated with BOT infrastructure projects, a country's general business legislation may have a far-reaching impact on the implementation of BOT projects. Such projects will not fare well where property rights are unclear, the enforcement of contract rights is uncertain, there is no protection of intellectual property and there are other legal impediments to business activities.

Ideally, a country's existing business legislation should be compatible with the government's BOT objectives. It is outside the scope of the *Guidelines* to examine the broad range of business laws and regulations that directly or indirectly influence BOT activities. However, it can be said that general business legislation, to be supportive of BOT projects, should include nine elements.

- **Laws protecting property rights**

  Most fundamentally, property rights (ownership of land and project facilities or contractual licence to use them) must be clearly defined and protected by law. Obviously a project company cannot carry out a BOT project unless its right to use the project site and the project facilities are protected by law against interference from third parties.

- **Protection of property rights against expropriation and nationalization**

  Obviously, expropriation and nationalization of private infrastructure projects are contrary to the basic intent of the BOT approach. Sponsors and lenders will ask whether, in the event of political change, a new government will maintain the agreements made by the preceding government. Since all countries reserve their right to expropriate for public purpose, expropriation of BOT infrastructure projects should be subject to judicial review, and fair compensation for the owners of such projects should be guaranteed. The guarantee should be expressly provided for in the law of the host country.

- **A legal framework for intellectual property protection**

  A legal framework for intellectual property protection may include ratification of international agreements on intellectual property protection. Some developing countries grant preferential treatment for the import and/or transfer of advanced technology. Intellectual property protection has become increasingly important for BOT projects.

- **Contract enforceability**

  Enforceable agreements are the legal cornerstone of BOT arrangements. The contract laws of the host country must ensure that the long-term agreements between the BOT parties are legally binding and enforceable, including against the host government. The enforceability of contracts is of particular concern in countries without well-developed legal systems and legal institutions. Since the success of any BOT project depends on a complex system of underlying contractual arrangements, sponsors and lenders may seek to reduce the enforceability risk by requesting protective provisions in the contracts and by additional non-legal measures (see the following section).

- **Adequate corporate laws**

  Laws defining the rights and obligations of companies should be in place. These laws should include provisions for the establishment of companies, foreign ownership, limited liability operation of the companies, minority protection and/or sale or transfer of shares.

Government's Role

4

- **Legislation on leasing and franchising**
  Legislation setting up special business mechanisms such as leasing may be an important vehicle to support private participation in the development of infrastructure projects. This is particularly true in countries that do not permit private ownership of infrastructure facilities. The project company must at least be entitled to lease or have a contractual licence to use and occupy the land needed to carry out the project for the concession period without interference from third parties.

- **Bankruptcy legislation**
  Commercial liquidation, bankruptcy and insolvency legislation should also be in place. Loan agreements generally protect BOT lenders against default well before the bankruptcy stage. Bankruptcy and insolvency legislation may, however, provide a second line of defence for the project company's creditor.

- **Commercial banking and insurance legislation**
  A proper legal framework for the host country's banking system and financial laws, such as credit and insurance legislation, will be of concern to potential sponsors and lenders. Banking legislation may, for instance, be needed to authorize the transfer of project revenues to offshore revenue and retention accounts.

- **Environmental laws and labour laws**
  BOT sponsors and lenders need to know the host country's environmental and labour laws and regulations, first of all because they will of course have to be complied with but also because they will be a cost factor. Of crucial importance to project sponsors and lenders is whether future changes in environmental legislation that cannot be anticipated when the sponsors enter into long-term BOT obligations will apply to the project and, if so, who will pay for the added cost of compliance. To attract foreign sponsors and lenders, governments often offer some protection against material changes in the environmental legislation or they provide adequate assurance that the cost of compliance with such changes will be for the account of the host government.

## Protection of contract rights under the governing law and by adequate legal institutions

Even if a BOT strategy is supported by an adequate legal framework, the question arises whether the many BOT contracts and the supportive legislation will be respected and can be enforced by investors, constructors and operators. This means that a country's judicial system and other institutions must ensure the rule of law.

Various devices are used to ensure the enforceability of BOT contracts. Among these are traditional legal instruments, such as provisions for the resolution of disputes by internationally recognized arbitration. Waiver of sovereign immunity from suit and judicial enforcement is required in some countries to ensure the efficient application of the law.

The protection of contract rights may also be addressed in a number of non-judicial ways:

- Multinational sponsorship, preferably by respected foreign sponsors and investors.

- Investment or loan guarantees from the World Bank or one of the regional development banks.

- Loans and/or guarantees from the government export credit agencies of industrialized nations.

- Loans to the project in which a broad range of international banks participate, some having other loans to the country with cross-default clauses. Such arrangements can be strengthened by closely associating the bank syndicate loan with a loan to the same project by the World Bank or a regional development bank. It is unlikely that a developing country would intentionally risk harming its international credit standing by not paying amounts due to international lending organizations like the World Bank or to international commercial banks.

## Special legislation

Whether a specific BOT law should be enacted depends largely on a country's existing legislative framework. It may be easier to amend and supplement existing laws to fill any perceived gap or it may be more efficient to introduce a new body of law.

Some countries (the Philippines, Turkey and Viet Nam, for instance) have enacted rather comprehensive BOT laws and regulations in con-

Government's Role

4

nection with their BOT programmes. These laws address most of the legal issues discussed in this chapter, including authorization, required government approvals, preferential tax treatment, procurement issues and the framework for BOT project agreements. An alternative approach is to develop BOT legislation by stages. As a first step, the host government may establish minimum enabling legislation for BOT projects. The first BOT projects (pilot projects) based on that minimum legislation may then set the stage for a more detailed legal and regulatory framework, if it is needed. This approach was adopted by China and Pakistan.

There are significant advantages to having a specific BOT law:

- It helps foreign investors to find, with relative ease and in one place, the main legal provisions related to BOT projects.

- It provides readily available answers to the essential issues, such as the rights of foreign investors, procurement procedures and security requirements, involved in BOT projects.

- It clarifies and gives legal effect to the support and incentives to be provided by governments.

- It sends a clear and positive signal to potential investors of the government's commitment to develop BOT projects and, possibly, to government departments and local authorities who might otherwise not give their full support.

- It reduces the cost of drafting project contracts and the time needed to do this by reducing the number of conditions that need to be included in the contracts.

- It may mandate the protection of national interests.

Many of these positive effects can also be achieved by legal approaches other than a specific BOT law, in particular by the mandatory use of standardized BOT contracts for each infrastructure sector.

## ■ Administrative framework for BOT projects

The host government must establish a credible and efficient administrative framework to successfully implement its BOT strategy. Complicated bureaucratic procedures and lack of authority for administrators to make decisions are often cited as serious obstacles to BOT operations.

Since potential sponsors and lenders will carefully evaluate the organization, experience and procedures of the procuring administrative entity in the host country, an efficient administrative framework will considerably accelerate private sector investments in BOT projects.

There is no single ideal framework for the development of all BOT projects, as each country has its own administrative system and administrative culture. An analysis of existing BOT policies, however, can illustrate some typical problems and solutions to administrative issues.

## Planning and coordination

At the institutional level, most governments have appointed an internal focal point to formulate and coordinate their BOT policy. In some countries this point is in the ministry that has taken the BOT lead, such as the Water and Power Department Authority in Pakistan, the Ministry of Public Works in Chile, the Ministry of Finance in Argentina, the State Planning Commission in China and the Office of the Prime Minister in Malaysia. In other countries, such as the Philippines and Sri Lanka, the Governments have established high-level, intergovernmental committees as institutional focal points to formulate and administer BOT policy.

The institutional focal points for BOT projects have a wide range of responsibilities:

- Formulating government BOT policy and selecting sectors suitable for BOT projects.

- Proposing legislation and setting up administrative regulations to promote and monitor BOT projects.

- Setting up rules to rationalize and coordinate administrative procedures with ministries, government agencies and local authorities.

- Ensuring proper economic and financial analysis of BOT projects.

- Initiating the drafting of model or standardized project agreements and approving any deviations from such agreements.

- Identifying and prioritizing appropriate BOT projects in cooperation with the implementing ministries, government agencies and local authorities.

- Deciding on the procurement method to be applied to BOT projects and initiating and approving the drafting of procurement regulations for BOT projects.

- Examining and approving the development and implementation of BOT projects, including the use of consulting companies.

- Cutting through bureaucratic entanglements to ensure prompt approval and implementation of BOT projects.

The focal points are usually composed of high-level representatives from the government and the relevant ministries and of civil servants with experience and training in the technical, financial and legal aspects of BOT projects.

## Administration of BOT projects

Insufficient administrative preparation and organization can substantially delay the development and implementation of BOT projects. Accordingly, before inviting BOT proposals, the government should provide a clear framework within which they will be considered. A considerable amount of work can be done in advance, including economic analysis, market statistics and forecasts, feasibility studies, preparation of facility designs, drafting of legal documents and other tasks designed to avoid or solve problems that can be anticipated. Development banks or international organizations such as UNIDO can provide guidance to the host government in this important preparatory phase.

Since a BOT project will require approvals, permits and licences from several ministries, agencies and local authorities, it is desirable for the host government to coordinate in advance the policies and responsibilities of those entities. If this is done, the authorization proceedings will be clear and easy for the private sponsors to follow, avoiding costly and unnecessary delays; if it is not, they may be extremely time-consuming and frustrating.

Some countries and sponsors believe that the so-called one-window system is the most efficient approach to the administration of BOT projects. Under such a system the project company needs to deal with only one government office to obtain and renew all necessary approvals, permits and consents for the construction and operation of the project. In addition, that government office usually coordinates the decision-making process to expedite the project company's applications. A one-window system has been applied to administrative project management in several countries, for example, Ecuador, Malaysia, Pakistan and the Philippines.

Another method (or an additional one) of avoiding delays in obtaining approvals, permits and consents is to require in the project agreement (as a condition precedent for the contract obligations of the project company) that all such approvals, permits and consents that can be obtained prior to the construction of the project shall be in place at a specific date.

To avoid or shorten the long development phase that has characterized many BOT projects, the government should select its project team carefully. It should give the team clear authority to develop the particular BOT project and to cut through administrative obstacles. Most important, it should ensure that the team stays with the project through the financial closing, avoiding personnel changes in the middle of project development. This will ensure consistency in the government's position and give the private sector confidence that the host government is committed to closing the transaction.

### BOT training programmes for administrative personnel

Many administrative problems arise because government officials or local authorities are not fully familiar with the BOT concept. Administrative procedures to cope with international project financing and private sector participation in public infrastructure have not yet been sufficiently developed in many countries.

Any government deciding to apply the BOT approach to infrastructure projects should, therefore, consider training its administrative personnel to understand and appraise BOT schemes as well as to tailor the project terms to meet government objectives.

## ▪ Government incentives and other forms of support

### The type and extent of government incentives and support

Host governments must recognize the need to provide incentives and some direct or indirect support in almost all BOT projects. The extent and type of support varies considerably, depending, among other things, on the country risks, the feasibility of the project, the country's need for the project and the competitive position of the host government. Although host governments do not normally provide equity, loans or direct guarantees for loans, they have used a wide range of indirect financial support mechanisms to advance BOT projects. Some of these mechanisms are discussed below.

## Tax incentives and concessions

Most foreign investment codes make special tax regimes available for private investors. Investors in BOT projects should, of course, enjoy the same tax concessions. The tax regime of a host country greatly influences the financing of BOT projects. While tax concessions are not a direct infusion of capital, they have many of the same effects by reducing cash flow needed for operating expenses.

It should, however, be recognized that tax concessions are not an inherent part of BOT arrangements. Private investors will naturally ask for tax exemptions, tax holidays and similar concessions for their BOT project. They have, for example, sought tax relief from host governments to compensate for taxes on dividends levied by their home country. Special tax concessions should be carefully analysed and offered only when they will benefit the BOT project or are needed to attract foreign investors.

Tax regimes for foreign-sponsored projects may include the following features:

- Exemption from corporate tax for the concession period (tax "holiday").

- Exemption from income tax for foreign project staff.

- Exemption from or reduction of real estate tax.

- Exemption from or reduction of import duties on equipment, raw materials and components for the construction, operation and maintenance of the project.

- Tax concession on royalties.

- Tax refunds for foreign investors reinvesting their profits in new infrastructure projects in the country.

- Deductions from taxable income for the cost of logistical supplies such as electricity, water and transport.

- Capital allowances in the form of depreciation and amortization.

- Tax concessions and the like must be assessed on a case-by-case basis. An important consideration for the host government when determining the type of tax relief to be granted is whether the taxes paid to it may be eligible for a tax credit in the home country of the sponsor. A host government should review the contents and applicability of the sponsor's national tax legislation so it can take them into account in a fair manner in its BOT strategy.

## Land and other logistical facilities to be provided by the government

In most BOT projects, the host government provides support in one or more of the following forms:

- Commonly, governments provide the land on which the project is to be built. Such land lease or land transfer provisions are important prerequisites for the financing of a BOT project. They should cover a term equal to the project's life and include all the easements over adjoining property necessary to provide full access to the project, including land for connecting roads, water supplies, energy transmission lines and so forth. Some BOT agreements provide for the reimbursement of the cost of this support over the concession period or after 10-15 years, that is at the end of the loan repayment period. In any case, it is advisable that the host government or its agencies acquire the land for the project.

- In some projects the host government constructs associated infrastructure facilities, including access roads, transmission lines and communications.

- The government may ensure the availability of labour during the construction and operating period, although the project company must of course comply with the labour laws of the host country.

- In some projects the government ensures that the building materials and raw materials needed for the construction and operation of the project are available. This is particularly important when there are local monopoly suppliers of cement, steel and other basic materials. Private sector sponsors may insist on a government guarantee for the allocation of sufficient supplies to the project at a reasonable price. Usually the government also ensures the supply of electricity and water and telecommunication facilities.

- Governments must normally ensure that the various private parties, sponsors, equipment suppliers and O&M contractors are free to import plant and materials and that duties and taxes are non-discriminatory.

## Contribution of existing assets by the host government

In some BOT projects the host governments have contributed to the projects by awarding the sponsors the right to operate and to earn revenues from existing assets. For instance, in the North-South Highway project in Malaysia, the sponsors were awarded the right to earn tolls from the existing 300-kilometre expressway. In the Bangkok Second-Stage Expressway project, it was agreed that tolls from the existing First-Stage Expressway would be shared between the private sponsors and the government at an agreed ratio.

In Thailand, a BOT proposal to build and operate a 60-kilometre elevated rail and toll road system for 38 years included the sponsor's right to develop commercial and residential complexes at stations through which the transport system was to run.

In the Sydney Harbour Tunnel project, the sponsors obtained the concession to operate the existing Sydney bridge as one of the incentives. To finance the new project, the bridge toll was increased to the same level as the toll for the tunnel.

Such incentives not only provide additional revenue but may also make it possible to have lower fares than would otherwise have been required to make the project economically viable.

## Power purchase agreement

The power purchase agreement (PPA) between the government utility or agency and the project company is a central contract in the vast majority of BOT power plant projects. From the obligations set forth in the PPA, basic resources (or cash flow) are provided to meet (a) debt service, (b) operation and maintenance costs and (c) return on investment. For this reason, the terms of the PPA and the creditworthiness of the power purchaser are key factors in the private sponsor's and the lender's assessment of the risk of a BOT power project in developing countries.

PPAs have usually been on take-or-pay terms equal to the life of the project or at least as long as the terms of the loans. A take-or-pay PPA is an unconditional obligation to make periodic payments for an agreed quantity of available electricity whether the purchaser takes the electricity or not. In other words, it is an obligation for the purchaser to pay for the capacity of a power plant.

The obligation to take or pay may be in a variety of forms. Typically the obligation to pay for the agreed capacity of the plant is not subject to counter-claims and exceptions. The termination rights of the utility and the project company are limited and subject to the rights of the lenders. Therefore take-or-pay contracts are called indirect guarantees.

If lenders to a BOT-financed power plant are relying on a take-or-pay PPA for repayment of the loans, the payment will be in an amount sufficient to both service the project company's debt and pay fixed and variable operating expenses of the plant.

The PPA and the terms and conditions of this contract heavily influence the lenders' risk evaluation of the project. The greater the risk or perceived risk to the projected revenue stream, the higher the price for the financing. Thus, to reduce the risk to the revenue stream, the take-or-pay term has become an important instrument.

The creditworthiness of the government utility signing a take-or-pay PPA has sometimes been supported by a performance guarantee from the host government at the request of the sponsors or lenders to the project.

The task of establishing and drafting the content of a PPA usually requires detailed economic analysis, reflecting the uniqueness and complexity of each power plant project. In general, the key issues of a PPA are capacity or quantity of available power; electricity (or power) purchase charge or price, normally in terms of a capacity charge for fixed costs and an energy charge for costs associated with operating the plant; tariff adjustment scheme; duration of contract; prolongation of contract; billing and payment procedure; and payment schedule.

A detailed power supply procedure, including dispatch principles, voltages control and monitoring, abnormal operation and accident management, operation records, communication systems and inspections, has to be arranged for, preferably in an appendix to the PPA.

When using a competitive bidding approach for BOT power plant projects, the PPA can be incorporated in the bidding documents as a supplement to the project agreement.

## Fuel supply support

The availability of fuel and the reliability of its supply during the concession period may be crucial to the revenue stability of BOT projects, particularly those in the energy sector. Normally the private sponsors and the lenders will require that the government commission an independent study on the availability of the particular fuel from national or regional sources, alternative foreign sources, import restrictions, adequacy of the delivery systems etc.

This issue, however, is of less concern to the sponsors and lenders if the central government signs a long-term fuel supply and transportation agreement. If either the supplier or transporter of fuel is a government agency, performance guarantees from the central government may be required.

## Government guarantees and stand-by financing

The host government in some cases provides indirect guarantees and stand-by financing to advance the project. In theory, the BOT concept is the opposite of traditional sovereign borrowing. However, to encourage foreign investors and to assist in the structuring of financial packages for BOT projects, host governments may provide indirect guarantees to sponsors and lenders, stand-by financing and even support loans on a case-by-case basis. In the Malaysian North-South Highway project, for example, the Government provided a stand-by loan for the first 17 years of the 30-year concession period, to be paid if there is any shortfall in the traffic volume forecast. In addition, it provided a stand-by loan to cover adverse exchange rates and interest movements in external loans.

The different forms of financial support that governments have provided to advance BOT projects are now described briefly.

### Indirect guarantee of operating income and stand-by loans

Indirect guarantees of revenue by means of long-term off-take agreements are common in certain countries and in certain BOT sectors, particularly the energy sector. A government may cover the risk of non-payment by a performance guarantee under which it guarantees the public utility's performance of its obligations to the project company as they fall due. The central bank of the country may need to approve the indirect performance guarantee. The government may also mobilize risk guarantee facilities for project finance from development banks to hedge its guarantee to sponsors and lenders covering non-performance of government contractual obligations.

Toll road, tunnel or bridge projects with a substantial demand risk may require some form of government support (a guarantee or risk-sharing). In the Sydney Harbour Tunnel project, the project company was guaranteed a minimum income from traffic tolls. Similarly, the Government of Pakistan guaranteed a fixed minimum percentage of the projected traffic level for a toll road project. Such guarantees are exceptions, but those that are given should be structured so that the return is dependent on operational efficiency. Provisions to share profits above a certain level may be included in the project agreement, thereby protecting the national interest.

In some BOT projects in Malaysia, Pakistan and Turkey, the host governments have agreed to make loans available on a stand-by basis over a certain period of time. The loans can be called on for senior debt service if revenues fall below a certain minimum. This was the mechanism used in the North-South Expressway project in Malaysia, referred to above. In Pakistan and Turkey, the governments have also agreed to make stand-by loans available to provide for senior debt service if and when the project company's cash flow is insufficient for such purpose owing to specific *force majeure* events.

### Protection against the loss of expected revenues due to competing projects

The host government may have to give the project company some protection from competition to ensure the expected revenues. This may be particularly important in toll road projects, where an additional road could undercut the revenue flow. Protection from the consequences of competition is briefly discussed in the section on assurance against a competing project.

### Guarantee of commercial freedom

In the Eurotunnel project, the project company was guaranteed commercial freedom, including the right to determine its tariffs. This appears to be an exception. Although the success of a BOT project is significantly affected by the government's willingness to allow the services of the project to be sold at a price sufficient to generate a reasonable return to investors, changes in agreed tariffs, tolls etc. are usually regulated by detailed contract terms subject to government approval.

### Subsidy support

An alternative to the full commercial freedom to determine tariffs, tolls etc. is for the government to provide revenue support to cover the difference between the full commercial price and the actual user charges. A project may be subsidized by revenue support so as to retain the incentive for private sector efficiency. However, the need for such subsidy financing may reduce the creditworthiness of a public sector project if the long-term sustainability of the subsidy guarantee is politically questionable. Revenue support, moreover, is somewhat difficult to manage in that it requires ongoing monitoring to measure and control project output and administer subsidy payments.

### Currency exchange protection

Loans to BOT projects in developing countries are often in foreign currency, and lenders usually expect repayment to be in the same currency. Sponsors and lenders therefore often require guarantees from the government:

- Convertibility: that it is permitted to change local currency for foreign currency.

- Availability: that sufficient foreign currency will be available in the host country.

- Transferability: that it is permitted to remit the foreign currency to foreign bank accounts.

A further risk is that the exchange rate will depreciate faster than the agreed increase in revenue (more precisely, that local inflation will increase faster than that of the currency of borrowing). Lenders will not normally accept this form of risk, particularly where turbulent macroeconomic conditions make it difficult to predict the future real exchange rate. The different methods of covering foreign exchange risks are discussed in Chapter 8.

### Interest rate reimbursement

High inflation in the host country will have a significant impact on the equity returns and preservation of the value of the sponsors' investment. In cases where the private sponsors were given an interest rate guarantee by the host government, they will be reimbursed if the interest rate increases by more than a stipulated percentage during the project period.

### Uninsurable force majeure events

*Force majeure* risks that cannot be covered by insurance at a reasonable premium may pose a difficult problem for BOT projects. Lenders are rarely willing to take *force majeure* risks, and sponsors are unwilling to protect the lenders against the economic effects of uninsured *force majeure* events exceeding their own equity investment. This means that some form of government support for uninsurable *force majeure* risks is usually required by sponsors and lenders.

One government remedy to mitigate the effects of some *force majeure* events is to provide the sponsors with an extension of the contract period equal in length to the time during which the *force majeure* event had an effect, provided, of course, that the effect was only for a limited period. If a *force majeure* event impedes or altogether prevents the operation of the project for a longer period, buy-out provisions or termination compensation provisions may provide adequate protection for the sponsors and their lenders.

Similar remedies, including compensation provisions, may provide some protection against political risks such as expropriation, military events and substantial and adverse changes of laws. Guarantee facilities from international financial institutions, such as the World Bank and the Multilateral Investment Guarantee Agency (MIGA), can hedge government guarantees for some uninsurable *force majeure* events and political risks.

### *Summary*

Governments can provide financial support and undertakings that are not formally government guarantees and sovereign loans but that are sufficient to provide credit support. When drafting provisions for the host government's support of the financing for a BOT project, much care should be taken to promote the incentives for private sector efficiency that are such an important part of the BOT concept.

## Loans and equity contributions

Very few BOT projects have received direct loans from host governments. In the Sydney Harbour Tunnel project, the Government provided a substantial loan to finance the construction costs. In the Malaysian Expressway project, a support loan was given by the host Government to bridge the loan repayment to the banks payable after 17 years. But these examples appear to be exceptions.

Direct equity investment from host governments, their agencies or local authorities has been proposed in some BOT projects. Such participation in project equity may have the advantage of assuring government involvement in and support for the implementation and operation of the project. It may also help to strengthen the government's monitoring of the projects.

If there is a shortage of foreign exchange for government equity, money from bilateral or multilateral aid may be used for this purpose. Shifting such aid from the straightforward funding of public sector projects to the financing of government equity contributions to private sector projects may overcome critical constraints on the financing of BOT infrastructure projects.

# Assurance of no competing projects

To analyse the feasibility of a BOT project and to obtain financing, private sponsors must be reasonably certain what the demand – and thus the revenue – will be once the project is completed. To ensure that the anticipated demand is not threatened by competition, the private sponsors and their lenders will seek assurance that competing public or private infrastructure projects will not be undertaken, at least until certain revenue thresholds are met. In a toll road project, for instance, sponsors and lenders often want assurance that no new parallel toll or non-toll roads will be built or no existing roads will be materially improved that would compete for the same traffic.

The point for the host government is to balance the sponsors' need for assurance and stability with the country's need to continue the development of infrastructure sectors. A BOT arrangement cannot be allowed to frustrate future improvements and expansions of a country's or a locality's transportation system. The private sponsors should therefore be offered protection against competing projects only as long as the BOT project can satisfy the current demand and continuously provide the quality of service required.

In offering the sponsors some protection from competition, host governments should also be careful not to create monopolies that put national consumers at a disadvantage.

# Completion and performance incentives and penalties

BOT projects can, and should, be structured to give the project company a strong incentive to meet its obligations and to achieve, if possible, a higher level of performance than forecast. One way to achieve this objective is to include a bonus arrangement in the project agreements based on the degree to which the project company exceeds projections. Bonus incentives, which can be lump sum or percentage payments made to the project company, are of different types:

- A signature bonus is a lump sum amount payable if the project agreement is signed by a date stipulated in the BOT proposal. This payment is an incentive to the sponsor to accelerate negotiation activity and tends to encourage compromise on issues that are not really material but that might otherwise unduly prolong the negotiation period.

- A completion bonus is a sum payable if construction of the project facilities is completed before the date stipulated in the project agreement. An earlier completion may improve the economic viability of the project to a degree that far outweighs the amount of the completion bonus. Such a bonus is not, however, an essential ingredient of BOT arrangements. Indeed, the BOT approach contains a strong, inherent incentive for the project company to complete construction ahead of schedule. Earlier completion simply means a longer operation period and thus more revenue for the project company. Indeed the construction time for a number of BOT projects has been considerably shorter than anticipated in the project agreements. In some projects, a longer-than-anticipated construction period may have been written into the project agreement in order to address the risk of delay. Governments are advised to carefully consider, on a case-by-case basis, whether an additional completion bonus should be offered to a project company.

- A performance bonus is an amount payable if the output of the project (for instance, the production of a water supply system or a power plant) exceeds a stipulated level. Some countries, like Pakistan, have made the performance bonus system for power infrastructure projects more attractive to sponsors by stipulating a rather low target for productivity in the project agreements. The project sponsors are thus able to obtain a higher return on investment as their productivity rises. Obviously, it is important that the incentives a host government offers are consistent with its main project objectives. Where earlier completion and higher productivity clearly bring economic and financial benefits to the country and facility users, the government may consider introducing an element of progressivity into the bonus provision.

Normally, completion and performance bonuses are balanced by penalties for failure to meet performance targets. Penalty provisions must be tailored to the individual contract. For example, it is not realistic to impose penalties far beyond the expected profits of the project company. In most cases penalties are stipulated as a percentage of the revenue from the project for the period in which performance falls below base-case expectations. For instance, in the Labuan Water Supply project in Malaysia, if the project company fails to supply the specified quality or the daily minimum quantity of water, it will have to pay to the host government a penalty equal to a certain percentage of the agreed monthly payment.

**Government's Role**

**4**

# Attractive risk-reward provisions

There is no better incentive than to give private BOT sponsors the possibility of an attractive return on their investments. The sponsors should be entitled to an attractive return, as determined by competitive market standards, if they succeed in meeting the BOT project's economic and contractual objectives.

The risk-reward issue raises two fundamental questions. The first involves the proper allocation and sharing of risk between the host government and the project sponsors. Unrealistic expectations of what can be accomplished by private sector participation in infrastructure projects may complicate the risk allocation. It is not uncommon for governments to propose BOT projects in the expectation that all project risks should rest entirely with the private sector until the date of the transfer of the project facility to the government. Governments tend to ignore or undervalue the risks they normally take in similar public sector projects. This has led to extreme government positions on risk issues in some cases, long delays in other cases and the abandonment of otherwise sound BOT proposals in still others. Obviously, achieving the right balance in risk allocation and arriving at a satisfactory basis for evaluating a BOT proposal requires a realistic valuation of the project risks.

In principle, the private sponsors of a BOT project should take all the basic project risks, i.e. the risks associated with construction, completion and performance. These would include cost overruns and operating failures as well as liquidated damages. However, serious private sponsors will normally be reluctant to take general risks beyond their control, such as country (political) risks. Host governments must therefore be willing to take or share risks such as expropriation and nationalization risks, foreign exchange risks, some uninsured *force majeure* risks and the consequence of changes in the legal regime. A rational risk allocation will greatly increase the attractiveness of a BOT project to sponsors, lenders and contractors. The issues of risk allocation and risk management in BOT projects are discussed in detail in chapter 8.

The second risk-reward question involves how to structure the level of return to the sponsors to give it some reasonable relationship to their assumptions of risk. Private investors are naturally unwilling to participate in a higher risk project at a lower-than-reasonable rate of return. On the other hand, an inflated rate of return that is not commensurate with the private risk assumption may create the perception that the sponsor is taking advantage of the host country. Possible solutions, including mechanisms that capture a portion of windfall (excess) profits but do not discourage high profitability, will be further discussed in chapter 11. One accepted mechanism is to allow the project company to earn a certain maximum on its equity investment (after taxes) and then to distribute excess revenue between the company and the government entity according to a pre-arranged formula. Thus, the public also benefits if the project is very successful. Such an arrangement may help to overcome the mistrust that can arise when public and private entities work together.

## ■ Government commitment to conclude BOT projects within a reasonable time

A government must be seen by project sponsors and lenders to have a credible commitment to conclude a BOT transaction within a reasonable time. Failure by host governments to adhere to reasonable time schedules for the development phases of BOT projects has caused enormous frustration among project sponsors, and many competent, well-financed sponsors have ruled out doing business in some developing countries for this reason.

Schedules need to be adhered to because the cost to sponsors of retaining a project team is very high and may increase the overall costs of the process considerably. Moreover, when the procurement process goes on beyond a reasonable time, lenders, contractors and suppliers become reluctant to extend lending commitments or give firm quotes for supplies and equipment, a serious drawback for the packaging of a BOT project. The basic assumptions underlying a BOT project may also change fundamentally during a lengthy development phase. An unduly protracted development phase often means starting all over again, with new bidders and all the delay and additional expense that entails.

A clearly defined and reasonably tight time schedule for the project development phase is therefore essential for BOT projects to attract sponsors and lenders. It is recommended that the host government should require firm bids and should set up and adhere to realistic target dates (milestones) in the BOT tender invitations for the bidding and the development process, leading up to the eventual signing date. This is also important in the exceptional cases where the procuring government entity engages in direct negotiations with a private sponsor company (single-source procurement). At an early stage of the negotiations, the host government, together with the sponsors, should agree on a schedule and then take all reasonable steps to meet it.

# ▪ Summary

The government's approach to the issues discussed in this chapter will determine to a large extent whether private sponsors and lenders decide to participate in BOT projects in a developing country. If the government takes a proactive approach, the private sector's interest will be considerably greater. The more encouragement and assistance private sponsors receive from a host government, the better able that government will be to compete for private sector participation in infrastructure projects in the face of growing demand worldwide.

# TRANSFER OF TECHNOLOGY AND CAPABILITY BUILDING THROUGH BOT PROJECTS

5

Technology Transfer

Chapter 5 discusses how the host government should seek to maximize two of the benefits of BOT projects: local capability building and the transfer of technology from the project company sponsors and contractors into the local economy. In these *Guidelines*, the term technology denotes the sum of knowledge, experience and skills necessary for planning, engineering, implementing and operating an infrastructure project, including the managerial and marketing aspects. The issue of technology transfer through such an infrastructure project is complex, because the transfer involves not only services, equipment and production processes but also capability building and research and development activities. Since the discussion here focuses on BOT projects in developing countries, it is framed in terms of the general relationship between foreign investment and transfer of technology.

Foreign investment has traditionally been a source of technology for manufacturing sectors in developing countries. A significant flow of new techniques and processes has followed in the wake of foreign capital investments, often made by large corporations, whether through wholly owned subsidiaries or controlled joint ventures. Allowing foreign companies full or at least controlling ownership of the enterprise is often a precondition for advanced and sophisticated foreign technology to be made available to developing countries.

Since legislation in most developing countries customarily required that infrastructure projects be publicly owned and operated, the infrastructure was implemented and run by the public utilities, and foreign private participation was on a much smaller scale than in the manufacturing sector, generally being limited to construction and the supply of equipment.

Foreign contractors and suppliers usually left a project after the works or installation was completed and their contractual obligations fulfilled. Under a turnkey arrangement, such obligations were usually fulfilled within a year or less of completion. The failure to secure a transfer of advanced technology from the contractors and suppliers over the long term and to implement capacity-building programmes might have contributed to the high rate of breakdowns, lengthy interruptions and high maintenance costs in infrastructure projects in some developing countries.

The BOT approach gives host countries an opportunity to promote effective technology transfer and capability building over the long term. In this approach, foreign contractors and equipment suppliers usually form part of the sponsor group and therefore are interested in the good performance of the project throughout the concession period. They are

**5**

**Technology Transfer**

motivated to provide advanced technology and training to the project company, as well as to local workers, subcontractors and suppliers, to ensure that local delivery and services meet the efficiency and quality standards needed to implement, operate and maintain the project.

Properly structured BOT projects can thus provide for the transfer of advanced technology, reducing developing countries' dependence on foreign technology and enhancing their technological self-reliance.

# ■ Overview

## The potential for technology transfer

The BOT concept provides a good opportunity for a country to obtain and use advanced technology. The sponsors and contractors make such technology available because it helps the project company to more precisely meet the project technical specifications, as well as to maximize the economic advantage of the project. The host country benefits, in turn, because power or other services are produced at a lower cost to industrial users and individual users.

However, certain sophisticated technology may not be made available to infrastructure projects in developing countries unless the company that owns it is assured of control over or protection of the technology, which is the case under the BOT concept.

The BOT concept ensures that a technology is upgraded throughout the long concession period, for doing so serves to increase revenue. The challenge to the host country is to ensure that the project agreement and other contracts require the project company to fully transfer the technology and all its improvements into the local economy during the concession period.

The BOT concept also provides an opportunity for employing and training nationals in the development, construction and operation of the infrastructure facilities. It is important for a project agreement to stipulate that such training must be carried out throughout the concession period, so that more and more national personnel are employed in all phases of a project and are ready to take over its operation at the end of the concession period.

Typically, a project agreement and the associated contracts will insist on participation by those local companies that are internationally competitive in the development, construction, operation and maintenance of project facilities. Such a requirement contributes to capability building and enhances the competitiveness of national industries and services. Similarly, provision may be made to transfer the project technology to the government at the end of the concession period. In particular, the operation and transfer obligations of the project company may include the obligation to use up-to-date technology on the project.

Certain BOT projects may be structured to provide for cooperation between the project company, which will be operating in the host country for the long concession period, and national companies in such downstream activities as research and development and joint ventures for manufacturing equipment and components. Technological cooperation of this sort may open the door for further profitable cooperation in the international market. This has been the case where advanced technology developed for local conditions in the host country proves to be appropriate to other countries as well.

In short, the use and transfer of advanced technology is one of the main benefits of the BOT concept. At least one country (Norway) has used the BOT concept systematically as a springboard to develop national technology at the highest level.

## Mechanisms for promoting technology transfer in BOT projects

The extent of technology transfer will depend on the nature of the particular BOT project and the care taken by the host government in structuring the project. A number of legal mechanisms should be considered in formulating a practical and progressive technology transfer strategy. One mechanism is to have in place legal and regulatory requirements such as the following:

- Minimum technical, safety and environmental standards for infrastructure projects.

- Protection and acquisition of technological innovations throughout the concession period, and transfer of the project technology at the end of the period.

- Competitive national companies as suppliers of goods and services to the BOT project.

- Training programmes for nationals at all levels throughout the concession period.

Obviously, legislation and regulations can do no more than provide a framework for the promotion of technology transfer, with the details being

**5**

**Technology Transfer**

left to the drafting of the project agreement and other related contracts. They may, however, strengthen the hand of the government unit engaged in BOT arrangements and ensure that all relevant technology transfer issues are considered by the parties.

The bidding procedures themselves may be structured so as to include criteria that promote the transfer of technology. Both the government's tender documents and the bidders' proposals can be made to address the government's technology transfer requirements. In addition, a bidder's past record for transfer of technology has in some countries been a factor in awarding the BOT concessions.

Another essential mechanism for realizing the potential of BOT projects for transfer of technology is, of course, the project agreement. The technology to be used for the project design and construction, maintenance and operation requirements, requirements for the use of national companies, capability building through training and employment, protection of innovations and so forth can all be set forth in reasonably precise terms in a project agreement. Examples of such provisions are provided in the sections that follow.

There is one further mechanism to promote the transfer of technology: a government may provide a range of incentives, including tax relief, preferred status for future projects and the right to downstream activities. It should be noted that the project sponsor's stay in the host country for a long concession period and the prospects of its participation in future infrastructure projects there may give it a very real incentive for cooperating with national companies on technology transfer, on the sharing of innovations and on research and development.


# ▪ Selection and acquisition of technology

## Suitability for local conditions

In principle, it is the government that sets the rules for selecting the technology for a BOT project. The selection process usually passes through several stages, from the feasibility study through the preliminary and detailed designs of the project, to the drafting of project specifications in the tender document and, finally, to the evaluation of bids.

Where a technology is fairly well known to the government, or where the government wants a particular technology because it is consistent with that used in other similar projects in the country, the government may give detailed instructions in its tender documents. If the technological requirements are not foreordained or the government is not fully aware of all the technological solutions and wants to draw on the prospective bidders' knowledge and innovative skills, the project requirements may be set out only broadly in the tender documents.

In any case, it is important for the government to ensure that the technology most appropriate to local conditions is adopted. The technology applied to an infrastructure project must be compatible with nationally available inputs and with the present and projected demands of the country. The most advanced and sophisticated technology sector may not be the most appropriate technology: less sophisticated techniques that rely on indigenous factor inputs and skills may better serve the national interest.

## Reliability of the technology

Lenders to a BOT project will usually insist that the project uses well-established technologies and engineering practices. The lack of experience with innovative and experimental technologies, the uncertainty associated with them and the risks they pose to the reliable operation of a project normally make lenders hesitant to finance them. New and unproven technology is therefore unlikely to be financed in the absence of a guarantee from a strong and credible sponsor.

This consideration aside, the selection of the most appropriate technology is still a key issue in BOT projects, because there are important differences even among standard and proven technologies that may have considerable impact on developing countries. In addition, there may always be some potential for innovative steps to be introduced into standard and proven technologies.

Finally, it should be noted that very innovative and advanced technology available has been applied to some projects financed by BOT arrangements, for example those for the exploration of oil in the North Sea. In the final analysis, the critical issue for the lenders may not so much be whether a technology is established or innovative but whether it can be proven to be reliable.

## Acquisition of the selected technology

The technology used in a BOT project is normally an integral part of the bid package. Sponsors are often established construction and equipment supply companies that have their own technological base and do not need to purchase technology. If they need to acquire technology for a project, it is mostly to cover specific gaps in their technological knowledge.

**5**

**Technology Transfer**

Host governments need to review the arrangements for transfer of technology from sponsors (or their parent company) to the project company, as they vary considerably. In some cases, there is no specific charge for supplying technology and ensuring the flow of technology service and components throughout the concession period. In others, the cost of the technology is considered to be a capital contribution to the project company. In still other cases, additional payment may be demanded for technology services provided during the operation of the project. While such demands for payment are not necessarily unfair, a government needs to scrutinize them to make sure it is not being overcharged.

# ▪Transfer of technology through the use of national goods and services

## Current BOT legislation and project agreement provisions

One way of transferring technology through BOT projects is to give domestic companies the opportunity to participate in BOT projects as suppliers of goods and services. Some concession codes and project agreements insist that the project company afford some measure of preference for national goods and services, provided that they are available on competitive terms and conditions. One such requirement is expressed in a Malaysian project agreement:

*"Local materials and services: Subject to satisfactory quality, availability and timely delivery, the Company shall use local materials and services in the construction and maintenance of the Works."*

Norwegian Concession Code for Petroleum Activities, Section 54.1, provides as follows:

*"In connection with activities covered by this act, competitive Norwegian suppliers shall be given genuine opportunities to secure orders for deliveries of goods and services."*

International procurement rules such as the Uruguay Round Agreement on Government Procurement and the World Bank Guidelines on Procurement provide some limits for the use of local suppliers. For example, World Bank procurement policy would allow, under certain conditions, a cost difference of 15 per cent in favour of domestically manufactured goods and of 7.5 per cent in favour of domestic contractors.

The objective of such provisions is clearly to encourage the participation of domestic companies, in order to strengthen their capabilities and their competitiveness. Experience suggests that the involvement of domestic suppliers in the development, construction, maintenance and operation of BOT projects may be a great help in national capability building and other forms of technology transfer.

## Four principles for increasing local participation

General calls for the participation of domestic companies in BOT projects have not always been heeded closely by foreign project companies. In a number of projects it appears that such companies have preferred to award subcontracts to suppliers of their own nationality. To underscore the importance of building national capability, some governments have acted to enforce four principles (see box 5):

- Domestic suppliers must be included in all invitations to tender for subcontracts provided they offer the goods and services required.

- The project company must award the contract to domestic bidders whenever they are competitive and must in any case take the domestic content into account when evaluating foreign bidders.

- The project company must report to the host government all tendering for subcontracts and the tendering and proposed awards to domestic suppliers so that the government can monitor national capability building through subcontracting.

- The monitored record of a project company will be an evaluation criterion when the project company is bidding for future BOT concessions.

**5**

**Technology Transfer**

"Article 12. Use of domestic goods and services

12.1    Companies shall use domestic goods and services in the performance of the work in so far as they are competitive with regard to quality, service, schedule of delivery and price.

12.2    Domestic contractors shall be included in invitations for tenders for subcontracts in so far as they provide goods or rent services of the kind required.

12.3    In evaluating offers given by domestic or foreign bidders for subcontracting portions of the work, oompanies shall take into account the extent to which bidders will use domestic goods and services.

1·2.4   Contractors shall be responsible for the observation of these provisions by their subcontractors.

12.5    When evaluating bids for future concessions, the ministry shall take into account the extent to which companies have used domestic goods and services."

# ■ Transfer of technology through training and employment of nationals

## Typical provisions in existing BOT project agreements

Another important benefit to be gained from BOT projects relates to the transfer of technology through training and employment of nationals. Given the importance of this issue for the operation of BOT projects after the concession period and for the adequate absorption of technology, surprisingly few project agreements include more than casual provisions on training and education of nationals. Such provisions, which are usually found in construction contracts, require only that the project company train and employ national subjects "as far as practical", or they give the project company "the right to select a number of nationals for training and education" or obligate it to grant scholarships to seminars or universities in the project company's home country. Procedures to monitor compliance or to impose sanctions in the case of non-compliance are rarely provided for or effectively used.

The following provision in a standard project agreement was drafted by an experienced government unit. It exemplifies a more thorough and serious approach to technology transfer through training and employment:

*"From the commencement of the construction work and continuing to the Transfer Date, the project company shall arrange for training of the government's personnel. Such training shall be both theoretical and practical and include technical, administrative, business, operational and other functions which the government may wish to cover. The government may in this connection nominate national personnel as counterparts to expatriates and demand that a reasonable number of its employees shall work in the project companies' organization, in order to have proper and relevant on-the-spot-training in all aspects of the activities. In such event, the government shall pay wages and other expenses such as board, lodging and travelling expenses for its personnel. To a reasonable extent, the government shall have access to the project companies' internal courses. The project company must inform the government of courses to be arranged in due time. If the project company fails to effect training referred to in this article (refer to the liquidated damages article)."*

This sort of provision adequately defines the project company's obligation to train and employ nationals. The next step, of course, is to ensure that compliance with the provision is monitored by the government.

## Drafting and implementing training and employment provisions

A host government's objectives for training and employment of nationals may be summarized as follows:

- Training and employment of national personnel in the construction and ongoing operations and maintenance of the project in order to build capabilities in the different phases of a BOT project.

- Training and employment of national personnel so that after the transfer they will be able to independently operate and maintain the project.

**5**

**Technology Transfer**

- Training and employment should pertain not only to personnel who manage and operate the project, but also to government personnel with supervisory responsibilities.

The need to employ and train the local workforce differs, of course, from country to country, depending on the extent to which personnel with the relevant skills and competence have already been developed, and from project to project. Certain basic principles may, however, be considered by host governments when drafting or negotiating employment and training provisions in BOT-related contracts:

- The government may require the project company to supply an organizational chart showing the personnel requirements for the development, construction, operation and maintenance of the project. The minimum technical and other qualifications for the personnel should be specified in sufficient detail for the government to determine the extent of training and employment required. If practical, the government's prequalification process should require such information.

- It is advisable for the government to clearly define in an appendix to the project agreement the categories and numbers of national personnel to be trained as well as the specific training obligations of the project company in relation to each category. It may also be advisable to define the qualifications of trainees for each category or position, including linguistic abilities. Experience suggests that later misunderstandings between the project company and the host government can be avoided by specifying the qualifications of trainees in the contract.

- The training should be undertaken as much as possible inside the host country and on-the-job. While training seminars in the sponsors' own facilities in their home countries may prove useful in certain circumstances, the skills needed to operate and maintain a BOT project are usually best acquired through on-the-job experience. The best concept for on-the-job training may be so-called "ghost" training, in which nationals are assigned as counterparts to expatriates in crucial operational and managerial positions.

- In formulating training obligations for BOT projects, time schedules are of paramount importance. The objective of the government is to ensure that the necessary training is completed well before the concession period ends, so that a competent national staff and workforce can take over the operation of the project. It can be achieved by systematically arranging the training of nationals throughout the duration of the project. The project company should, in addition, be obligated to prove prior to transfer that the project's technology has been mastered efficiently and effectively by the national personnel who will assume responsibility for operation and maintenance.

- The technological information needed to operate and maintain a BOT project is also conveyed in technical documentation, including drawings, manuals, quality assurance programmes and computer programmes. Adequate training of nationals requires their participation in developing, organizing and utilizing such documentation. The project documentation should be available to government personnel for operating and maintaining the project and as future reference for similar projects.

- A yearly audit of training and employment programmes and special reports on important aspects of such programmes will emphasize their importance and ensure that they are faithfully carried out.

## ■ Transfer of project technology at the expiry of the concession period

### Technology transfer as part of the transfer of ownership

The technology pertaining to a BOT project is normally transferred along with the ownership at the end of the concession period. The government will naturally receive the right to use the project technology, including the technology embodied in the machinery and equipment. This is an adequate solution for the government, providing that national employees have been trained to operate and maintain the equipment and technology.

In BOT projects that involve patented or otherwise protected technology, the government may insist on a transfer provision in the project agreement, whereby the project company is obligated to grant, free of charge, a licence to use the technology after the transfer of the project. One may find such provisions in the project agreements under the heading "Patents" or "Licences and patents". A typical provision reads:

*"The project company grants the government an irrevocable, royalty-free, non-exclusive licence, under all patents now or hereafter owned or controlled by the project company, to the extent necessary for the operation, maintenance, repair or alternation of the project."*

In very exceptional cases, where the technology is highly complex and constantly being upgraded, additional transfer mechanisms or contract provisions may be necessary.

## Conditions restricting the use of transferred technology

A host government should scrutinize a project agreement for any direct or implied restrictions in the use of the transferred technology. Examples of such restrictions are discussed below.

### Post-transfer supply of components

Some project companies may seek to arrange the supply of technology so that the government, after transfer of the ownership, will be dependent on the project company for components and spare parts needed to operate the technology. (It is common knowledge that apart from lump-sum fees and royalties, the most significant source of income to companies possessing technology often comes from supplying components and spare parts.) Such an arrangement may be disadvantageous to the government, particularly if it can obtain components and spare parts of the same quality from other suppliers on more favourable terms.

To reconcile this conflict of interests, it is usually recommended to provide in the project agreement that the government is obligated to purchase components and spare parts from a supplier designated by the project company, but that the supplier in turn is obligated to supply these on terms not less favourable than it offers to any other of its customers, or on terms not less favourable than those on which the government can secure components and spare parts of the same quality from another supplier.

### Confidentiality provisions

Most project agreements provide that the project company and the government must treat technology information, drawings, materials and all other similar matters in connection with the BOT project as strictly confidential. The parties are not allowed to disclose any technical information to a third party. The project agreement may, moreover, impose confidentiality requirements long after the expiry of the concession period, particularly where technical know-how applied to the project is proprietary but not patented.

During the concession period, confidentiality provisions are fairly easy to live with. However, problems often arise after the transfer of ownership of the project to the government, when such provisions may unduly restrict the government's ability to contract with a new concessioner for the project. Accordingly, it is critical for all parties to consider at the contracting stage how to balance the legitimate need to protect proprietary technology, on the one hand, against the need for long-term projects to proceed efficiently and effectively after the initial concession period has ended.

### Indemnification provision

Finally, the government should include in the project agreement an undertaking by the project company that the use of the technology transferred will not infringe any industrial property rights or result in any claims against the government by a third party alleging infringement by the use of the project technology. The government can protect itself by an indemnification provision such as the following:

*"Patent, design and copyright indemnification. The project company hereby agrees to defend, indemnify and keep the government harmless from and against all claims, losses, costs, damages and expenses incurred by the government as a result of, or in connection with, any alleged patent, design or copyright infringement asserted against the government and arising out of the construction, operation or maintenance of the project."*

The government and the project company may include additional contract provisions that establish a procedure to be followed in case of a claim by a third party alleging that his industrial property rights have been infringed.

# ■ Rights to improvements and innovations

During the long concession period of a BOT project, the technology might be improved and technological innovations developed. The rights, title and interest to such improvements and innovations may be addressed in the project agreement (see box 6).

When the improvements or innovations are made during project construction and operation under the responsibility of the project company, the company will probably insist that all rights, title and interest in the improvements or innovations belong to it. This may be reasonable and

**5**

**Technology Transfer**

acceptable if the improvement or innovation stems solely or mainly from technology programmes and engineering skills provided by the project company. If, however, it results solely or mainly from the efforts of national contractors to the project, a different result may be appropriate.

There are several practical solutions for dealing with this issue. Since both the project company and the local contractor usually have an interest in obtaining the use of the improvement or innovation made by the other party, the project agreement should provide that each party is obligated to inform the other party about any improvement or innovation made in connection with the project during the concession period. Both parties should have the right to use the improvement or innovation to perform their obligations on the BOT project.

In any case, improvements and innovations made by the project company or by domestic contractors during the concession period may afford an opportunity for the parties to arrange for joint research and technology development. This opportunity is discussed in more detail in the next section.

# ■ Transfer of technology through R and D projects, joint ventures and other downstream activities

BOT projects may provide the opportunity for technology transfer and development through downstream activities in the host country. In the petroleum sector, for example, cooperation in research and development between foreign project companies and national institutions and companies, joint ventures for construction service and manufacturing of equipment and other downstream activities have been quite common and productive for all parties involved.

Three different methods appear to have been used by governments to promote technology transfer from foreign project companies to nationals through downstream activities. First, it is not uncommon for project agreements to contain general statements by the project companies about their intention to enter into or assist in the establishment of project-related downstream activities. Experience suggests, however, that such general statements are difficult to implement in practice. Good intentions, here as elsewhere, are no substitute for legal obligations.

Secondly, the bidding procedure has proved to be an efficient instrument for the host government to promote transfer of technology through downstream activities. Criteria for awarding BOT concessions should take into account foreign bidders' willingness to transfer technology to the host country by participating in local manufacturing, R and D projects and other activities in conjunction with the technology selected for a BOT project, as well as their track record in this matter. The fulfilment of these criteria is made a condition for the concession and defined in detail in the project agreement. A reporting or tracking system should be implemented to ensure that the project company fulfils its downstream obligations.

The government's objectives should be stated clearly in the tender documents. One such host government evaluation of bidders' proposals for downstream activities reads as follows:

*"Special emphasis shall at all times be given to initiating projects which entail a transfer of technology and have a general scope technologically."*

---

**Box 6. Example of a provision for dealing with improvements and innovations during the concession period**

"Improvements and innovations made during the concession period

1.1     Improvements and innovations made by a contractor during the performance of his obligations shall be the property of the contractor. This does not apply, however, to improvements and innovations mainly based on technology, programmes and documents received from the project company, which shall be the property of the project company.

1.2     The parties shall notify each other of all such improvements and innovations.

1.3     The project company shall grant to the contractor an irrevocable, royalty-free, not-exclusive licence to improvements and innovations, which are the project company's property in accordance with Art. (1.1) to the extent necessary for the contractor to perform or to improve the performance of his obligations to the project company.

1.4     The contractor shall grant to the project company an irrevocable, royalty-free, non-exclusive licence to improvements and innovations, which are the contractor's property in accordance with Art. (1.1) to the extent necessary for the project company to perform or to improve the performance of its obligation to construct, maintain and operate the project during the concession period."

---

**5**

**Technology Transfer**

The bidder's obligation to transfer technology downstream will normally be specified in the project agreement. The standard term used by one host government reads as follows:

*"In undertaking the . . . project in . . . , the Company will ensure that relevant technology and know-how which is at the Company's disposal will be made available for the performance of the project."*

A third approach to the transfer of technology from the project company to the host country has been to negotiate joint ventures between the project company and national companies to exploit technology applied to the BOT project. For instance, the establishment of production facilities for spare parts has often benefited the entire project and all parties concerned. This approach has helped domestic suppliers to improve their technological and quality standards.

## ■ Summary

BOT projects offer a valuable opportunity for host governments to enhance their country's technological capabilities and to secure the transfer of technology to their local companies and institutions. Moreover, they can be a springboard for developing downstream R and D and other technical activities to the mutual benefit of the foreign sponsors and local companies and institutions. Countries with considerable experience in BOT projects have welcomed foreign-sponsored BOT projects, particularly in sectors where technological experience is scarce or not available locally.

BOT projects are not, of course, a cure-all. Host governments cannot expect to obtain technological benefit in every BOT project, given the competition in the world economy. Some infrastructure projects may use conventional technology that is of limited impact for the technological development of a particular country. Policies and instruments that have proved advantageous in one country may be difficult to apply in others. The main point, however, is that a government planning its infrastructure policy is well advised to give close attention to the technology transfer and capability building that are possible within the framework of a BOT project and that are one of the most significant advantages of the BOT concept.

# PROCUREMENT ISSUES AND SELECTION OF SPONSORS

**6**

# ■ Procurement strategies

An adequate procurement strategy or procedure must be in place before a country's BOT policy can be carried out. The success of a BOT project will depend to a large extent on what occurred before the sponsor group was selected. By then key issues should have been identified and dealt with. If not, the project will either limp to its conclusion at an unacceptable cost or, more likely, fail.

Procurement procedures for BOT projects will be influenced by a variety of factors, including the host country's existing legislation governing public procurement of construction work, internationally accepted rules for public procurement, the business environment, the overall infrastructure policy and the nature of the particular BOT project. The fundamental issue, however, is the choice between the two contrasting approaches to procurement, that is, between a competitive tendering system or a negotiated system.

In choosing a procurement procedure for BOT projects, a host government should consider if the procedure will achieve the following objectives:

- *Satisfy the needs of the particular BOT project.* A host government's overriding purpose in designing a BOT procurement system is to ensure that each project is in accord with the country's development plans and that it is authorized, approved and built as rapidly and economically as possible. This requires, among other things, a procurement system whereby the project proposals and the selection criteria are tailored to the government's particular economic and social objectives for the BOT project under consideration and the content and the value of each proposal is fully assessed. Project objectives must be clearly defined: the government must decide, before it selects a particular procurement method and requests proposals, what it wants and how a BOT approach can best achieve those objectives.

- *Ensure procedural clarity, fairness and transparency.* An orderly procurement process is imperative if foreign BOT sponsors are to be attracted. Integrity, equal treatment and transparency are the key elements of an orderly process and are essential for curbing abuses. Sponsors can be expected to embark on lengthy and expensive project development and bidding only if they are confident that the process for awarding the project is well known, orderly and fair. The signposts along the path to success must be well lit.

- *Promote competition.* One essential objective of a BOT procurement process is to encourage competition, which in turn will foster the effectiveness and efficiency of the private sector, a cornerstone of the BOT approach. The need to promote competition may be particularly strong in countries where existing procurement regulation excludes international participation in public projects or favours local contractors by way of preference criteria. In a wider sense, a procurement method that encourages competition for public infrastructure projects will help to increase the market orientation of a country's economy. Ways to encourage competition in infrastructure procurement include public announcement of the project, procurement laws and regulations that are accessible to the public, transparency, as few restrictions as possible for participation in the procurement process, solicitation documents that provide a common basis for preparing and evaluating proposals, and objective, non-discriminatory evaluation criteria made known to the private sector in advance.

- *Encourage private sector innovation and alternative solutions.* A fundamental reason for applying the BOT concept to public infrastructure projects is to take advantage of the private sector's capability for innovation and creativity in design, technology, management and financing. The procurement method should therefore allow flexibility and provide incentives that encourage the private sector to present alternative and innovative project solutions. It should encourage recommendations for better specifications, improvements in construction methods, technical innovations and other proposals that may reduce cost, accelerate the schedule and introduce efficiencies. The government must take care to ensure the protection of intellectual property in innovations and ideas sought from the private sector. Qualified sponsors will not continue to compete for BOT projects if they see their entrepreneurial ideas and innovations being copied in tender documents sent to rivals.

- *Assure investors, lenders and other parties that the government has selected the right BOT proposal.* Whether a BOT project is financeable is to some extent influenced by how investors and lenders react to the procurement method used by the government entity doing the procuring. In general, competitive tendering based on internationally recognized principles is the preferred method of procurement for contracts financed by the development banks. Lenders feel that transparent and orderly procurement procedures are most likely to result in cost-effective projects with the least risk of abuse and default.

- *Strengthen public confidence in the BOT approach to infrastructure development.* A transparent, fair and orderly procurement process will strengthen public confidence in private sector financing of public infrastructure. BOT infrastructure projects usually have a high public profile because they involve large sums of money and many different, and often competing, interests. A transparent process whereby private sponsors are chosen pursuant to publicly available procurement regulations and on the basis of objective evaluation criteria made known in advance will encourage both private sector interest and public confidence. Public announcement of the list of infrastructure projects to be awarded on a BOT basis, dissemination to the public of information about tenders and awards and requiring that a record be made of the key decisions taken by the procuring government entity: these are some of the other mechanisms that promote adherence to the procurement rules as well as confidence in the integrity of the procurement process.

- *Promote an early award of the project.* An efficient and early award process greatly improves the chances for firm proposals and for a smooth conclusion of the many contractual arrangements needed to finalize a BOT project. Experience shows that participants find it difficult to prepare firm proposals and to arrange firm commitments from lenders, construction companies and suppliers when the procurement process is lengthy and fraught with uncertainty as to the time of its conclusion. The solution is to design a procurement process based on a clear timetable with specific milestones for the key phases. Clarity and predictability in the contract award process, with the final award made on a timely basis, are characteristics experienced BOT investors look for.

- *Minimize the time and costs of developing BOT projects.* The time- and cost-intensiveness of developing a typical BOT project (see box 7) is widely regarded as such a project's greatest disadvantage. The development costs of BOT projects, especially the professional fees, have frequently been much higher than under the procurement of construction contracts for government-financed infrastructure projects. High development costs and the length of the process may have kept a number of BOT projects from moving forward and/or limited the number of qualified bidders, thus reducing the competition and efficiency governments wish to harness from the private sector. Experience shows that one main cause of heavy development costs and a lengthy procurement process is the lack of adequate, streamlined BOT procurement procedures, including standardized contracts and other standard documents.

A competitive tendering system would seem to be best suited to meet most of these suggested objectives. Such a system helps to foster efficiency and competition, which are the hallmark of private sector participation in infrastructure projects. There is a danger in any negotiated system that the award may be based on arbitrary judgement or undue influence.

The integrity, equal treatment and transparency of the procuring process, which are of paramount importance when it comes to attracting a number of foreign sponsors, is certainly better secured through a formal tendering system than through a negotiated system, the outcome of which may be unpredictable for the sponsors.

Competitive tendering may also be the best method of encouraging the private sector's innovative ability and efficiency. Moreover, a transparent competitive tendering system is probably the only procurement method that can strengthen public confidence in the BOT approach in politically sensitive infrastructure areas and reduce suspicion of undue influence. Competitive tendering systems that follow international principles are preferred-even required-by lenders and investors for basically the same reasons as mentioned above.

Obviously the cost- and time-driving factors (all but the first three items in box 7) are all obstacles that can be mitigated by adequate procurement methods, that is, they are not inherent in the BOT approach. Fortunately, with experience, some countries have found creative ways to minimize the high development costs and the lengthy procurement process. Sponsors confirm that the costs (and time) of project development are much less in countries with well-established BOT or similar arrangements, such as independent power projects in the United States and Norwegian petroleum projects in the North Sea.

Competitive tendering systems are not, however, without possible drawbacks. At the policy level, the advantages of competitive tendering for BOT projects must be weighed against the fact that such tendering may at times be more rigid and time-consuming than direct negotiations with one or two selected sponsors. Another problem is that the costs of preparing bids for projects of the size and complexity of most BOT projects can be very high. Qualified and serious companies are known to have considered the bidding risk for BOT projects to be too high and have accordingly lost interest in the projects. This indicates a pressing need for some form of prequalification or limited tendering procedures for procuring BOT projects.

## Box 7. Some causes of high development costs for BOT projects

- The complex contractual and financial structure of BOT projects and the large number of parties involved in the development process.

- The relative inexperience of some of the parties and of government officials in developing and packaging BOT projects.

- The lack of adequate legislation to allow private sector participation in public infrastructure projects and the inability of the government to provide necessary regulatory and administrative support.

- The lack of a clearly defined project framework, including a lack of clear government objectives.

- The lack of clear criteria for evaluating bids.

- The lack of independently commissioned feasibility studies to confirm that the project is viable and to help the government solicit realistic project proposals.

- The lack of standardized project agreements and standardized bidding documents.

- The lack of established methods of prequalifying bidders, in order to limit the number of bidders and thus reduce the high bidding risk.

- The lack of a clearly established procurement procedure and schedule.

- Prolonged and uncertain negotiations with preferred bidder(s) before final acceptance (closing) of a tender.

# ■ The current legal and regulatory frameworks for BOT procurement

A brief survey of the current legislative framework in countries with established BOT experience may help to place some of the above observations in the correct context.

Legislation in two countries, the Philippines (1989) and Viet Nam (1993), authorizing BOT infrastructure projects requires public bidding of the projects. Both pieces of legislation and the implementing regulations prescribe in great detail a prequalification, bidding and awarding procedure, including criteria and guidelines for evaluating bid proposals. Direct negotiations may be resorted to only under special circumstances, for instance if only one bidder meets the prequalification requirements.

In Chile, the Public Works Concession Law Regulations prescribe competitive tendering for BOT infrastructure projects and stipulate in detail the items to be covered in bid specifications, evaluation criteria etc. In Ecuador, the Modernization Law of 1993 and the implementing General Regulations require competitive bidding for all private concessions including BOT concessions; in addition, the Ecuadorian authorities have developed specific bidding regulations for BOT concessions within the energy sector (1995).

Government provisions and guidelines for awarding BOT projects in Pakistan (power plants) and in Sri Lanka also provide for a competitive tendering process and requiring all government-solicited BOT proposals to be made public. The evaluation of proposals in Sri Lanka attaches importance to a broader range of criteria than does the legislation of the Philippines or Viet Nam, including, as it does, factors such as reinvestment in the country and the training of nationals. The award procedure in Sri Lanka includes a detailed negotiation stage after bid evaluation, based on a letter of intent. In Malaysia, Hong Kong and Thailand, the authorizing ministries usually prefer a competitive bidding procedure for BOT projects. Examples are the Second Stage Expressway System in Greater Bangkok and the Shah Alam Expressway in Malaysia.

Statutory provisions requiring competitive tendering for the public purchase of construction work, goods and services are found in most American and European countries. The principles of competitive and transparent awarding of public projects, which underline such statutory provisions, may apply to BOT projects. The European Union (EU) has adopted directives that require competitive bidding for the public contracting of construction work, goods and services over a certain threshold value. Basically, the EU procurement system requires that the governments advertise and award relevant contracts (i.e. those above the established threshold) only after a transparent, competitive bidding process. Contracts must be awarded on the basis of either the lowest price or the most economically advantageous tender.

The new General Agreement on Tariffs and Trade (Uruguay Round Agreement on Government Procedures), generally applicable from 1996, has established a procurement system rather similar to the EU rules for procurement "by any contractual means", which may be applicable to BOT projects. The new agreement on government procurement will replace the old government procurement code of GATT. It provides for expanding coverage to the procurement of services and construction and, to a certain extent, to state and local governments. It also establishes a number of criteria for procurements, designed to improve transparency, fairness and due process.

The worldwide acceptance of competitive tendering as the preferred procurement method for BOT infrastructure projects does not imply that a BOT tendering procedure has been laid down in one universal set of rules. On the contrary, the tendering procedures vary not only from country to country but also to some extent by infrastructure sector and type of project. For example, governments differ as to how specific they get in defining the project in the invitation to tender. At one extreme, the procuring government entity specifies in great detail what is wanted. At the other, it specifies very little, leaving it to the ingenuity of the bidders as to how best to meet the project needs.

Governments use different prequalification strategies. Some prescribe a detailed prequalification process in advance of the invitation to tender. Others specify only minimal prequalification criteria in the invitation to tender and require bidders to supply only modest information about their qualifications and capabilities.

There are a variety of accepted procedures for clarification of and modification to the bid documents, as well as for how bidders may propose alternative commercial and technical solutions. The evaluation criteria governments use for selecting bids also vary greatly. Some are detailed, objective and quantifiable; others simply call for the "best" proposals; sometimes no criteria are specified.

There are different approaches as to whether the procuring government entity may engage in direct negotiations with a "provisionally selected" bidder to obtain the most favourable offer in a final procurement phase. The procurement regulations in some countries provide for awarding a letter of intent after the best bid has been selected and approved in principle, while those in the majority of countries appear to move automatically from the selection process to the final award. Formal rules of procedure and the extent to which they are followed (for example, the procedures for advertisement, time schedules, period of effectiveness of tenders, submission and opening of tenders and so forth) also vary from country to country.

To take into account the diversity of circumstances that may be encountered and the different procurement procedures that may be applied, the United Nations Commission on International Trade Law (UNCITRAL) has produced the UNCITRAL Model Law on Procurement, with an accompanying Guide to Enactment for legislators using the Model Law.

## ■ Specific issues for procurement of BOT projects

The procurement methods in use for BOT infrastructure projects reflect two characteristics of BOT projects. First, the internationally recognized principles for competitive bidding normally used for traditional construction contracts appear not to have been suitable for contracts for BOT projects. Indeed, the contrast between the tendering procedures for traditional public sector projects and those for BOT projects can be substantial:

- Traditionally, the public procuring entity produces in the bidding documents comprehensive descriptions and specifications of the construction work to be procured. The invitation to bid for a BOT project, in contrast, may precede any design work and may outline only in very broad terms the need or performance criteria the project should fulfil. While this approach may have the advantage of drawing on each bidder's expertise and innovative ability in proposing solutions to meet the prescribed need, it hardly provides the solid common basis on which bidders for traditional public sector projects are accustomed to preparing their bids and having them evaluated.

- Financial and legal issues typically take precedence over technical issues in structuring a BOT project. When preparing the bid documents, it is crucial for the procuring government entity to understand what investors and lenders are prepared to accept. For the bidders the ability to arrange an attractive financial package has been the decisive factor in winning the bid for a number of BOT projects. The unique and complex financial and legal issues of BOT projects are, naturally, not covered by the rules for procurement of traditional public construction contracts.

- Unlike traditional tendering processes, the BOT tendering process does not necessarily aim to maximize the number of competitors: to ensure the quality of a limited number of competitors is a more important objective. Bidding for BOT projects can be very expensive, particularly if the project description in the bid document is open-ended, requiring potential bidders to present their own concepts for design, construction, financing and operation. The need for a strict prequalification proceeding, to reduce the cost of unsuccessful tendering for BOT projects, is therefore considerable, as mentioned above.

- Negotiations or "discussions" with bidders during the evaluation period on, for instance, technical or financial solutions have not been uncommon in BOT proceedings in some countries. This is clearly inconsistent with the traditional prohibition against negotiation with respect to tenders submitted.

- For the same reasons it is not unusual that, as the procuring government entity evaluates the different BOT concepts and solutions proposed, it becomes aware of a need to change the scope of the project. In such a case, it does not normally reject all bids and start the tendering process again. The practical approach appears to be to negotiate the changed scope of the BOT project with a single bidder or to present it to a short list of bidders. This approach, which is not uncommon for other large construction works, is not fully consistent with the principle of equal opportunity for all bidders.

- The project to be performed and the required content of the bids is more comprehensive for BOT projects than for conventional construction contracts, reflecting the more extensive obligations of the contractors under a BOT scheme. This again influences the criteria used in evaluating and comparing BOT tenders, making them less rigid and more varied than the traditional criteria. Not only the tender price, or a combination of that price and other criteria closely related to the construction work, but also such criteria as the attractiveness of the financial package, the economic strength of the sponsor group, the transfer of technology and capability building, and the soundness of the operating plans may be used to compare and evaluate BOT tenders.

Moreover, there have been a number of BOT projects where it apparently has not been practical or possible for the procuring government entity to apply a competitive bidding system. There are a number of reasons why this can be so:

- A financial package that includes favourable bilateral loans to developing countries may exclude competitive bidding if the host country is obliged to use contractors from the donor country.

- The technical or operational character of a BOT project may require a direct approach to a particular private company, for instance if there is a need to continue with a standardized technology that is the property of that company, or if that company is already involved in operating the specific infrastructure sector in the country or locality.

- An urgent need for a BOT project can make competitive bidding impractical because of the time it entails.

- In some developing countries, particularly where it appears to be extremely difficult to secure competitive bidding, the procuring entity has decided to directly negotiate with a chosen private sponsor because the entity has considered it unlikely that a sufficient number of bidders would engage in competitive proceedings for the project. In countries where no capital market exists, where regulatory parameters are not well established and where the political risks are great, it may be unrealistic to expect to obtain competitive bids for a BOT project within a definite time. In such environments the only practical solution may be to negotiate directly with one or a few chosen sponsor(s) in accordance with some established benchmarks, or to use some form of limited competition.

- In countries where the BOT approach to infrastructure projects is well established, the private sector is often encouraged to take the initiative to identify projects and come forward with detailed project proposals. Although private, unsolicited BOT projects have been submitted to competitive bidding proceedings, a procuring government entity may consider it more practical to negotiate with the company that originated the project proposal.

Some of these procurement issues are inherent in the BOT concept. Others may simply reflect problems that crop up with any rather new and complex project concept. Whatever the reasons, the types of procurement proceedings used so far and the issues encountered have to be considered when deciding on an adequate procurement method for a BOT project.

The next section suggests a basic procedure for conducting procurement in BOT projects. The use of competitive tendering is recommended as it is generally the most effective way to promote the objectives set forth at the beginning of the chapter.

# ▪ A basic procedure for procuring BOT projects

The stages in BOT procurement, discussed below, are summarized in figure III and described in detail in the flow chart in figure IV.

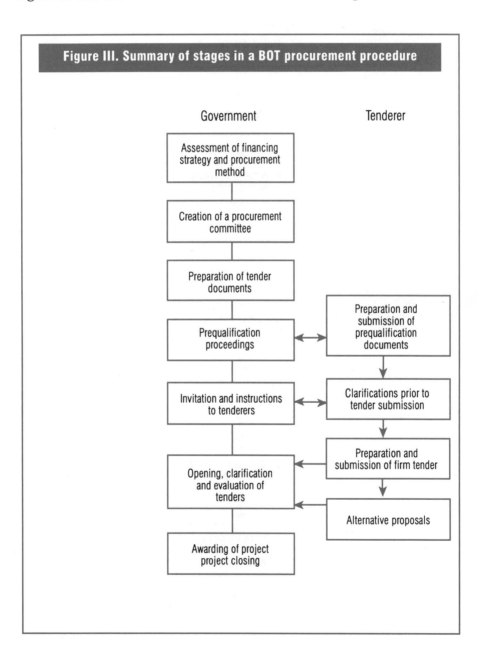

**Figure III. Summary of stages in a BOT procurement procedure**

Government      Tenderer

Assessment of financing strategy and procurement method

Creation of a procurement committee

Preparation of tender documents

Prequalification proceedings ⟷ Preparation and submission of prequalification documents

Invitation and instructions to tenderers ⟷ Clarifications prior to tender submission

Preparation and submission of firm tender

Opening, clarification and evaluation of tenders ← Alternative proposals

Awarding of project project closing

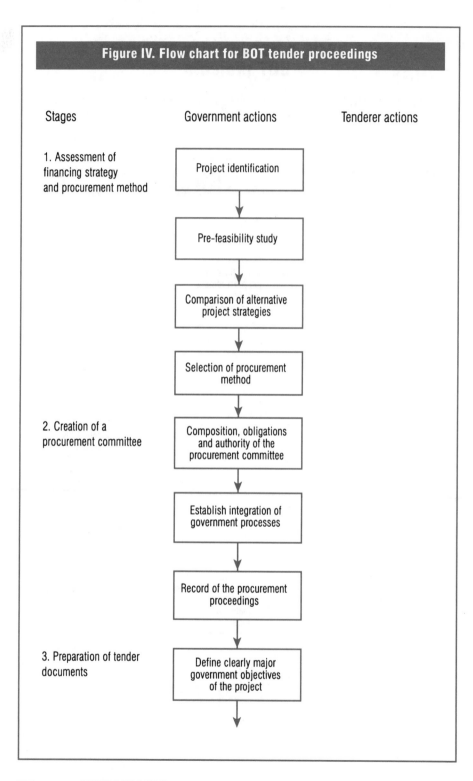

**Figure IV. Flow chart for BOT tender proceedings**

| Stages | Government actions | Tenderer actions |
| --- | --- | --- |

1. Assessment of financing strategy and procurement method

Project identification

Pre-feasibility study

Comparison of alternative project strategies

Selection of procurement method

2. Creation of a procurement committee

Composition, obligations and authority of the procurement committee

Establish integration of government processes

Record of the procurement proceedings

3. Preparation of tender documents

Define clearly major government objectives of the project

Stages　　　　Government actions　　　　Tenderer actions

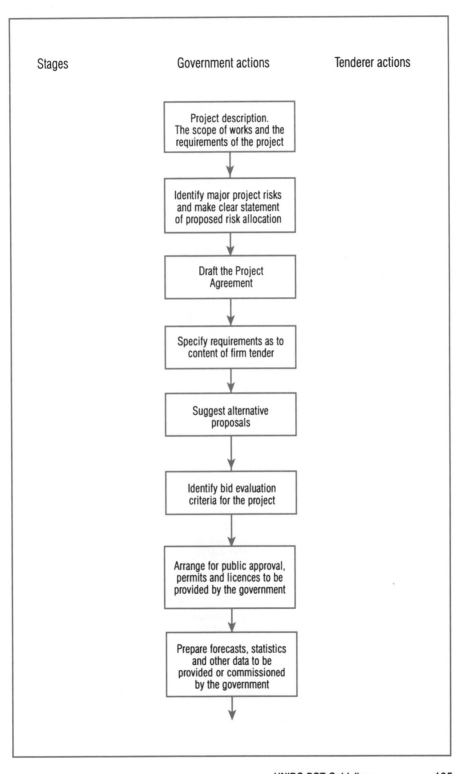

Project description.
The scope of works and the
requirements of the project

Identify major project risks
and make clear statement
of proposed risk allocation

Draft the Project
Agreement

Specify requirements as to
content of firm tender

Suggest alternative
proposals

Identify bid evaluation
criteria for the project

Arrange for public approval,
permits and licences to be
provided by the government

Prepare forecasts, statistics
and other data to be
provided or commissioned
by the government

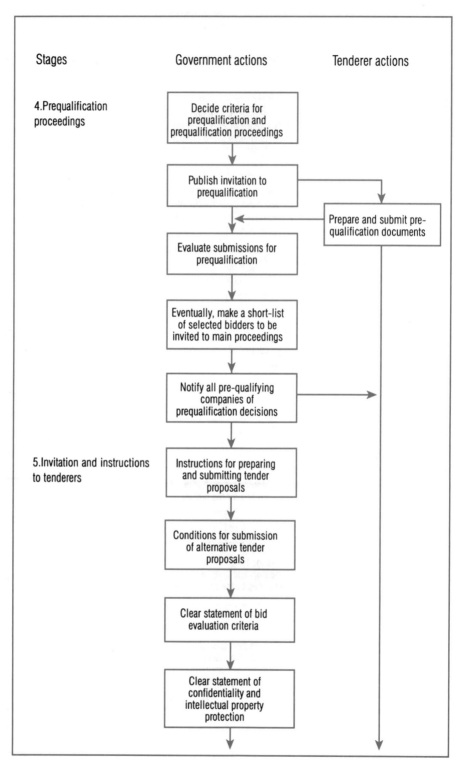

| Stages | Government actions | Tenderer actions |
|---|---|---|
| **4. Prequalification proceedings** | Decide criteria for prequalification and prequalification proceedings | |
| | Publish invitation to prequalification | |
| | Evaluate submissions for prequalification | Prepare and submit pre-qualification documents |
| | Eventually, make a short-list of selected bidders to be invited to main proceedings | |
| | Notify all pre-qualifying companies of prequalification decisions | |
| **5. Invitation and instructions to tenderers** | Instructions for preparing and submitting tender proposals | |
| | Conditions for submission of alternative tender proposals | |
| | Clear statement of bid evaluation criteria | |
| | Clear statement of confidentiality and intellectual property protection | |

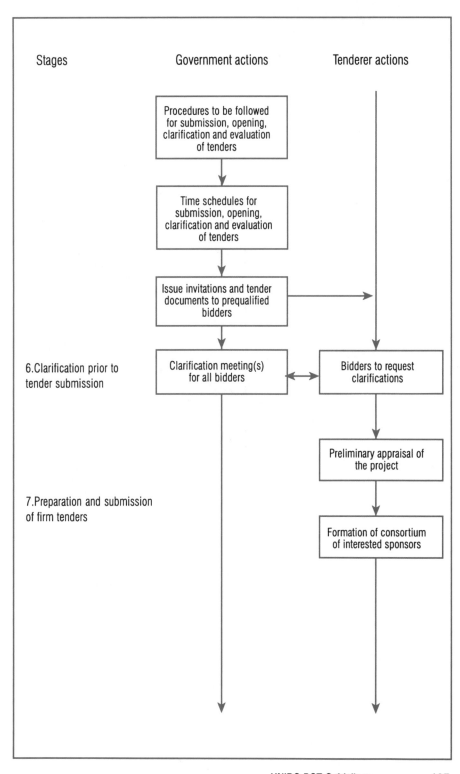

| Stages | Government actions | Tenderer actions |
|---|---|---|
| | Procedures to be followed for submission, opening, clarification and evaluation of tenders | |
| | Time schedules for submission, opening, clarification and evaluation of tenders | |
| | Issue invitations and tender documents to prequalified bidders | |
| 6. Clarification prior to tender submission | Clarification meeting(s) for all bidders | Bidders to request clarifications |
| | | Preliminary appraisal of the project |
| 7. Preparation and submission of firm tenders | | Formation of consortium of interested sponsors |

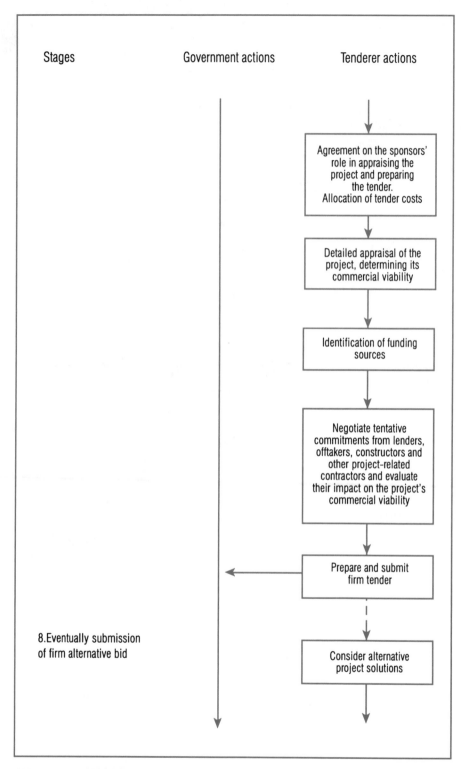

| Stages | Government actions | Tenderer actions |
|---|---|---|

Agreement on the sponsors' role in appraising the project and preparing the tender. Allocation of tender costs

Detailed appraisal of the project, determining its commercial viability

Identification of funding sources

Negotiate tentative commitments from lenders, offtakers, constructors and other project-related contractors and evaluate their impact on the project's commercial viability

Prepare and submit firm tender

8. Eventually submission of firm alternative bid

Consider alternative project solutions

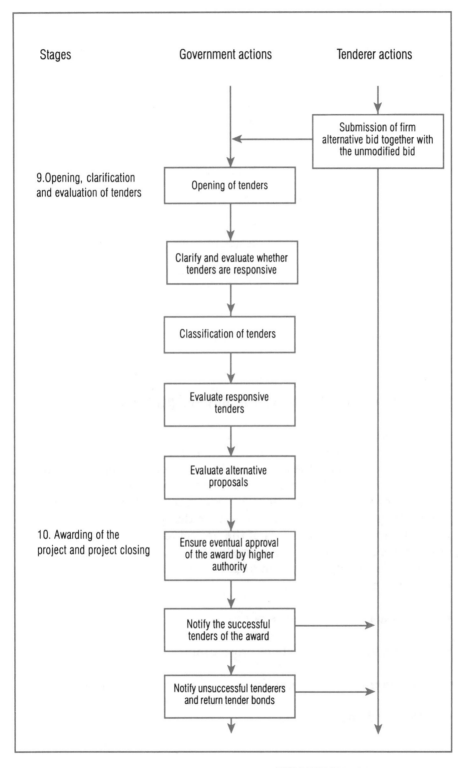

| Stages | Government actions | Tenderer actions |
|---|---|---|

Submission of firm alternative bid together with the unmodified bid

9. Opening, clarification and evaluation of tenders

Opening of tenders

Clarify and evaluate whether tenders are responsive

Classification of tenders

Evaluate responsive tenders

Evaluate alternative proposals

10. Awarding of the project and project closing

Ensure eventual approval of the award by higher authority

Notify the successful tenders of the award

Notify unsuccessful tenderers and return tender bonds

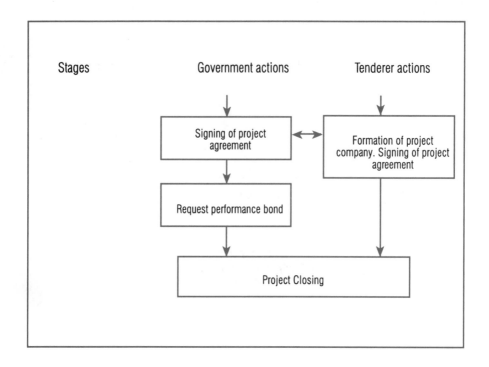

## Assessment of financing strategy and procurement method

After a project has been identified and the need for it has been demonstrated, a government will normally conduct a prefeasibility study for it. The study establishes the basic requirements of the project, weighs the pros and cons of BOT financing and government financing and serves as the basis for project procurement. Without a comprehensive prefeasibility study, the government will not be able to design a procurement framework that meets the objectives of the project and will not be in a strong position *vis-à-vis* potential sponsors.

The prefeasibility study should as a minimum establish and evaluate the following:

- The basic characteristics of the project.

- Sources and availability of project input.

- Location, geological and soil conditions and access to site.

- Environmental impacts.

- Preliminary engineering and technology possibilities.

- Implementation schedule (it should be flexible enough to allow responding to changing conditions and construction delays).

- Allocation of risk between the private and public sectors.

- Financial appraisal of the project profitability, including sensibility analysis using different assumptions for key variables.

The prefeasibility study may also serve as the basis for a final feasibility study, which is usually prepared by the sponsors at the request of the lenders and-eventually-as part of the required content of the tender.

Once the prefeasibility study has been analysed and a BOT approach selected for the project, it is time to decide on the procurement method. Ideally, the government entity doing the procuring should choose the procurement method best suited to the project. Competitive tendering is normally chosen to promote competition, to prevent negative public perceptions, to attract qualified private investors and to satisfy the lenders.

If competitive tendering is chosen, the findings contained in the prefeasibility study will serve as a basis for the drafting of the bidding documents, in particular for laying down minimum performance standards as well as the economic parameters to be observed by the bidder in preparing the bid and, if successful, in building and operating the project facilities. The prefeasibility study should also be used for defining the evaluation criteria for the bids.

## Creation of a procurement committee

Before the procuring government entity begins the procurement proceedings, it is advisable to establish a procurement committee or a project team that will be responsible for preparing and conducting the procurement proceedings. This committee should have, as a minimum, the following composition:

- A high-ranking official of the procuring government entity.

- A legal official with experience in the particular type of BOT procurement and contracting.

- A technical official knowledgeable about the project.

- A financial management official experienced in project financing.

The procurement committee may be authorized to use the services of consultants with appropriate experience in the procurement and implementation of BOT projects.

The procuring government entity may, additionally, consider nominating or inviting a facility user to join the committee (for example, a representative of a consumer organization or a union) to improve transparency and strengthen public confidence in the proceedings. Another way to promote transparency and accountability is to require that the committee keep a record of the proceedings. The record may contain information such as a summary of the prequalification proceedings, the principal terms of each tender and a summary of the evaluation of the bids. It should be made public for inspection after a bid has been accepted or the procurement proceedings terminated without the project having been awarded, provided that it does not disclose confidential information from the tenderers. An adequate procurement record may also facilitate the work of the central government in supervising and controlling BOT projects developed by government agencies or local authorities.

## Preparation of tender documents

The procurement committee should prepare the tender documents before prequalification is initiated. These documents should set forth clearly and precisely the work to be accomplished, the operating and maintenance conditions, the proposed tariff structure and the proposed concession period. To promote transparency and international competition, the tender documents for BOT projects may include the following:

- Detailed instruction to bidders on bidding proceedings and the form of tender.

- The prefeasibility study undertaken for the project.

- The required minimum content of the bid.

- The text of the project agreement.

- The type of facility(ies) to be constructed and the proposed technology, including design standards, technical specifications and performance requirements.

- International and national standards governing the work, equipment and materials and a statement as to which equipment and materials meeting other standards that ensure the same or better quality will also be accepted.

- Technical specifications based on performance criteria.

- Description of the site location and access to the site.

- Specification of the facilities to be provided by the government authority.

- Timetable for completion of the construction work.

- Maximum concession period.

- Statement of the financial requirements, including the minimum committed equity.

- Proposed tariff, toll or fee structure and revenue-sharing arrangements, if any.

- Information about rules and regulations governing foreign exchange remittances.

- Nature, amount, period of validity and other principal terms and conditions of security and warranties.

- The criteria to be taken into account in evaluating and comparing bids, including how such factors may be quantified or otherwise evaluated and the method for evaluating alternative proposals.

- Environmental performance norms and the environmental impact assessment (EIA).

- (For power projects) power purchase agreement and, possibly, fuel supply agreement.

- Information about the market conditions in the sector.

- Other provisions that need to be included in the bidding documents.

To provide a uniform basis for preparing the bids and on which the procuring government entity can compare them on a net present value basis, the procuring entity may also consider prescribing the following economic parameters:

- The currency in which bids may be expressed.

- The procedures and foreign exchange rates for conversion of currencies to a common base for comparison.

- Inflation and discounting rates.

- Maximum period for project construction.

- Timetable for project operation.

- Formulae and price indices to be used in the collection and adjustment of tariffs, tolls or fees.

The tender documents for a BOT project are in many ways comparable to the tender documents for international competitive bidding for public works and construction. Some additions and adjustments are, however, necessitated by the character of the BOT scheme. The procuring government entity must decide whether the bidders shall be required to submit their bids in response to a specific and detailed set of technical criteria or whether the bid documents shall specify only the basic project performance criteria, leaving the choice of technology, construction method, project schedule etc. to be proposed by the bidders. The two different BOT procurement approaches are usually described as, respectively, a structured approach and an unstructured approach. The structured approach can streamline the procurement process, saving costs and time. The unstructured approach encourages innovation but at the same time makes the bids more time-consuming and expensive to prepare and evaluate. Since the single biggest challenge for BOT projects is to reduce the time- and cost-intensiveness of their development, it may be advisable to opt for a structured approach under most circumstances. If the procuring government entity wants to encourage project ideas and creativity, it may allow bidders the option of submitting an alternative bid in addition to a structured bid.

In case the procuring entity is unable to formulate detailed specifications for a BOT project, it may use a two-stage (or several-stage) bidding process to arrive at the optimal project proposals.

# Prequalification proceedings

Competent prospective bidders may be reluctant to participate in the cost- and time-intensive procurement proceedings for BOT contracts if they risk having to compete with unrealistic tenders submitted by unqualified or disreputable companies or if they think the number of bidders is too large. To ensure that experienced and serious sponsors with the ability to develop the particular BOT project are invited to submit tenders and re- duce the bidding risk, it is advisable to limit the number of bidders at the pre-tender stage by a mechanism known as prequalification.

Prequalification proceedings are normally subject to a number of pro- cedural requirements and conditions, including advertisement of the invitation to prequalify, prequalification criteria, minimum period for preparation of prequalification applications and notification to the ap- plicants of the result of the prequalification. Such procedural safeguards ensure that the proceedings are transparent and non-discriminatory. Unlike conventional methods of prequalification that may consider con- tractors for a number of future projects (bidders list), prequalification for a BOT project is normally based on the ability of the prospective bidders to perform the particular BOT project satisfactorily and on their resources. Typical prequalification information-and criteria-for BOT projects include the following:

- *The financial capability of the applicant.* The applicant must provide evidence that it has the resources to finance the engineering, con- struction, operation and maintenance of the project. Typically, it must document its financing capability by submitting the following:

  □ A report on the state of its financial situation.
  □ A report on the proposed financing structure of the project.
  □ A statement from a reputable financial institution or bank on the intention to extend a line of credit to the applicant for the implementation of the project.

- *The experience and track record of the applicant.* Typically, the pro- spective bidder must provide the following evidence:

  □ That, by itself or with others, it has undertaken one or more projects that are similar or related to the BOT project to be bid.
  □ That its key personnel and those of its contractors have suffi- cient practical experience in the relevant phases of the BOT project to be bid.

- *Management structures and operational capabilities of the applicant.*
  The prospective bidder typically provides information about its personnel, the equipment and construction facilities to be applied to the project, quality assurance systems, health and safety records and-normally-its existing workload and that of its contractors.

- *Legal requirements.* There is typically an undertaking from the participants in the joint venture or consortium that, if awarded the BOT contract, they will bind themselves jointly to perform the obligations under the contract. They also give evidence that they are not insolvent or in receivership and state that they have not committed any criminal offence related to professional conduct. Information about any pending legal claims against the applicants may also be requested.

Most international rules on the procurement of public works and services require that all applicants meeting the specified prequalification criteria be allowed to bid. This principle may be less satisfactory for BOT projects, where project development and the evaluation of tenders are much more complicated, costly and time-consuming. Since experience also shows that qualified developers may not participate in procurement proceedings for BOT projects if the competitive field is too large, it is often recommended to limit the number of BOT project bidders to fewer than five qualified companies or consortia. The procuring government entity may adopt a quantitative rating system for the prequalification criteria to achieve such a short list of qualified bidders. The possible elimination of some prospective bidders for this purpose and the application of a rating system must be clearly stated in the invitation to prequalify.

Finally, it is advisable that the procurement regulations require a prequalified bidder to reconfirm its qualifications at the time a BOT contract is awarded, in accordance with the same criteria utilized for the prequalification. A post-qualification requirement is particularly important for complex and high-value BOT infrastructure projects. To safeguard national interests, the procuring entity must be sure that the qualification information submitted by a developer at the time of prequalification remains valid.

## Invitation and instructions to tenderers

The bid document package sent to the prequalified bidders will contain instructions to the bidders and a tender form in addition to a number of documents and information as specified above under preparation of tender documents. The fee charged for the bid document package should be reasonable, reflecting only the cost of its printing and delivery to the bidders. Unreasonably high fees for BOT bidding documents could discourage qualified prospective bidders from participating in the bidding.

While the whole bid document package is interlinked, the tender proceedings will basically be continued in the instructions to bidders, which outline, among other things, the required content of the bid, the procedures for clarification of bidding documents and for submission of bids, security requirements, how the bids will be opened and evaluated and the procedures to be followed for the award of the project.

The instructions to the bidders for a BOT project contain mainly the same provisions as the instructions to bidders for conventional large industrial projects. The instructions as to the content of the bid are, however, different in so far as BOT projects are more comprehensive and complex than traditional government-financed infrastructure projects. Normally, a bid for a BOT project includes the following data:

- Technical proposal

  □ Operating programme and costs, including the quality of service to be offered.
  □ Maintenance programme and costs.
  □ Environmental protection plan.
  □ Plans for operation and maintenance of additional facilities.
  □ Evidence of the capability of committed or proposed construction contractors, equipment suppliers and O&M contractors.

- Financial proposal

  □ Feasibility study prepared by the tenderer.
  □ Investment proposal, including financial structure and security package.
  □ Pricing (tariffs, tolls or fees) proposal, including any adjustment formulae.
  □ Escrow account schedule.
  □ Period for completing construction of the project.
  □ Proposed concession period.
  □ Expected period over which the project facilities are to be depreciated.
  □ National capability building and transfer of technology offered.
  □ Any offer to reduce charges to consumers if the return on net worth or assets exceeds a certain maximum (profit sharing).

- Legal proposal

  □ Acceptance of the terms of the project agreement.
  □ Acceptance of the land conveyance agreement.
  □ Draft shareholder's agreement, consortium agreement, joint venture agreement or a similar contract by which the sponsors commit themselves to perform the project agreement if they are awarded the BOT project.
  □ Acceptance of the terms of the purchase agreement (for energy projects).
  □ Acceptance of the terms of a supply agreement.
  □ Evidence of other contractual commitments.
  □ Letter of conveyance signed by the authorized representatives of the company or consortium submitting the bid.

From a legal point of view, the instructions concerning the content of the bid should read as a minimum requirement so as not to preclude the bidder from including additional information that it considers relevant.

## Clarifications prior to tender submission

The ideal situation is that the bidding documents and annexes comprise a complete set of provisions covering all technical, financial and legal aspects of the project. The bidders are then to enter their tenders in conformity with these provisions so that all tenders will be based on the same obligations and therefore directly comparable.

Because it is often difficult to adequately describe and cover all the factors in a complex infrastructure project in the bidding documents, there must be a way to have unclear provisions or omissions from the bidding documents clarified and to have errors corrected.

The instructions to the bidders will normally specify a procedure permitting the bidder to ask for clarification or correction of the bidding documents. To preserve the principles of transparency and fairness in the bidding proceedings, there should be procedural safeguards to ensure that all bidders are given the same clarifications and corrections. Usually clarifications and corrections must be communicated to all potential bidders in writing without, however, disclosing the source of the request.

The procuring government entity may conduct a pre-bid conference in reasonable time before the deadline for submission of bids to clarify and correct the bidding documents or any related matter that the bidders may raise. The salient results of a pre-bid conference should be put down in writing in a bid bulletin and sent promptly to all bidders.

Most instructions to bidders state the name of a person on the procurement committee who is to receive the questions from bidders during tender preparation and require that the questions be in writing. There may also be a strict prohibition on informal contacts to ensure equal treatment of bidders.

Since BOT infrastructure contracts often involve considerable sums of money (and for other reasons as well), the competition may be severe. Some BOT procurement regulations and project agreements contain detailed and rather strict provisions against inducements and other undue contacts with current or former officers or employees of the procuring government entity.

## Preparation and submission of firm tender

An important element in fostering participation and competition is to give bidders sufficient time to prepare their tenders. The time allowed for this will be determined by the circumstances of the BOT project, in particular by the level of preparation provided by the procuring government entity and by the size and complexity of the project. Generally, however, 90-120 days from the date of the invitation to bid-or, if later, the date on which the bidding documents become available-should be allowed for preparation and submission of tenders for BOT projects. Instructions to the bidders must clearly indicate the deadline for the submission of tenders, including the place for their receipt.

Tenders must usually be submitted on standard forms provided by the procuring government entity as part of the bidding documents. This considerably eases the process of data assembly and analysis during the complex evaluation process.

To ensure the transparent, fair and reasonably efficient conduct of the procurement proceeding, the tenders that are submitted must be firm. The bidders are not allowed to consider the bids as admission tickets to the procurement committee's negotiation table. Most international procurement regulations and instructions to bidders therefore request a bidder to submit its definite and binding terms and conditions, together with a cover letter in which the bidder explicitly verifies or validates that the bidding documents are fully understood, the period of effectiveness of the bid and its completeness. According to the prevailing procurement rules, a bidder is not permitted to alter its bid after the deadline for the submission of bids.

The request for firm bids for BOT projects will not normally prevent a bidder from using an escalation formula to compensate an increase in financing, material or labour costs during the procurement proceedings.

The effects of escalation formulae will, however, be calculated by the procuring entity and considered when bids without such formulae are being compared.

To secure due performance by the bidder of the firm obligations undertaken in the bid and to afford the procuring government entity reasonable protection against irresponsible bids, the bid is normally accompanied by a bid security, usually in the form of a letter of credit or a bank guaranty from an acceptable bank. As already mentioned, the bid security required for a BOT project should not be set so high as to discourage bidders. Security equal to approximately 2 per cent of the expected total capital costs of the project appears to be quite normal for BOT projects. The bid security should remain valid at least for the same period as the effectiveness of the bid.

A tenderer submitting a bid may be an individual, a sole proprietorship, a corporation, a joint venture, a consortium or a general or a limited partnership. Whatever the case, the submitted bid must provide suitable evidence of the legal form of the bidder and that the individuals managing the tendering proceedings are authorized by the bidder. In most BOT projects, the project company has not been formally established at the time the bid is submitted. A preliminary cooperation agreement or a draft proposal of a shareholder agreement, a joint venture agreement or consortium agreement by which the bidders commit themselves to perform the project agreement if they are awarded the BOT contract should therefore be submitted as part of the bid, and the bid should preferably be signed by all prospective partners.

## Alternative proposals

To enhance the comparability of bids for BOT projects and to reduce the time and costs of the evaluation process, it is generally required that the bids comply fully with the terms and conditions of the bidding documents. If a bid is incomplete or if it is not substantially responsive, that is if it contains material deviations from or reservations to the specifications, contract terms and other conditions in the bidding documents, it will be rejected.

The required conformity of the bids may have a negative impact on the creativity of the private bidders, which is generally supposed to be one of the advantages of the BOT concept. A prospective bidder may have the knowledge to offer a solution to the implementation of a BOT project that is different from the solution described in the bidding documents. Of special importance to the government is that the bidder may be able to come up with changes in the construction method, in the project specifications or in the O&M methods that could save time and/or reduce costs to the benefit of the consumers.

The practical solution will generally be to invite the bidders to present alternative bids, provided that such bids will reduce costs, shorten the development schedule or allow better implementation or operation of the project. Alternative bids must be accompanied by a detailed description of the proposed methodology, technical specifications, a price breakdown and other relevant details. Alternative bids that are not fully detailed and priced should not be considered.

For reasons of comparability it is generally stated in the instructions to bidders that no alternative bid will be considered by the procurement committee unless the bidder also submits an unmodified bid in accordance with the bidding documents.

## Opening, clarification and evaluation of tenders

To prevent a time gap between the deadline for the submission of BOT tenders and the opening of the tenders, it is recommended that the tenders be opened at the time specified as the deadline for submission of tenders. Otherwise a time gap may create opportunities for misconduct (e.g. disclosure of the content of bids prior to the opening time) and deprive bidders of the opportunity to minimize that risk by submitting a tender at the last minute, immediately prior to the opening of tenders.

The bid opening procedure for BOT tenders usually follows internationally recognized principles, often with some formality. This includes, among other things, the principle that the tenders are opened in public and the name and address of each bidder are announced together with the total amount of each bid. Bids received after the deadline for submission of bids, as well as those not opened and announced at the bid opening, are not considered.

The procurement committee may ask bidders to clarify their bids to help in its examination, evaluation and comparison of those bids. Requests for clarification and the bidder's final response should be made and confirmed in writing. Such clarification or discussion exercises are quite normal for BOT procurement proceedings owing to the size and complexity of most BOT projects. It is very important for the procuring government entity to make certain that both parties have an identical and full understanding of all the provisions and issues in the bids.

As mentioned above, however, subsequent negotiations or bargaining between the procuring entity and the bidders to change, for example, proposed tariffs, concession period, risk allocation and other matters of substance in a submitted tender are not uncommon in BOT procurement proceedings. Such negotiations after the bids have been submitted are clearly contrary to most internationally recognized procurement rules and guidelines. The Organisation for Economic Co-operation and Development (OECD) Rules on Good Procurement Practice, article 7; the United Nations Commission on International Trade Law (UNCITRAL) Model Law on Procurement, article 31; EU Directive 90/531, article 15; and World Bank Procurement Guidelines 2.45 all clearly prohibit negotiations between a procuring entity and a bidder concerning a tender submitted. For example, the UNCITRAL Model Law on Procurement, article 31, stipulates as follows:

*"No negotiation shall take place between the procuring entity and a supplier or contractor with respect to a tender submitted by the supplier or contractor."*

The Model Law does, however, provide methods of procurement that allow technical discussions and negotiations between the procuring entity and bidders (e.g. two-stage tendering and request for proposals).

The Uruguay Round Agreement on Government Procurement does not fully prohibit subsequent negotiation of bids; but the scope and procedure for such negotiation are rather strict. Thus, subsequent negotiations of bids are permitted only if such negotiations have been indicated in the invitation to tenderers or if it appears from the evaluation that no single tender is obviously the most advantageous. They should primarily be used to identify the strengths and weaknesses of the bids and should neither discriminate between the bidders nor provide information that would help a bidder to raise its bid to the level of other bidders. In particular, the procuring entity should ensure that any elimination of bidders is carried out in accordance with the evaluation criteria set forth in the bidding documents, that all modifications to the criteria and to the technical requirements are transmitted to all remaining bidders and that when the negotiations are concluded, all remaining bidders are permitted to submit final tenders on the basis of the revised requirements and in accordance with a common deadline (see the Uruguay Round Agreement on Government Procurement, article XIV).

The general prohibition or strict limitation of subsequent negotiations between the procuring entity and the bidders is intended to protect the transparency of the proceedings and to prevent discrimination and opportunities for misconduct. There seems to be a definite feeling among large construction companies that subsequent negotiations or the opportunity to "re-bid" might result in an "auction", in which a tender offer by one bidder is used to apply pressure on another bidder to offer a more favourable tender. Negotiations between the procuring government entity and the bidders on bids already submitted is known also to have delayed the procurement proceedings for BOT projects considerably.

There may be differences of opinion on both the negotiation of BOT tenders after the submission of the tenders and how far such negotiations may go in relation to substantial terms and conditions of the bid. However, in the light not only of international procurement rules but also of the critical need to reduce the expenses and time needed for BOT procurement proceedings, it may be advisable to prohibit-or strictly limit-negotiations between the procuring government entity and the bidders concerning tenders submitted.

The evaluation process requires two steps. The first is to determine whether a bid is "responsive". Bids that are not responsive are rejected. This first step is handled more or less like any traditional procurement of construction works. Once responsiveness has been determined, the second step is to evaluate the bids on the basis of the evaluation criteria stated in the bidding documents. Price and non-price evaluation criteria for BOT projects and the method of objectively assessing the relative attractiveness of the bids are discussed in chapter 7 in the section on evaluating bids.

## Awarding of project and project closing

The instructions to the bidders are usually worded to give the procuring government entity a free hand in choosing between the submitted bids or rejecting all the bids. This means that a bidder, even after having submitted the most favourable bid, has no claim to have his tender accepted.

Normally, however, the procuring government entity will award the BOT contract to the complying bidder with the highest number of evaluation points well within the period of effectiveness of the bids. In some countries the award of the BOT contract will not be effective until it has been approved officially by a higher governmental authority. The instructions to the bidders should specify a time limit for such approval.

Having awarded the BOT contract, the procuring entity will notify the unsuccessful bidders about the award and return their bid securities. The project agreement will usually be signed promptly or within a specified number of days of the announcement of the award, probably after approval by the higher governmental authority.

After the award, the successful bidder has to finalize and execute a number of arrangements and agreements before project implementation can take place. This process includes the following:

- Binding financial commitments from the lenders and equity investors (financial closing).

- Execution of the project contracts and documents that are needed before the financial closing can take place, including construction and equipment supply contracts, insurance contracts and security agreements and assignments.

- Approved studies and reports including feasibility studies and environmental reports required by the lenders.

- The establishment and incorporation of the project company in the host country.

- Certification of a number of corporate documents.

- Obtainment of approvals such as construction permits, import licenses and environmental permits.

- Legal opinions from local counsel and project counsel.

- A performance bond issued by a reputable financial institution to the government entity.

These final steps prior to project implementation are crucial in the development process of any BOT project. Although most of the onus is on the winning bidder, not even the most experienced developer will be able to complete this final phase of the project development successfully and in time without support and flexibility from the procuring government entity.

The legal framework for the project closing process is typically embodied in the project agreement. The obligations of the successful bidder to take the project to financial close and to finalize other steps before project implementation are usually worded as conditions precedent to the effectiveness of the project agreement. The date when all the conditions precedent have been complied with is defined in the project agreement as the "effective date" of the contract, from which date the concession period shall begin. If the conditions precedent are not satisfied by the deadline agreed on in the project agreement, the procuring government entity may terminate the project agreement and award the BOT project to the second best bidder.

## Unsolicited proposals

An unsolicited proposal is one prepared and submitted solely at the initiative of a private developer and not in response to an official request for proposals. Unsolicited BOT proposals are sometimes discouraged, in particular by lenders. The validity and seriousness of unsolicited proposals can be difficult to determine. Experience indicates that unsolicited proposals may not lead to the cheapest infrastructure projects or the best service to the community. On the other hand, encouraging the private sector to identify and structure BOT infrastructure projects on their own initiative may help a country's BOT programme to succeed. The private sector may have better knowledge of new technologies or may have better insight than the public sector into local solutions to infrastructure problems. BOT agreements based on unsolicited proposals are normally reached on the basis of negotiations between the private proposer and the authorized government entity. Such negotiations need to be conducted on a case-by-case basis. To make sure that unsolicited proposals are evaluated following approximately the same criteria as are followed for officially initiated proposals, the government should consider setting up rules for this in the general procurement regulations for BOT projects. Such rules typically stipulate the following conditions:

- An unsolicited proposal should be consistent with the government's infrastructure policy and with its general plans for solicited proposals in order to be considered.

- It should meet the same criteria for BOT projects as solicited proposals, including financial viability, economic viability and environmental and social impact assessments.

- It should meet the usual prequalification criteria, that is, provide evidence that the proposing entity has the financial and operational capability, the experience and the resources to successfully implement the proposed BOT project and that it fulfils the legal requirements.

If an unsolicited proposal meets these initial conditions, the proponent should be required to provide a detailed project proposal based on the (minimum) requirements for the content of bidding documents and bids set forth in the general procurement regulations.

The detailed project proposal should then be evaluated against the cost and other criteria for similar BOT infrastructure projects, for example, against a benchmark toll tariff or a benchmark price per kilowatt-hour established by existing projects or other proposals.

To promote transparency and integrity, it is recommended that the government entity announce the receipt of an unsolicited proposal, the request for a detailed project proposal and the agreement and that it record the stages of the negotiations.

Although unsolicited proposals for BOT projects are normally negotiated between the parties, some unsolicited proposals have been submitted to competitive bidding by the government entities (a well-known example is the Hong Kong Harbour Tunnel project). It might be better, however, to avoid negotiating unsolicited proposals in countries that have established a competitive bidding process for BOT projects, since such negotiations may seriously undermine competitive bidding (if private proposers know that their proposals will be considered on an unsolicited, negotiated basis they will have little incentive to submit to the rigors of competition). If unsolicited proposals are submitted to competitive bidding, the government may consider reimbursing a portion of the cost incurred by the proposer of preparing the unsolicited proposal and/or encouraging private initiative by rewarding the proposer, in the course of the evaluation process, with some additional points for its initiative.

# FINANCIAL AND ECONOMIC APPRAISAL OF BOT PROJECTS

**Appraisal**

**7**

Chapter 7 focuses on how to assess the financial and economic viability of a BOT project. It also covers commercial, technical and environmental appraisals and prequalification assessment studies. It is not intended to provide detailed guidance on project feasibility, which is available in the UNIDO publication *Manual for the Preparation of Industrial Feasibility Studies*.[2] Instead, it outlines a methodology by which a government can appraise BOT schemes. It points out the key differences in the way governments and sponsors assess projects.

In particular, the chapter does the following:

- Briefly describes the different project appraisal techniques, suggests those that are appropriate for the various parties to a BOT project at different stages in the project cycle and compares the appraisal of BOT projects with that of more traditional projects funded through government borrowing.

- Provides a framework for a government's financial and economic appraisal of BOT projects.

- Discusses how the sponsor's financial considerations are likely to differ from the government's considerations and how different parties in a BOT contract are likely to assess risk and evaluate expected costs and revenues from their own perspectives.

- Shows how a financial and economic appraisal framework can be used to evaluate bids.

---

[2] W. Behrens and P. M. Hawranek, *Manual for the Preparation of Industrial Feasibility Studies* (UNIDO publication, Sales No. E.91.III.E.18). See also *Guidelines for Project Evaluation* (United Nations publication, Sales No. 72.II.B.11); *Guide to Practical Project Appraisal: Social Benefit-Cost Analysis in Developing Countries* (United Nations publication, Sales No. 78.II.B.3); L. Squire and H. G.van der Tak, *Economic Analysis of Projects* (Baltimore, published for the World Bank by Johns Hopkins University Press, 1975); I.M.D. Little and J. A. Mirrlees, *Project Appraisal and Planning for Developing Countries* (London, Heinemann Educational Books, 1974); M. Bridier and S. Michailof, *Guide pratique d'analyse de projets: analyse économique et financière de projet dans les pays en voie de développement,* 3rd ed. (Paris, Economica, 1984); and J. Dickey and L. Miller, *Road Project Appraisal for Developing Countries* (New York, John Wiley, 1984).

- Outlines some of the means by which a government may improve the financial viability of a BOT project to encourage private sector participation.

# ▪ Types of appraisal

Appraisal of a BOT project will be carried out by different parties during the various stages of the project cycle: project identification, feasibility study, analysis of options, bid evaluation, project implementation and final evaluation. The host government will focus primarily on the economic appraisal of the project, which is concerned with national costs and benefits and the best use of the country's resources. In preparing an economic appraisal, the government will, however, need to draw on information from the technical appraisal and the financial appraisal and from an analysis of the project's likely social and environmental impact.

The key differences between the sponsor's and the government's criteria are that the sponsor will usually emphasize financial rather than economic issues, will use a higher discount rate to reflect its higher cost of capital and will place a higher cost on risks.

The key difference between the appraisal of a BOT project and that of a more traditional public sector scheme are that the former tends to focus more on risk, so the project's financial viability will be more important than for a scheme financed entirely by the public sector.

Five types of appraisal are usually carried out in connection with a BOT project: commercial, technical, environmental, financial and economic. The five types are summarized below, and their relevance for BOT projects is discussed.

## Commercial appraisal

In preparing a commercial appraisal, the government or the BOT sponsor will conduct research on the markets for the output of the facility, including the following:

- The identification and location of potential customers/users.

- Historical trends in prices, production and demand.

- Current and future government tariff policies.

- The actual or expected regulatory framework.

- The present and projected capacity of potential competitor facilities.

- Competitive characteristics of the sector.

This market information is used to generate demand and revenue forecasts and to project the market share of the proposed facility and also in a risk and sensitivity analysis. For a BOT transport project, traffic or passenger forecasts will be required and the elasticity of demand with respect to fares or tolls must be assessed.

It is essential to clarify the assumptions underlying the market projections, including the basis for the output, demand and price projections, operating and administrative costs, the debt profile, insurance costs, tax rates, dividend policy, inflation and exchange rate assumptions and the government's expected regulatory policy, in particular price regulation. The effects of likely variances, particularly downside ones, in demand and income levels on the financial viability of the project must also be tested, given the tendency to optimistic bias in appraisals.

## Technical appraisal

The objectives of a technical appraisal are to ensure that the BOT project is soundly designed, uses the appropriate technology and meets international design and engineering standards. It is based on a technical description of the project and information provided by engineers and other technical specialists. The appraisal is used by governments, sponsors and lenders to assess the likelihood that the project will be completed on time and within budget, that it will be capable of operating at the design performance level and that its operation will not be constrained by technical factors. It provides essential information on construction and operating costs for the financial and economic appraisals.

The BOT technical appraisal will consider, among other topics, the following:

- The suitability of various technologies, including equipment and processes, to national, local and environmental conditions.

- The likelihood of achieving the planned performance level, including capacity and quality of output.

- Location, scale and layout of the infrastructure facility, including analysis of the terrain and ground conditions.

- Acquisition of land for the project, including, where relevant, transmission lines and access roads.

- Procurement arrangements, including the availability and supply of raw materials and utilities.

- Availability of a suitable, experienced management team.

- Availability of a skilled workforce and additional training of project personnel.

- Details of the construction works involved.

- Assessment of whether the construction schedule is realistic.

- Review of the cost estimates for construction and operation and the underlying engineering data on which they are based.

- Trade-offs between initial construction costs and later maintenance and renewal costs.

## Environmental assessment

In developing and implementing most BOT projects, as is normally the case in conventional infrastructure projects, environmental screening, environmental impact assessment and the specification of environmental performance norms assume special importance. Incorporating environmental assessment into the relevant phases of the project satisfies three objectives:

- Identification of environmental risks from the inception of the project.

- Definition of an acceptable environmental impact.

- Establishment of environmental norms and standards to which the BOT contractor is expected to conform while developing, constructing and operating the project.

Environmental assessment is the subject of a vast body of literature. This section identifies only the most important tasks in the various phases of the project:

- During project identification, the host government or agency responsible for developing the project should incorporate the results of an environmental screening into the specification. The screening should verify the likely impact of the project on all environmental media (air, water, soil) and also on concerned parties such as communities and impacted or displaced populations.[3]

- When developing the project to the stage of an invitation to bid, the host government or agency usually undertakes a cost-benefit analysis of the project. Along with the cost-benefit analysis, an environmental impact assessment (EIA) should be undertaken. The EIA should specify and evaluate the likely environmental impacts of the option and project specification finally chosen. It should establish that all alternatives have been examined and that the project has maximized benefits in relation to social and environmental costs. The EIA and prevailing environmental legislation should allow establishing a set of environmental performance norms, which should then be specified in the invitation to bid. This would enable the bidder to incorporate the desired norms into the project design and the technology proposed. It would also enable the bidder to identify strategic choices that would mitigate the project's foreseen environmental impact, i.e. to use cleaner technologies rather than end-of-pipe treatment.

- In analysing the bids, the host government or the procuring agency should verify the following:

  - That environmental performance norms have been respected in the specifications provided by the bidder.
  - That those norms can, indeed, be met with the proposed project design and the chosen technology.

- The project agreement should establish an environmental performance reporting system. Such a provision would ensure that project design, construction and operation can be verified as conforming to the agreed environmental norms. The project company should be obliged to include this provision in all relevant contracts, such as construction contracts and O&M contracts.

---

[3] At the screening stage, projects are usually categorized according to the degree of their environmental impact. Projects that are viewed as having major environmental impact would obviously require more rigorous analysis and specification than projects that have a marginal impact.

- For projects that can have a substantial impact on the environment, the project agreement and the construction and O&M contracts should specify the obligations of the contracting parties to evaluate, treat and/or remedy unforeseen environmental impacts.

## Financial appraisal

A financial appraisal ensures that the BOT project is a financially viable entity and that there are sufficient funds to cover the costs of implementing the project according to the planned schedule. The financial viability of a BOT project depends on many factors, including the cost of construction and operation, the project's overall expected financial return, the cost of raising the finance required for the project. A financial appraisal is also necessary to determine which of various options would achieve the greatest financial return.

A financial appraisal of a BOT scheme evaluates the monetary costs of project implementation and operation and the projected monetary revenues associated with the project over the contract period. It focuses on the annual cash flows arising from a project, although a sponsor will also need to forecast annual balance sheets and profit and loss accounts in order to calculate profit and tax implications with greater accuracy. The net cash flow is then discounted by an appropriate discount rate reflecting the cost of capital, to arrive at the project's net present value (NPV) and internal rate of return (IRR). The purpose of the NPV and IRR calculation is to assess whether the investor can expect to earn a return on the project that would be greater than the return that could be earned from alternative investment opportunities, taking into account the relative risks of each. All of the interested parties in a BOT project are likely to carry out some form of financial appraisal:

- The government needs to estimate the monetary costs and benefits as a first stage in an economic appraisal. A financial appraisal will also allow it to test whether project cash flows alone are likely to give a sufficient financial return to a private sector sponsor or whether a contribution will be required from the public sector. The government may also require a financial model to evaluate the bids in the competitive tender.

- Potential sponsors look at both operational and financial cash flows to check the project's financial viability and to assess whether the project company will be able to meet all its financial obligations, including debt service. From the financial appraisal, the sponsor can estimate the size of any funding gap that may have to be met by a public sector contribution, the impact of different proportions of debt and equity, and the risk and return to each form of finance.

- Other equity investors need to be satisfied that the project's expected equity return on investment is acceptable in comparison with returns they could obtain from other investments with the same or less risk.

- Lenders want to be satisfied that the project can service its debt with a sufficient allowance to cover any contingencies. They normally require that sensitivity analysis considering different risk structures should show a sufficient debt service coverage ratio to ensure uninterrupted debt servicing for the term of the loan. While some lenders may be content to examine the sponsor's financial appraisal and test the underlying assumptions, some international financial institutions will undertake their own independent appraisal.

## Economic appraisal

The key purpose of an economic appraisal is to assess a BOT project's potential contribution to the government's development objectives for the whole economy and, accordingly, the project's priority in the country's infrastructure development programme. Economic appraisal is concerned with the best use of a country's resources rather than with just the monetary return to the project company. It therefore includes an appraisal of alternative ways to achieve the development objectives.

An economic appraisal of a BOT project does the following:

- Starts with the monetary costs and revenues identified by the technical appraisal, the commercial appraisal and the financial appraisal, including capital and operating costs and revenues from user charges, but excluding financing-related cash flows. The market research prepared for the commercial appraisal is also required for both a financial appraisal and an economic appraisal.

- Adjusts these monetary costs and revenues to reflect economic costs and benefits. Where market prices do not reflect the true resource costs because of distortions such as subsidies, foreign exchange controls and trade restriction, shadow prices (see section on shadow prices, below), are used to value costs and revenues.

- Assesses and, where possible, assigns monetary values to the wider economic costs and benefits of the project. These include the effect on the host country's economic development, by virtue of the project's effect on growth and employment in other industries, technology transfer, labour force skills and the environment.

- Considers the distribution of the costs and benefits (gains and losses) between different sectors and income groups. This can help the government to determine measures required to compensate groups that lose from a project.

- Assesses how the outcome of the project and its impact on the economy could change as a result of plausible variations in key factors such as capital costs, demand and income profiles and environmental conditions. These variations will be used later in a sensitivity analysis.

Of the parties to a BOT contract, the government is the one most interested in the economic appraisal, because this appraisal is concerned with the real economic return to the country as a whole rather than with the financial return to the project company. However, the sponsor may carry out an economic analysis to support its bid, or it will at least examine the government's appraisal, and it will be aware that the economic benefits of the project are part of the government's criteria for deciding a competitive tender. Financial variables such as toll levels can have a significant impact on the economic benefits of the project, so sponsors may wish to model the impact of different toll structures or construction timetables on net economic benefits.

# ■ A framework for the government's financial and economic appraisal

## Introduction

There is no single correct model for the financial and economic appraisal of infrastructure projects. Any model will have to be adapted to the circumstances of the particular project. This section sets out an appraisal framework for a host government consisting of general principles and a systematic process for applying those principles to BOT projects. The framework is intended to ensure that better decisions are made and value for money achieved from the use of the country's internal resources and foreign investment funds. This analysis should be carried out before inviting proposals.

Given the importance of infrastructure investment to national development, it is essential to assess the net economic value of a BOT project. The wider costs and benefits will not all be reflected in the financial return to a private sector investor, and corporate objectives may conflict with national objectives and priorities. In addition, the government will also need to consider the social and distributional effects of infrastructure investment, that is, the impact of investment on income distribution and on the welfare of different social groups and the populations of different localities.

This section first sets out the principles underlying the financial and economic appraisal framework and then describes the key steps in the BOT appraisal process: identification of project objectives and options, the financial appraisal, the social and economic appraisal and the sensitivity analysis. Box 8 contains a check-list for this process.

## Framework principles

The appraisal framework proposed in the *Guidelines* is based on a cost-benefit analysis, which sets a monetary value where possible on all financial, economic and social costs and benefits over the lifetime of the BOT project. The underlying principles for this analysis are as follows:

- In most cases, the relevant project lifetime to consider is set by the expected life of the longest-lived major asset to be created by the project. A discount rate is then applied to future costs and benefits to arrive at the NPV of the project.

- The elements of the analysis that can be expressed in monetary terms should be set out on a spreadsheet with separate lines for each type of cost and benefit.

- In principle, local currency should be used in the analysis, but another currency could be used if required as long as it is consistently used throughout the analysis and as long as the exchange rates used are also consistent.

- The analysis should be conducted in real terms (constant prices), but with an allowance made for relative price inflation. This is because it is the real value that matters in an investment appraisal. General inflation simply raises all cash values by a given percentage,

1.  Determine objectives of project within overall infrastructure plan.

2.  Define options for both public and private finance and different technical options.

3.  Is a BOT contract suitable for this project?

    □ Does the government require long-term strategic control over the facility?
    □ Is significant initial investment required?
    □ Is there an opportunity for efficiency gains in construction and/or operation?
    □ Can the financial outlay be recouped largely through user charges?
    □ Would such charges be publicly and politically acceptable and easy to levy?

4.  Determine lifetime of the project for appraisal.

5.  Determine appropriate discount rate.

6.  Set up spreadsheet model.

7.  Calculate project costs and revenues in financial terms, drawing on background commercial analysis and the technical appraisal.

8.  Do market prices reflect the economic value of project costs and revenues? If not, calculate the appropriate shadow prices.

9.  Identify wider economic costs and benefits and attach monetary values where possible.

10. Consider the environmental and social impact of each option and the net advantage for different regions and income groups.

11. Identify the key risks and carry out a sensitivity analysis to estimate the potential impact on economic and financial feasibility.

12. Compare options and make recommendations after weighing the advantages and disadvantages.

although financial cash flow may remain constant if the debt has been incurred at a fixed interest rate.

- The discount rate should also be expressed in real terms. For a government, the discount rate should represent the public sector's real cost of capital, reflected by the real rate of return that could be earned at the margin by similar projects in the private sector.

- Project costs and revenues should be based on central estimates, taking care to avoid the common bias towards optimism. Ideally, the values should represent the expected value of each variable, calculated from the sum of its possible values weighted by the probability of that outcome occurring. However, an expert estimate of the "most likely" outcome will be accepted if there is insufficient information to calculate an accurate probability distribution.

## Project objectives and options

The first steps in the BOT appraisal process are the following:

- Define clearly the objectives of the project. The government must decide what it is trying to achieve by the project and how this relates to its overall infrastructure strategy, capital formation and economic development policies. A subset of these objectives may be made public at a later stage to provide guidelines for potential sponsors, bidders and project managers.

- Identify the different alternative options to meet the objectives. Where possible, this should include a conventionally financed project as well as a BOT project.

## Direct financial costs and benefits

The next stage in the process is to estimate the financial costs and benefits expected from each option over the lifetime of the project and the year in which they will be incurred. These include the following:

- Initial capital expenditure on land, equipment, licences etc. Any residual values for these assets should be shown as a negative expenditure at the end of the appraisal period.

- Other construction costs, including labour and materials.

- Operating costs over the lifetime of the assets, including maintenance.

- Revenues expected from user charges, based on a forecast of the number of users, at different charge levels.

- Other receipts or revenue expected, such as contributions from land-owners benefiting from development gain.

The appraisal model should sum the expected financial costs and benefits to identify the financial NPV and IRR for the central case for each option, which will broadly indicate the net benefits of the project to a private promoter.

## Shadow prices

The next step in the appraisal process is to adjust any costs and benefits calculated in the financial appraisal to reflect their economic value, that is the opportunity cost to the country in which the facility is to be located. This is often reflected in the market price for the resources involved. However, market distortions such as an overvalued exchange rate, overstated wage rates, taxes and subsidies may cause economic and market values to differ. In these circumstances, shadow prices, which reflect true national scarcities, should be used in the appraisal.

The analysis of shadow prices is complex and whether it is worth calculating the true economic value for a particular project cost depends on the relative importance of these shadow prices to overall project viability.

## Wider costs and benefits

The next step is to identify the non-monetary costs and benefits of a BOT project, expressing them in monetary terms where possible. Guidance on methods of quantifying wider costs and benefits, such as the multiplier effect, time savings and environmental impacts, is widely available. Double-counting must be avoided: some of the costs and benefits will already be reflected in the revenues from user charges.

Wider costs and benefits of BOT projects include the following:

- The impact on industrial development of removing blockages, enhancing reliability of the infrastructure, increasing the use of local products and services or of the multiplier effects of investment.

- Effect on consumer savings of lower or higher user charges.

- Environmental impacts related to the facility itself and induced in other sectors (for example, telecommunications systems may reduce the need for transport).

- Potential for better safety standards, with consequent avoidance of death, injury and losses.

- Generation of employment during construction and operation.

- Impact on improving the supply of basic needs.

- Impact on the consumption of energy and other natural resources.

This analysis of non-monetary costs and benefits allows the government to capture the indirect impacts of the BOT project on the national economy.

## Social impact and economic net present value

The next step is to consider the impact of the BOT project on different sectors of the community and different income groups. This impact may not be quantifiable but should at least be reported on clearly so it can be taken into account by the decision maker.

The economic NPV can then be calculated for each option for the proposed BOT project as the sum of the net financial benefits, adjusted to reflect their economic value, plus the net non-financial benefits, plus any quantifiable social impact. This indicates the net benefits of the project to the country as a whole.

## Sensitivity analysis

The next step is to identify the key risks in a BOT project and conduct a sensitivity analysis. This involves modelling the impact of changes in assumptions on the values assigned to certain costs and revenues to see how the changes affect the project's overall financial and economic viability. A simple sensitivity analysis would consider the impact of, say, a possible percentile variation up or down from the expected value. A better method would be to consider a likely range of variation based on past experience or engineering estimates. A third, and more powerful, method is to calculate the "switching value", that is, the change in a variable required to make the NPV negative and the project unviable. The likelihood of a change of this magnitude may then be assessed.

The analysis should be used to assess the sensitivity of the project's financial and economic indicators to changes in the underlying assumptions. If project viability is particularly sensitive to certain risks, ways of avoiding or reducing the risk should be considered, including other technical solutions.

Key uncertainties in a BOT project are likely to be in the following areas:

- Possibility or likelihood of construction cost overruns or late completion of the project.

- Shortfalls in actual capacity compared to design capacity.

- Forecasts of the number of users and overall revenues at different levels of user charges.

- An increase in the cost of borrowing.

- Actual operating and maintenance costs.

- Residual value at the end of the concession period.

- Possibility or likelihood of project abandonment.

An important key advantage of BOT projects is that some risks are wholly or partially transferred to the private sector, including the risk of cost overruns in construction and the risk that revenues will be less than expected. The issue of risk identification and management is discussed in more detail in chapter 8. In any case the quantification of the value of risk transfer is one of the most difficult elements of the economic appraisal process.

One way of presenting the results of a sensitivity analysis is shown in table 1. This table illustrates the sensitivity of appraisal indicators to variations in the base case of a BOT toll-road project. Table 2 shows the switching values for the selected variables.

## Table 1. Sensitivity of appraisal indicators to variations from the base case

| | Appraisal indicator | | | |
| | Financial | | Economic | |
| Base case and | NPV | IRR | NPV | IRR |
| variations from it | *(thousands of US$)* | *(%)* | *(thousands of US$)* | *(%)* |
| Base case | 1 200 | 15.6 | 1 600 | 18.0 |
| 20% construction cost overrun | 880 | 13.9 | 1 290 | 15.1 |
| Shortfall of capacity by 10% | 912 | 14.3 | 1 330 | 16.9 |
| Completion delay of 6 months | 838 | 13.0 | 1 250 | 16.3 |
| Demand 10% less than expected | 840 | 13.1 | 1 260 | 15.9 |

## Table 2. Switching values (NPV = 0)

| Area of risk | Financial viability | Economic viability |
|---|---|---|
| Construction costs | 75% higher | 100% higher |
| Capacity | 39% lower | 35% lower |
| Completion delay | 2 years | 2.5 years |
| Demand shortfall | 25% lower | 35% lower |

## Comparison of options

The final stage is to compare the different options for the project. A choice between options not only should consider financial and economic NPV but also should take account of uncertainties attached to the central case and any unquantifiable benefits, such as the impact on income distribution and then carefully and systematically assess the balance of advantage.

# ▪ Evaluating bids

The government may use a financial and economic appraisal framework (for example, the one described earlier in this chapter under a framework for the government's financial and economic appraisal) to evaluate the impact of the bids on the economic NPV, varying its assessment of the cost assumptions and revenue projections in line with information contained in the bid documents. It will need to make its bid evaluation criteria clear in the bid documents, as discussed in chapter 6. Decision factors will include the following:

- The proposed initial level of user charges and the formula proposed for varying charges over time.

- The length of the concession period.

- The degree of project risk transferred from the government and the taxpayer to the sponsor.

There will be a trade-off between these factors. For example, a sponsor might be willing to settle for a lower initial user charge in return for a longer concession period or a lesser degree of risk transfer. It is difficult for the government to value the trade-offs in advance and arrive at the combination of factors that maximizes the benefit of the BOT project to the economy. One approach to the competitive tender process would be to specify the concession period and risks to be transferred to the private sector in the tender documents and require the tenderer to make a conforming bid. This would make it easy to compare the bids. However, the tenderer would also be allowed to make non-conforming bids that varied these specifications or provided for risk-sharing between the public and private sector. This would allow the government to assess the value of the trade-offs and of risk transfer and to validate or amend the initial specification. The setting of the initial concession period and the evaluation of risk transfer are discussed in more detail below.

## The concession period

The government will need to specify an initial BOT concession period for the conforming bids and also an acceptable range for non-conforming bids. Tenderers will generally prefer a long contract period to allow time to repay debts and earn a return on equity investment. A short concession period is likely to enhance the political acceptability of private involvement, particularly where a foreign sponsor is involved. At the end of the concession period, the government may be able to agree to a new operating and maintenance contract at a lower price than in the project agreement and with a shorter duration, to allow frequent market testing. This could lead to lower user charges, and if the new operator is a domestic firm, it may stem foreign exchange outflows.

However, a short concession period may adversely affect the maintenance profile during operation. The requirement to transfer the asset in a fit condition may be difficult to apply in practice, and there will inevitably be an incentive for the promoter to "patch and mend" towards the end of the contract period. The public sector therefore takes the risk that the residual value will be less than expected if the concession period is less than the economic life of the facility.

A government should take the following factors into account when specifying the length of the BOT concession period for conforming bids:

- The economic life of the infrastructure facility.

- The expected profile of renewals and maintenance expenditure.

- The likely financing structure for the private sector operator, in particular the point at which loans will be repaid.

The government can make an initial assessment of the likely trade-off between the BOT concession period and user charges by varying the assumptions in its financial and economic appraisal model. It can then use the model to assess the trade-offs made by sponsors that decide to vary the concession period in a non-conforming bid.

## Cost of risks

The key risks faced by the parties of a BOT scheme are described in more detail in chapter 8. The cost of the risks is calculated first by estimating the cost of transferring the risks where possible, for instance to insurance companies or constructors and secondly by estimating both the likelihood and the impact of each type of risk retained.

The likelihood of the risks can be assessed from:

- Past experience of the average and the maximum adverse variance in costs and revenues for similar projects.

- Engineering estimates of uncertainty in costing or the potential impact of adverse ground conditions, which should be contained in the technical appraisal.

- Estimates of the range of uncertainty of demand and revenue projections based on the market analysis.

- Previous volatility in exchange rates, inflation and economic growth in the host country and forecasts of future volatility.

The impact of an adverse outcome on the project NPV can be assessed from the economic or financial appraisal model by a sensitivity analysis as described in the section on sensitivity analysis. The impact on the project company or sponsor should also be estimated; this might damage the company's reputation or chances of securing future work as much as a financial penalty. Combining the probability and the impact for each risk allows a broad estimate to be made of the value to the government of transferring the risks to the private sector and the cost to the sponsor of accepting the risks.

The government and the sponsor are likely to assess the cost of each risk differently, for one or more of the following reasons:

- Views may differ on the likelihood of an adverse outcome. For example, the sponsor may be more certain than the government of being able to control construction cost overruns but less sanguine about political risks.

- The impact of a given risk will be different for the different parties. A large increase in construction costs could have a catastrophic impact on the project company and a significant impact on its sponsors, threatening the survival of the former and the profitability and reputation of the latter.

The tender documents should outline an initial arrangement for risk-sharing, with sponsors required to make a conforming bid against this specification and, preferably, to price the specific risks in the tender.

# ▪ Financially non-viable BOT projects

The economic rather than financial viability of a BOT project should be the overriding concern for the government. However, some projects that offer significant net economic benefits may not be financially viable for a private sector promoter under a BOT scheme. This may reflect the existence of significant economic benefits that do not generate financial returns or large uncertainties attached to the estimates of financial costs and revenues.

In these circumstances, the government may wish to consider improving the risk-reward balance for the private promoter by one of the following means:

- *Creating a national framework for infrastructure investments.* A clear legislative and regulatory framework that sets the government's objectives, strategies and long-term plans will encourage BOT sponsors by reducing the role of uncertainty and risk in their investment decisions.

- *Providing a financial contribution to reflect the wider benefits of the project.* The contribution may be in the form of a grant, loan or equity share, or it may consist of public funding for an element of the project (for example, approach roads or junctions in the case of road schemes). The contribution should not exceed the estimated value of the non-monetary benefits and should be focused at the front end of the project, where financing risk is greatest. It should be transparent and structured to provide incentives for the sponsor to improve efficiency and provide a quality service (it could, for example, grant a subsidy per unit of output).

- *Reducing bidding risk.* This could be done by limiting the number of tenders, clearly specifying project award criteria and protecting the intellectual property rights of bidders. In exceptional circumstances, the government may consider a single tender where this would clearly maximize economic benefits.

- *Sharing demand and other risks.* In road schemes, this may be achieved by allowing a variable concession period or by providing a government-guaranteed income to the private operator while creating an incentive to maintain an economically efficient toll-charging structure. In the power industry, this may involve government guarantees for power sales and fuel purchases that would give investors an adequate return on capital.

- *Establishing a regulatory authority.* Such an authority would enforce fair competition between private sector operators and publicly owned entities within the industry.

- *Providing a range of BOT projects.* In this way investors and promoters could spread risk across a portfolio of projects.

## ■ Key differences between public and private sector appraisals

Understanding the private sector's viewpoint, which may differ from its own, will help the government in its relationship with potential sponsors. There is no universally accepted financial appraisal model used by all private sponsors. In fact, there are likely differences in the approach to project appraisal and the evaluation of risks, costs and benefits by most governments and sponsors, and these warrant brief discussion:

- The government normally focuses more on the economic appraisal, while the sponsor and lenders will focus on the financial appraisal. A government is concerned with the returns to the economy as a whole and the impact of a project on industry. The sponsor is chiefly concerned with the profitability of the project company and in particular on the returns to equity finance, while the lender is concerned with the security of its lending and thus the debt service ratio.

- The government uses a lower discount rate to calculate the net present value of future project cash flows. The government's discount rate usually reflects its ability in general to borrow at lower rates than private sector companies and to raise money by taxation. The discount rate used by the private sector reflects the project company's weighted average cost of capital, that is, the opportunity cost of each type of capital (debt and equity) weighted by the relative contribution to the total capital of the company. The higher the discount rate, the lower the net present value for projects that have high up-front capital expenditures and long-term revenue flows.

- The government calculates financial cash flows before tax while the sponsor and lenders are more interested in after-tax cash flow. The government is interested in returns to the economy as a whole, including tax revenues, and will thus conduct its analysis gross of tax. The sponsor is interested in net cash flow after tax.

- The government usually carries out its appraisal in real terms (constant prices) while the sponsor considers current or nominal prices. The government is interested in the real economic return, so public sector appraisals are usually conducted in real terms. However, the private sector tends to use nominal cash flows, for a number of reasons:

  □ Most private sector managers think in terms of nominal rather than real measures.
  □ The timing of tax payments (usually paid in the year after the liability is incurred) complicates the calculation of real costs.
  □ Interest rates are usually quoted in nominal terms.
  □ The sponsor and lenders want to assess the potential impact on project cash flows of variations in inflation rates, nominal interest and exchange rates.

- The government tends to be less risk-adverse than the private sector and therefore tends to place a higher value on expected cash flow than the private sector. It generally has a broad range of activities over which to spread risk and is protected to some extent against inflationary risk by fiscal drag (the tendency of tax revenues to rise faster than inflation as allowances are eroded in real terms). The sponsor, by contrast, also has to face political risk, which can dramatically reduce the expected values assigned to project revenues, reflecting, for example, the perceived risk of expropriation or civil disorder.

- The sponsor estimates financing cash flows as well as operational cash flows. The categories of financial costs and revenues in a sponsor's appraisal are the same as shown in the government's appraisal, with the exception that, as discussed above, the sponsor deducts all tax payments from the financial cash flow.

- The government takes account of costs borne, and benefits incurred, by parties other than the sponsor.

- The government generally places a greater weight than the sponsor on non-monetary benefits and costs, such as environmental and health impacts.

# RISK IDENTIFICATION
# AND MANAGEMENT

**Risk Management**

**8**

Chapter 8 identifies the main risks that investors and lenders are concerned with when appraising BOT schemes, especially in the context of developing countries. It also describes some of the ways in which investors and lenders attempt to mitigate those risks. The private sector is generally willing to undertake those risks that it considers it can best control, while seeking maximum government support for those risks it feels it is least able to control. The annex presents four case-studies of risk management in BOT projects.

# ■ Introduction

Identification and management of risks is fundamental to any project. There is no such thing as absolute certainty in any venture. Before undertaking a project, all participants will want to identify the risks involved, as well as the steps that may be taken to manage them. Whether an infrastructure project is structured and financed under a BOT scheme or a non-BOT scheme does not alter the fundamental risks associated with it. The key difference is the participation of the private sector in BOT projects and hence the transfer of risks from the public to the private sector. Risks in infrastructure projects are heightened by the large capital outlays, by the long lead-times typically associated with such projects and-for BOT projects-by lenders and investors having to rely primarily, if not exclusively, on the project cash flow for their returns. The identification and management of risks therefore plays a key role in the structuring and financing of BOT projects and has to be handled in a well-organized and disciplined manner. This chapter presents basic principles and techniques of risk identification, risk allocation and risk management for BOT projects.

**Risk Identification**

**8**

# ▪ Risk Identification

It is difficult to generalize about the risk characteristics of BOT infrastructure projects. Each host country, each infrastructure sector, indeed each specific BOT project has its own risk profile. The different types of risks BOT projects are exposed to may, however, be divided into two broad categories for the purpose of risk identification:

- General (or country) risks, which are associated with the political, economic and legal environment of the host country and over which the project sponsors generally have little or no control.

- Specific project risks, which to some extent are controllable by the project sponsors.

A check-list of general risks and specific project risks for BOT projects is set forth in table 3.

## General (or country) risks

General or country risks refer to factors such as a country's economic growth, its political environment, the tax code, the legal system and the prevailing currency exchange regime. Such factors will affect demand for the output and services of BOT projects, that is, demand for power, water and transport services as well as their ability to meet their contractual obligations. But while the operators of BOT projects can control the level and quality of a project's output, they are not in a position to influence a country's growth rate, which is more a function of macroeconomic management. Similarly, unfavourable inflation, interest or exchange rate movements can result in rapid deterioration of a project's cash flow if the project company is unable to respond rapidly by adjusting the tariffs it charges.

The general risks may be divided into three major categories:

- *Political risks.* These are related to the internal and external political situation and the stability of the host country, the government's attitude towards allowing the private sector profits from infrastructure projects, changes in the host country's fiscal regime, including taxation, the risk of expropriation and nationalization of the projects by the host country, cancellation of the concession, and similar factors.

## Table 3. Worksheet for risk identification and risk allocation

| | Project company | Insurance company | Other contractors | Host government |
|---|---|---|---|---|
| **Political risks** | | | | |
| Political support risks | | | | |
| Taxation risks | | | | |
| Expropriation/nationalization risks | | | | |
| Forced buy-out risks | | | | |
| Cancellation of concession | | | | |
| Import/export restrictions | | | | |
| Failure to obtain or renew approvals | | | | |
| **Country commercial risks** | | | | |
| Currency inconvertibility risks | | | | |
| Foreign exchange risks | | | | |
| Devaluation risks | | | | |
| Inflation risks | | | | |
| Interest rate risk | | | | |
| **Country legal risks** | | | | |
| Changes in laws and regulations | | | | |
| Law enforcement risk | | | | |
| Delays in calculating compensation | | | | |
| **Development risks** | | | | |
| Bidding risks | | | | |
| Planning delay risks | | | | |
| Approval risks | | | | |
| Transnational risks | | | | |
| **Construction/completion risks** | | | | |
| Delay risk | | | | |
| Cost overrun risks | | | | |
| Re-performance risk | | | | |
| Completion risk | | | | |
| *Force majeure* risk | | | | |
| Loss or damage to work | | | | |
| Liability risk | | | | |
| **Operating risks** | | | | |
| Associated infrastructure risks | | | | |
| Technical risks | | | | |
| Demand risk (volume and price) | | | | |
| Supply risk (volume and price) | | | | |
| Cost escalation risks | | | | |
| Management risks | | | | |
| *Force majeure* risk | | | | |
| Loss or damage to project facilities | | | | |
| Liability risk | | | | |

Risk Management

8

- *Country commercial risks.* These are risks related to the convertibility of revenue from the project into foreign currencies, foreign exchange and interest fluctuation and inflation. They have their impact on the cost of finance, which is usually high for infrastructure projects.

- *Country legal risks.* BOT schemes rely heavily on contractual arrangements and the legal framework supporting project financing arrangements. The risks to sponsors and lenders is that legislation that is relevant to the BOT project (for instance, environmental legislation or property legislation) may change after a BOT scheme has been implemented. Such changes may substantially undermine the long-term viability of the project if the sponsors are not compensated for them.

The importance of these risks can vary substantially from country to country and from project to project.

## Specific project risks

Specific project risks, which sponsors and lenders face in addition to the general risks discussed above, refer to risks that are generally within the control of the sponsors, such as the management capabilities of project operators. The specific project risks may be broadly divided into the following categories in accordance with the phases of a project cycle:

- *Development risks.* These are risks associated with the bidding competition that occurs in the initial stage of the BOT process, e.g. the bidder's risk of losing the tender to another bidder or of failing to sign the project agreement, resulting in the loss of development expenditures. For large BOT projects, development and bidding costs can be very high, as such projects require detailed design, comprehensive planning, preparation of extensive bid documents and lengthy clarifications.

The development risks may also include losses caused by delays in planning and approval, which can be particularly acute in the case of transnational projects, where project sponsors have to deal with the authorities of two or more governments.

- *Construction/completion risks.* The primary risks here are the following:

□ The actual cost of construction may be higher than projected (cost overruns).

□ Completion takes longer than projected (completion delays).

□ The construction of the project is not completed.

In the last case, funds invested in a partially completed infrastructure project may be lost, while the return on investment will certainly suffer in the two first cases. The degree of construction/completion risk differs from project to project. For example, it can be considerable for the design and construction of a nuclear power plant or a distant off-the-road project site, while it is not very high for a conventional motorway in an urban area.

- *Operating risks.* Operating risks result from insufficiency in performance, revenue income, material supply etc. and from higher-than-expected operating costs. They may be divided into six main categories:

    □ *Associated-infrastructure risks.* These risks are associated with facilities outside the project, such as approach roads (in a highway project) and transmission lines (in a power project), for which construction responsibility lies with third parties rather than the project sponsors themselves. While such facilities may not specifically be part of a BOT scheme, they are nevertheless essential to the operational success of the scheme. This being the case, the BOT scheme in question is subject to the risk that the associated facilities may not be constructed or completed in time, thus jeopardizing its operations. Associated-infrastructure risks can be especially high in transnational projects.

    □ *Technical risks.* These include design defects and latent defects in project equipment. BOT projects are usually required to meet certain performance targets specified by the government, the relevant authority or the contracted purchaser of the project's output. (Examples of performance targets are the quality of water discharged from a water treatment plant and the level of electricity supplied from a power station.) Design, construction or equipment defects may be important risks, particularly in BOT projects that involve highly sophisticated technologies.

    □ *Demand risks.* Most BOT projects that rely on market-based revenues face demand risks related to volume and/or prices, in case the actual demand for output or services generated by the project may be lower than forecast, thereby lowering the rate of return of the project. Unless the BOT project is a local natural monopoly or the forecasting models can be demonstrated to have a high degree of accuracy, the lenders will normally perceive the demand risks as considerable.

□ *Supply risks.* Because they are also market risks, supply risks have two components, volume and price. Some BOT projects face the risk of an uncertain supply of critical raw materials (e.g. fuel supply to a power plant). If the raw material supply is uncertain or insufficient to meet the needs of a project, the project's ability to meet output commitments and debt repayment obligations will be compromised. In some cases, raw material supply is controlled by either the State or a monopoly, which means that projects being supplied would be at the mercy of sudden increases in price over which they have little or no control, but which would nevertheless have an adverse impact on the operations of the project.

□ *Management risks.* The quality of management in every project is always a critical success factor.

□ Force majeure *risks. Force majeure* risks denote losses from certain exceptional types of events beyond the control of the parties to the BOT project that impede the performance of their obligations. The losses include casualty losses from events such as fire, flood and earthquake and non-casualty losses from events such as war, civil disturbance, strikes and lockouts. If a *force majeure* event occurs and continues for a long period, the concession may be terminated. *Force majeure* risks may also be borne by key suppliers of raw materials or services such as transportation. Parties required to take the service or the output of the project under a long-term take-or-pay contract are also subject to such risks. Some *force majeure* risks may be covered by insurance from private or government sources. The main issue in relation to BOT projects is, therefore, the allocation of those *force majeure* events and losses that are not insurable.

## Special risk challenges facing BOT projects in developing countries

All BOT project participants are confronted with a wide range of general risks and specific project risks. These risks may be magnified in some countries, depending on whether one or more of the following conditions prevail:

- The local currency is convertible at fair rates and foreign exchange is available in the country. If not, BOT projects, which generate local currency revenues, may not be able to meet their obligations to foreign investors.

- The legal system is developed enough to support private and foreign investment in infrastructure projects, including whether contractual obligations are enforceable on a consistent and predictable basis.

- Data for the preparation of bids, development of projects and forecasting of demand are available and reliable.

- There are domestic contractors or operators that have recognized track records and that can give creditworthy performance guarantees. If not, internationally recognized contractors and operators may need to participate.

- There is an adequate transport infrastructure for construction of the project and for raw material suppliers, who must be able to deliver on a steady and reliable basis.

## ■ Risk allocation and risk management in BOT projects

### Basic principles

All the above-mentioned risks need to be allocated and managed efficiently to ensure the success of a BOT project. There are three overriding considerations when designing the risk allocation and management structure of a BOT project. First, it is the cost of the project in its entirety that should decide any particular risk allocation. Naturally, the host government wants to transfer most of the risks to the private sector. The private sector, on the other hand, is anxious to reduce its exposure to the risks. In any particular risk allocation, however, both parties should be concerned with the efficiency gains and costs of the project in its entirety. This means that a particular risk should be borne by the party most suited to deal with it, in terms of control or influence and costs. In some cases, the party in the best position to financially bear a particular risk may prefer some method of risk allocation that, in the interest of the project, does not reduce the other party's incentive to performance efficiently.

Secondly, since the solutions to the risk management of a BOT project do not in principle rely on unconditional guarantees from any one party alone, the financial structure of the project (also called the credit structure) must meet the following requirements:

- All substantial project risks have to be identified, allocated and managed.

- The project risks have to be managed by a combination of financial resources and firm contractual commitments.

Thirdly, the risk structure has to be sufficiently sound to cope with a combination of pessimistic scenarios for the project.

It follows that risk in a BOT project has to be allocated and managed on a case-by-case basis. Normally, however, the private sponsors will agree to bear risks that are familiar to them, such as most development risks, construction and completion risks and operating risks. The sponsors will hesitate to agree to bear uninsurable risks that are unquantifiable and outside their control, such as some political risks and country commercial risks, indeterminate demand risks and uninsurable *force majeure* risks. If a government still wishes to transfer some of these risks to the private sector, it must be prepared to accept the consequences of a higher cost of services.

## The contractual structure for risk allocation and risk management

The basic risk allocation is defined in the project agreement between the project company and the government entity that awards the BOT concession. This agreement defines the commitments of each party, including how risks are to be allocated or shared between them.

With the project agreement in hand, the project company will proceed to negotiate and sign a series of contracts with other project participants. These contracts will also define how the risks allocated to the project company by the government will be distributed between the sponsors and the other project participants. The set of contracts relevant for risk allocation normally include the following:

- The shareholders agreement.

- Various credit agreements with project lenders.

- The construction contract.

- Equipment supply contracts.

- Where applicable, fuel and long-term materials supply contracts.

- The off-take contract with the project's long-term output purchaser, if there is one, or the tariff agreement with the relevant regulatory authority.

- The operations and maintenance contract with the project operator.

- s.

The combination of the project agreement and all these agreements will define the basic risk structure of the project. How risks are allocated among the project participants is presented below.

### Risk borne by the host government

Usually, the host government will be able to devolve most risks related to the development, construction, management and operation of a BOT project to the project company. If the project company defaults in the performance of any of these obligations, these risks become project lenders' risks.

The picture is less clear in the case of demand and revenue risks. If the purchaser of off-take contracted services is a creditworthy public utility, which normally is the case in power, water and sewerage treatment projects, the project company normally accepts these risks; that is, the project lenders accept the risks, usually on the basis of a covenant by the project company that a reasonable debt to revenue ratio is maintained. If the revenues are paid by the public, e.g. toll roads, airport charges or electricity charges, the project company takes a much higher risk on revenue generation, and this is then borne by the project lenders. The lenders may seek to have part of the risk passed on to the government by means of guarantees for a minimum demand/revenue level or by stand-by loans. The demand and revenue risks could also be mitigated by a governmental undertaking that no alternative road, airport or energy source will compete with the project for a specified period.

When a government first embarks on a BOT approach it may find it necessary to provide some kind of support to the project company if a minimum level of demand/revenue is not met. In such an instance, that is, where BOT structures are untested, the private sector perceives the

Risk Management

8

risk as correspondingly greater. As the precedent for successful BOT schemes is established and the concept matures, a government will be in a position to reduce its support and to impose more stringent demands on the private sector. A good example of this is the Mexican Government's highway concession programme (see case-study 1 in the annex to this chapter). When the programme was first implemented, it effectively guaranteed traffic volumes (if actual traffic volume was below that forecast by the Government, the project company had the right to request an extension of the concession period to cover the shortfall in traffic). Once it was successfully established, extensions were no longer granted automatically and the Government retained the right to shorten the concession period if a certain rate of return on investment was exceeded.

Political risks such as delays and cost increases caused by the government or governmental authorities, including delays in obtaining required approvals, permits and licences, are normally considered to be borne by the government as it is the government that would ordinarily pay any compensation. Alternatively, in some cases prolongation of the concession period is provided for in the project agreement.

As for allocating the risk of taxes, tariffs or customs duties being increased or imposed as part of a general increase or imposition, there is no general rule. Obviously, no government will give an assurance or guarantee that such taxes or duties will not be increased or imposed. If a compensation is not provided for in the project agreement, the risks are borne by the project company.

Governments may bear or share BOT risks through performance guarantees, stand-by loan arrangements or compensation provisions, including assurances that:

- Certain minimum purchases will be made, at certain prices, thus assuring certain levels of project revenues.

- Certain minimum supplies of raw materials will be available, at certain prices, thus helping to ensure that project costs are predictable.

- Foreign exchange will be available for conversion of project revenues to repay offshore loans and to repatriate the dividends of foreign investors.

- Conversion into foreign exchange will be at certain predetermined exchange rates, thus avoiding exchange risks.

Governments may give such assurances to project sponsors to reduce uncertainty surrounding the repayment of project loans. Loan repayment will depend on the ability of management to operate the BOT
facilities efficiently enough to generate a sufficient surplus for the repayment of project loans. The level and type of risk borne by the government will be an important indication to the financial community of the
government's commitment to the project.

## Risks borne by the project company

The merit of the sponsors of the project company is the single most
important factor looked at by both host governments and lenders when
evaluating the risks of a BOT project:

- Their experience and ability to undertake such projects.

- Their creditworthiness and commitment to the project, i.e. their
  ability to bear risks in case the project does not proceed according
  to plan.

- The experience, capability and creditworthiness of the partners that
  the sponsors choose to associate with (e.g. the prime contractor,
  equipment suppliers, the project operator, raw material suppliers).

No matter how good a project is in terms of design and economic
viability, these factors mean nothing if the project is badly executed or if
the sponsors and their partners are unable to cover any shortfalls as the
project progresses. While reputation is not a guarantee of loan repayment or returns on investment, financiers will nevertheless seek comfort in the credibility of the sponsors and their partners. Lenders will
want to know that they can be relied on to deliver the project on time,
within budget and to the required technical standards and that in case
of failure they will have the ability to make good any shortfalls.

Governments and financing institutions will want sponsors to bear a
significant part of the project risks, as the sponsors' returns will be linked
to the long-term success of the project. Four kinds of risks are typically
undertaken by the project sponsors through the project company.

- *Construction and completion risks*
  Construction and completion risks would include responsibility for
  all project development costs, construction cost overruns and the
  cost of delays. To ensure adequate management of the construction

risks, the project agreement normally requires that the sponsors do the following:

- Provide completion guarantees, including additional sponsors' funds (equity or subordinated debt) where necessary.
- Make certain minimum levels of equity investment.
- Provide loan repayment guarantees during construction or some other specified period of time.
- Maintain certain minimum debt-equity and debt service coverage ratios for the project company.
- Sign fixed-price turnkey contracts with the prime contractor that include completion and performance guarantees and stipulate liquidated damages payable in the event that a defined level of performance is not met.
- Arrange for similar guarantees from the equipment suppliers and subcontractors assigned to the sponsors and their lenders.
- Use proven technology.
- Arrange for insurance during the construction period.

If a contractor or equipment supplier defaults in performance, the consequence is to the project sponsors.

- *Operating risks*
  The risks of a failure to operate or maintain the project in accordance with the project agreement are to be borne by the sponsors. The sponsors may manage these risks by transferring part of them to the O&M operator of the project in the O&M agreement. The project agreement requires that the sponsors cover insurable operating risks through an insurance package, including insurance of loss and damage to the project facilities and liability insurance. The project lenders may also require proceed retention accounts.
  To ensure that the project operator is performing satisfactorily, government, sponsors and lenders normally require monitoring and measurement of its performance (e.g. quality and quantity of output). This also facilitates the linkage of compensation and penalties to actual performance. Monitoring of BOT schemes is also necessary to ensure that an adequate investment programme and a defined maintenance schedule are followed.
  Some lenders require the establishment of technical assistance agreements between the project company and equipment suppliers.

- *Supply risks*
  The sponsors normally have to bear the supply risks. To protect themselves from these risks, they usually enter into contracts to

secure long-term supplies of basic inputs of the appropriate quality and at stable prices. The supply contracts should therefore include the following:

- Supply of raw materials, fuel and spare parts on a long-term basis.
- Commitments as to availability, quality and price, with appropriate penalties for failure to meet these conditions.
- An appropriate price escalation formula to allow for such factors as inflation and exchange rate movements.
- Supplies matched to project output to minimize the risk of market disparity between cost and availability of feedstock on the one hand and price of and demand for output on the other.

Where long-term supply contracts are not obtainable, lenders may require additional equity commitments from the sponsors, as either collateral accounts or equity subscription obligations, to ensure that lenders' security is maintained.

- *Currency and interest rate risks*
  A wide range of capital market instruments, such as swaps, options and futures, is now available for the management and hedging of currency and interest rate risks. What these instruments offer are the following:

  - Where there are many capital market participants, each will seek to transform its risk exposure into one that matches its own risk-reward profile. It is often possible to find complementary pairs of participants who can achieve their desired risk-reward profiles by swapping their respective exposures. For instance, one party may have United States dollar liabilities while generating German mark revenues and the other, German mark liabilities while generating United States dollar revenues. Clearly, both parties are exposed to exchange risk. If the two were to swap their liabilities, however, both would end up with liabilities that matched their revenues and exchange risk would be mitigated. A similar logic can be applied to the swapping of fixed and floating interest rates, to avoid interest rate risk.
  - There are market participants who are willing to bet on interest and exchange rate movements. These participants sell exchange rate options and future contracts to any party averse to exchange risk and seeking to lock in certain exchange rates. The parties selling the contracts take the risk that they may be wrong, in which case they incur a loss, but they also have the

potential for substantial profits if they are right. By contrast, the parties buying the contracts are fully protected, irrespective of exchange rate movements: they are protected from losses if exchange rates move against them, but they also stand to make no gains if exchange rates move in their favour.

## Emerging instruments for risk management in project finance

Swaps, options and futures offer project participants the means to remove uncertainty from currency and interest rate movements. As such, they allow project participants to adjust their risk-reward profiles to better suit their own absorption capabilities.

The reluctance of banks to lend in some countries without government guarantees presents a major problem in arranging financing. To address this problem, the export guarantee agencies of various countries, as well as international financial institutions such as the World Bank and, associated with it, the Multilateral Investment Guarantee Agency (MIGA) and the International Finance Corporation (IFC), increasingly provide protection against political and exchange risks where commercial insurance is very expensive and where capital market hedging instruments are not available.

In September 1994, the World Bank replaced its extended cofinancing facility (ECO) by bank guarantees to be used for infrastructure financing. These guarantees are designed to cover specific risks (the partial risk guarantee) or part of the financing (the partial credit guarantee). A partial risk guarantee covers risks arising from the non-performance of host government obligations spelt out in agreements with the project company or from *force majeure* events resulting in debt service default to the lenders. They are most appropriate for limited recourse financing as used in BOT and similar projects. A partial credit guarantee covers all events of non-payment for a designated part of the financing scheme with the exception of equity capital. It typically extends maturities beyond what private creditors could otherwise provide. Unlike IFC and MIGA, the World Bank requires a government counter-guarantee, which normally consists of an indemnity agreement for any payments the Bank makes under its guarantee.

A MIGA guarantee predominantly covers equity investments and can cover debt extended by equity investors. It provides coverage against political risks, such as currency convertibility, war and civil disturbance, and expropriation, and has specific project and country limits on its exposure. It does not enter into formal counter-guarantee arrangements with the host government.

# FOUR CASE-STUDIES

## CASE STUDY 1: LA VENTA-COLEGIO MILITAR HIGHWAY
## MEXICO CITY, MEXICO[4]

Grupo Tribasa S.A. is a Mexican construction company engaged in the construction of large-scale infrastructure projects. It specializes in highway construction but also engages in the construction of other projects, including tunnels, drainage systems, railways, airport runways, dams, water distribution systems, bridges and industrial facilities. On the basis of revenues, Tribasa is the second largest construction company in Mexico.

### Concessions

Since 1989, Tribasa has been engaged in the development, construction and operation of highways under the Mexican Government's highway concession programme. Until the end of 1993, all of Tribasa's highway concessions entitled the concessionaire to request extensions of the concession period in the event that traffic volumes were below levels specified in the concession, i.e. the Government took responsibility for estimating traffic volumes and bore the risk that those estimates might be wrong. Under this arrangement, Tribasa was protected from downside risks by the possibility of extending the term of the concession and also had unlimited upside potential, that is, if volumes were higher than forecast, then the additional benefits accrued entirely to it.

However, the terms of the concessions have been altered significantly in concessions granted since the beginning of 1994. Not only are extension provisions no longer included in concession agreements, but the concession periods are subject to reduction once the concessions produce a specified rate of return on investment. This change effectively shifts the burden of risk from the Government to the project sponsors; it puts an upper limit on the concessionaire's returns while giving it no downside protection. Tribasa's latest BOT concession is for the La Venta-Colegio Militar Highway. The term of the concession is 25 years, there is no extension provision but there is a stipulation that if traffic volumes exceed those set forth in the concession agreement, the term may be reduced or Tribasa may be required to pay a portion of earnings to the Government. Furthermore, the Government retains the right to revoke or terminate the highway concession without compensation before expiration of its term, in the event Tribasa fails to perform its obligations or to comply with the terms of the concession or applicable law. The BOT structure for the La Venta-Colegio Militar Highway is illustrated in figure V.

---

[4]*Source*: Extracted from Public Debt Offering Memorandum for Tribasa Toll Road 1, November 1993.

**Risk Management**

**8**

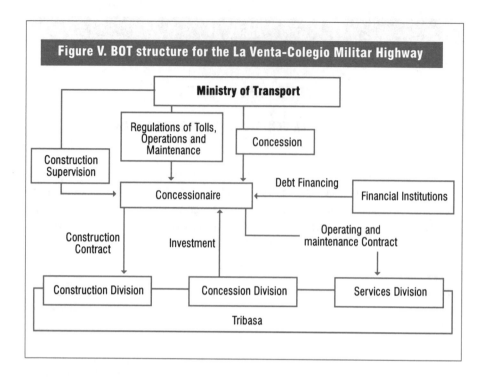

Figure V. BOT structure for the La Venta-Colegio Militar Highway

## Construction

As a construction company, Tribasa acts as the lead contractor for its own projects. To the extent that a fixed term and specific traffic volume forecasts are set out in the concession agreement, the Mexican authorities are not concerned with the actual construction cost of the project. The onus is on Tribasa, as the lead sponsor, to ensure that construction costs are kept as low as possible, since there is no assurance that a cost overrun will be protected by an extension of the concession period. In this case, lenders will be looking to the credibility of Tribasa to bring the project in on time and within budget and hence maximize the chances of the project loans being repaid.

## Operation

Tribasa has committed itself to perform operating and maintenance services for the highway at a specified management fee price. In addition, revenues are generated from tolls collected on the concession highway. The tolls to be charged are regulated, with the schedule of starting (base) tolls set out in the concession agreements and increased every six months, in accordance with the national consumer price index (NCPI) or whenever the NCPI increases by 5 per cent or more since the last adjustment. The toll for any one period is therefore calculated as follows:

$$\boxed{\text{Highway Toll}} = \boxed{\text{Base Toll}} \quad X \quad \boxed{\begin{array}{c} 1 + \text{percentage increase in NPCI} \\ \text{between last adjustment date and} \\ \text{Base Date} \end{array}}$$

The toll increases may be made without government approval, although supporting documentation has to be filed with the Ministry of Transport. Other toll increases above the levels set forth in the concession agreement would require specific government approval. Tribasa, however, is free to offer discounts or other special pricing arrangements to stimulate traffic volume, subject to the maximum levels set out in the concession agreement.

### Creditors

To raise debt financing for the La Venta-Colegio Militar Highway, Tribasa offered the revenues from the existing toll roads that it owns and operates as security, to the extent that those revenues were not already pledged for other purposes. In this way, financing was obtained without recourse to Tribasa, and the obligations do not appear as liabilities on the company's consolidated balance sheet.

### CASE-STUDY 2: DOSWELL INDEPENDENT POWER PROJECT, STATE OF VIRGINIA, UNITED STATES[5]

In 1986, the Virginia Electric and Power Company (Virginia Power) solicited proposals for co-generation power production facilities to supply power to meet its projected needs in the 1990s. The Intercontinental Energy Corporation (IEC) was one of the successful bidders. In June 1987, IEC and Virginia Power drew up two agreements (including power purchase agreements, or PPAs) for the development and supply of power to Virginia Power, each for a term of 25 years and for approximately 300 megawatts (MW) per annum capacity. In June 1989, the Doswell Limited Partnership, a limited partnership established to develop independent power, acquired the rights to develop the project from IEC.

### Concession

The Doswell project consists of a natural-gas-fired, two-unit combined-cycle power generation plant using proven technology. The combined capacity of the two units varies by season, between 724 MW per annum in winter and 603 MW per annum in summer. The original estimated dependable capacity (EDC) of the plant is 605 MW per annum, although the partnership has the option, under the PPA, to deliver up to 110 per cent of the original EDC (i.e. 663 MW per annum) to Virginia Power. However, the PPA also specifies that the partnership

[5] *Source*: Extracted from Financing Memorandum for Doswell Limited Partnership, 1989.

Risk Management

8

is liable for liquidated damages in the event that: (a) tests at commissioning indicate actual dependable capacity to be less than the original EDC and (b) subsequent semi-annual tests indicate actual dependable capacity to be less than 85 per cent of the original EDC.

Fuel for the Doswell project is natural gas supplied by Virginia Natural Gas (VNG) through a pipeline constructed by VNG, which is in turn connected to a pipeline constructed by CNG Transmission Corporation (CNG). CNG provides underground storage facilities for natural gas for use during the winter months. In addition, there is on-site oil storage sufficient for 15 days of continuous operation.

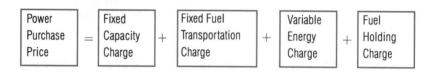

### Power purchase agreements

The power purchase price consists of four components based on the parameters of an existing 214,000-kilowatt (kW) power plant in Chesterfield County (Chesterfield 7):
The details of the four components are as follows:

- *A fixed capacity charge*. This is the fixed cost of having the Doswell plant available to supply power to Virginia Power, irrespective of actual sales. It is designed to cover salaries, overheads, depreciation, interest expense etc., repay creditors, recover the investment of investors and make a small profit, even if no consumption takes place. The fixed capacity charge is calculated to be US$ 10.2567 per kW for the first 15 years (the loan repayment period) and US$ 5.8933 per kW for the remainder of the concession period.

- *A variable energy charge*. This charge is designed to cover the cost of fuel used to generate electricity and is calculated as follows:

The energy purchase price per kilowatt-hour (kWh) is calculated monthly, using the following formula:

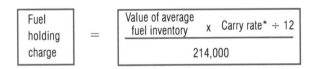

$$\begin{array}{|c|}\hline \text{Energy} \\ \text{Purchase} \\ \text{Price} \\ \hline \end{array} = \begin{array}{|c|}\hline \text{Fuel Price} \\ \text{(US\$ / mBTU)} \\ \hline \end{array} \text{X} \begin{array}{|c|}\hline \dfrac{\text{7,700 BTU / kWH}}{\text{1,000,000}} \\ \hline \end{array} \text{x 1.1 x 1.0115 x} \begin{array}{|c|}\hline \text{O\&M} \\ \text{Costs} \\ \hline \end{array}$$

The number of BTUs required to generate 1 kWh was calculated to be 7,700. The index of 1.1 reflects the fact that the actual quantity of power generated is expected to be 10 per cent more than the EDC. The index of 1.0115 reflects the fact that the pipe loss for gas transport is expected to be 1.15 per cent. Operating and maintenance costs are included in the energy price and were initially calculated to be 0.131 cents per kWh. They have since been escalated annually by the GNP implicit price deflator.

- A fuel holding charge. This is the working capital cost of holding fuel in storage and is calculated by the following formula:

$$\begin{array}{|c|}\hline \text{Fuel} \\ \text{holding} \\ \text{charge} \\ \hline \end{array} = \begin{array}{|c|}\hline \dfrac{\text{Value of average fuel inventory} \quad \text{x} \quad \text{Carry rate* } \div \text{ 12}}{\text{214,000}} \\ \hline \end{array}$$

\* (The carry rate refers to the prime interest rate, as announced from time to time by the Chase Manhattan Bank.)

The fixed capacity and fuel transportation charges give Doswell downside protection. To the extent that the energy charge is based on the market price of fuel, the partnership is protected from input cost inflation. The return on investment to the partnership therefore depends entirely on how efficiently the plant is operated. Exchange risks are not an issue in this case, since the project is 100 per cent United States dollar funded, with all project revenues in United States dollars.

## CASE-STUDY 3: SHAJIAO B POWER STATION, GUANGDONG PROVINCE, CHINA[6]

Hopewell Power China Limited (HPCL) signed a joint venture contract with the Shenzhen Power Corporation on 8 March 1985 to implement a BOT power project in Shenzhen, Guangdong Province. The contract provides for a cooperation period of 10 years, during which all facilities, machinery and equipment comprising Shajiao B are owned by HPCL. During the cooperation period, Hopewell Power has the right to operate and manage the power station and to sell the electricity generated thereby, as stipulated in the off-take agreement. At the end of the cooperation period, HPCL is obliged to transfer Shajiao B to Shenzhen Power in normal and operational condition for no consideration.

### Management agreement

Under the terms of the joint venture contract, HPCL has contracted Shajiao B's operational and management responsibilities to Shenzhen Power. The management fee has both foreign (United States dollar) and local (yuan renminbi) currency components. The schedule of payments to Shenzhen Power is US$ 0.0046675 and Y 0.0013069 per kWh for sales up to the minimum quantity (see below) specified in the off-take agreement and US$ 0.0021795 and Y 0.0006102 per kWh for sales in excess of the minimum quantity.

### Coal supply agreement

A coal supply agreement was executed on 6 December 1985 between Shenzhen Power, HPCL and Citicorp International. Under this agreement, Shenzhen Power is responsible for delivering coal of a certain specification to HPCL at the site of Shajiao B to meet the requirements of the power plant. The coal is to be purchased by HPCL at a fixed price of Y 90 per metric ton, subject to adjustments for quality. If Shenzhen is unable to supply coal as required by the supply agreement and HPCL is required to purchase the coal outside China, then Shenzhen is obliged to reimburse HPCL in foreign exchange for the cost of these imports. In addition, Shenzhen must assist HPCL to obtain all relevant approvals so that the imports can be brought in free of import duties.

### Off-take agreement

The off-take agreement was executed on the same date as the coal supply agreement and between the same three parties. Under this agreement, Shenzhen Power is obliged to take-or-pay for not less than 60 per cent of the installed capacity of Shajiao B (the minimum quantity). Prior to 1 January 1992, the price of electricity was Y 0.001148 per kWh for all sales up to the minimum quantity and Y 0.0006 per kWh for all sales above the minimum quantity. Starting from 1 January 1992, however, the price for all electricity sales was unified at Y 0.001148 per kWh. Shenzhen is obliged to pay for its power purchases, 50 per cent in local currency and 50 per cent in foreign currencies. For purposes of calculating the foreign currency component,

---

[6] *Source*: Extracted from Public Equity Offering Memorandum for the listing of Consolidated Electric Power Asia Limited shares on the Hong Kong Stock Exchange.

yuan renminbi are converted at predetermined exchange rates, that is, all exchange risks are borne by Shenzhen. Furthermore, in the event that HPCL is unable to meet certain project expenses as a result of factors other than an act, omission or breach by Shenzhen, the latter is obliged to make a subordinated loan up to a maximum aggregate amount of US$ 500 million to HPCL.

The preceding arrangements effectively give HPCL the following protection:

- Downside protection by virtue of a minimum take-or-pay obligation.

- Protection against fuel price inflation by virtue of a fixed price.

- Exchange risks protection by virtue of partial payment for power in foreign exchange at a predetermined fixed exchange rate.

## Guarantees

In addition, Shenzhen payments to HPCL under the coal supply and off-take agreements are guaranteed by the Guangdong International Trust and Investment Corporation (GITIC), i.e. performance guarantees, not full repayment guarantees. To obtain this guarantee, HPCL has to pay GITIC a fee of US$ 20 million per annum.

## Syndicated facilities agreement

A syndicated facilities agreement (SFA) was executed between HPCL and certain financial institutions, with Citicorp International as agent. Under the agreement, HPCL was granted loan facilities of US$ 600 million and Y 11 billion and a guarantee facility of up to Y 52 billion for the benefit of the turnkey contract for Shajiao B. The two loan facilities have since been repaid in full and the guarantee facility refinanced pursuant to a supplemental syndicated facilities agreement, under which Hopewell was granted a syndicated loan facility of Y 49 billion, repayable in 25 quarterly instalments. The terms of the supplemental agreement prohibit the payment by HPCL of any dividend or other distribution and the repayment of any share capital before the loan is fully repaid.

---

[7] *Source*: Extracted from Public Equity Offering Memorandum for the listing of Consolidated Electric Power Asia Limited shares on the Hong Kong Stock Exchange.

## CASE-STUDY 4: NAVOTAS I POWER STATION, METRO MANILA, PHILIPPINES[7]

A project agreement was entered into on 16 November 1988 between Hopewell Project Management Company Limited (HPML) and the National Power Company (NAPOCOR), a State-owned entity responsible for generating practically all electric power in the Philippines.

### Project agreement

The project agreement entitled HPML to carry out the design, development, construction, completion, testing and commissioning of the Navotas I Power Plant and to be responsible for the financing of the project, the obtaining of all necessary approvals and the import of all necessary equipment. Under the project agreement, NAPOCOR was responsible for making the project site available at no cost, for ensuring the provision of all necessary utilities and for the construction, installation and connection of the transmission line. Testing of the plant was successfully completed on 22 March 1991. The cooperation period is 12 years, during which HPML owns the power station together with all fixtures, fittings, machinery and equipment. HPML is also responsible for the management, operation, maintenance and repair of the power station.

NAPOCOR is obliged to supply and deliver, at its own cost, all fuel (in accordance with specifications set out in the project agreement) for the power station and to purchase all the electricity generated at its request. During the cooperation period it is further obliged to pay, on a monthly basis, the following: (a) a capacity fee, payable in United States dollars, based on the contracted capacity for each year following completion of the power station (as nominated by HPML, but not exceeding 210,000 kW unless NAPOCOR agrees) and a base rate of US$ 3.225 per kW per month, but subject to adjustment in the event of reduction in the available capacity of the power station, during the relevant month; (b) an energy fee, based on the amount of electricity generated pursuant to requests from NAPOCOR, payable partly in United States dollars (US$ 0.003 per kWh) and partly in Philippine pesos (P 0.023 per kWH), with the portion payable in Philippine pesos being subject to adjustment for inflation; (c) start-up fees, payable partly in United States dollars and partly in Philippine pesos, in each case calculated in accordance with formulae specified in the project agreement. At the end of the cooperation period, HPML is obliged to transfer the power station to NAPOCOR for no consideration, on an as-is basis, with NAPOCOR responsible for all costs and expenses incurred in connection with the transfer.

The pricing formula, as described above, effectively gives HPML the following protection:

- Downside protection by virtue of a capacity charge.

- Protection against fuel price inflation by virtue of free fuel.

- Exchange risks protection by virtue of capacity charge payments and partial energy payments in United States dollars.

- Protection against inflation by virtue of indexation of Philippine peso payments to inflation.

## Financing

A project company, Hopewell Energy Philippines Corporation, was established to implement the project with four shareholders: HPML for 60.1 per cent of the shares; Citicorp for 19.9 per cent of the shares; the Asian Development Bank (ADB) for 10 per cent of the shares; and the International Finance Corporation (IFC) for 10 per cent of the shares. Under the investment agreements with ADB and IFC, each also granted loans to Hopewell Energy Philippines: two US$ 10 million loans from ADB (one for its own account and one for the account of participating commercial banks) and one US$ 10 million loan from IFC. The agreements contain covenants restricting, *inter alia,* the ability of Hopewell Energy Philippines to pay dividends and to incur further indebtedness.

# FINANCIAL STRUCTURING OF BOT PROJECTS

Financial Structuring

**9**

Chapter 9 explains how funds are mobilized for BOT projects. In particular, it describes the types and sources of capital available, in terms of the level of risk that each type of capital undertakes and the types of risks that different providers of capital are willing to bear. By means of various financing techniques and legal instruments, different types of capital are matched to different project risks. This process is commonly referred to as financial structuring, or assembling the financial package. The financial techniques and legal instruments used in BOT projects are well established and commonly used in other financial transactions.

# ▪ Project financing

The types of financing available to developing countries have evolved substantially since the Bretton Woods Agreement (1944). Initially, financing consisted largely of bilateral and multilateral loans and grants to governments. Commercial lending to developing country governments was limited, and to the private sector even more so. Given the choice, creditors were inclined to undertake governments rather than corporate risks. Only when the strongest private sector companies were able to demonstrate consistent performance over an extended period of time did international commercial lenders begin to consider lending to them without recourse to sovereign guarantees.

Lending against corporate assets alone represented an important step forward for developing countries. However, the financing of new projects continued to be a problem, since corporate guarantees would usually be required for loans to finance these projects. Companies were therefore exposed to the extent of their total assets if a project in a developing country failed. The need for companies to shield themselves from such risks led to the further development of project financing. The essence of project financing is that creditors provide financing to a project solely based on the merits of the project itself, with limited or no recourse to the companies sponsoring the project (i.e. non-recourse or limited recourse financing). Typically in such financing, a separate project company is established by the project sponsors to implement the project. Such an arrangement has several advantages for the sponsors:

Financial Structuring

9

- It allows the sponsors to borrow funds to finance a project without increasing their liabilities beyond their investment in the project. On the sponsor's balance sheets, therefore, their exposure to the project is the amount of their equity contribution to the project and nothing more.

- Lenders to the project assume a part of the project risks, since they are lending without full recourse and primarily on the basis of project assets.

To the maximum extent possible, therefore, sponsors will seek to avoid financing a project on anything other than a non-recourse basis. Nevertheless, to put economic pressure on sponsors to perform, governments and creditors often require some exposure of the sponsors' balance sheets to project risks in the form of performance bonds and other liability instruments.

## BOT financing

While the use of different organizational forms does not alter the inherent risk of a project, the BOT format does alter the way in which risk is allocated among project participants. To the extent that private sector sponsorship replaces that of the public sector, the primary responsibility for financing and assuming risks is also shifted from the public to the private sector. Given this situation, private sector participants in turn will naturally want to minimize their risk exposure.

Private sector sponsors need to carefully analyse the financial feasibility of projects, in the light of the risks involved and their proposed distribution, before submitting bids or proposals for BOT schemes. They also have to consider how to allocate risks to other participants in their consortium. For instance, if the initial project sponsors have limited or no previous experience in the operation and management of BOT schemes, they will want to find co-sponsors with the appropriate operating experience or to subcontract the work to specialized private operators.

BOT financing, like project financing, involves the funding of projects on the merits of the projects themselves. But to a much greater degree than conventional financing for manufacturing projects, lenders will seek loan repayment security from a project's cash flow and the contractual agreements making up the project's security package, rather than from the physical assets of the project. This is because the physical assets of infrastructure projects are of relatively limited interest to lenders. Their ownership by the private sector is usually for a finite period, after which they have to be transferred to the host government. Also, most infrastructure fixed assets are only useful as built on a specific site. It is usually not practical to dismantle infrastructure facilities and then sell their parts piecemeal. BOT financing, therefore, is essentially contract financing, which focuses on the viability and security of a given project's revenue stream.

In effect, BOT financing is a specialized form of project financing. Some of the more common features of BOT financing are as follows:

- It involves the financing of a discrete venture that is more often defined by its revenue stream than by its products or markets.

- It involves several interrelated contracts with third parties, such as suppliers, purchasers/consumers and government agencies, which are crucial to the credit support for the project.

- Project loan repayments are secured by project cash flows, as specified in contractual agreements or as indicated by demand forecasts, rather than by project assets. The enforceability of these contracts and the reliability of demand forecasts are therefore of greater importance to lenders than the creditworthiness of the BOT sponsors *per se.*

- Similarly, project sponsors will rely primarily on contract enforceability (or guarantees) to minimize their exposure to project risks and uncertainty.

Because a web of contracts is the backbone of a BOT project, sponsors, banks and financial advisers tend to be involved in the negotiation of project documents at a much earlier stage than is normally the case in conventional financing schemes.

The basic financial flows that are relevant for BOT projects are indicated in figure VI.

## ▪ Types of capital

Financing, or capital, is required for the implementation of all projects. BOT schemes are in large part a means for a government to mobilize private financing for infrastructure projects. Broadly speaking, there are three types of capital available to all projects: equity, debt and mezzanine

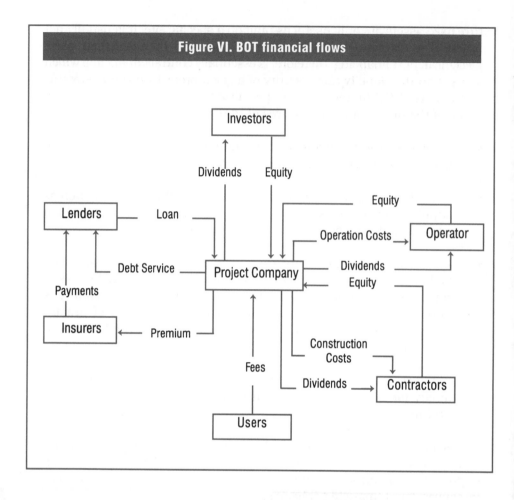

**Figure VI. BOT financial flows**

capital. Each plays a specific role in project financing and has its own risk characteristics. The return on each type of capital is determined largely by its risk characteristics.

## Equity capital

Equity is the lowest-ranking capital of all in terms of its claims on the assets of a project. It represents the funds injected by the owners of the project. Normally, all other project obligations must be satisfied before any distributions can be made to equity investors. If a project fails, therefore, all other claims must be met before any claims can be made by equity investors. Moreover, if after all other obligations are met, the value of the remaining assets is less than the initial equity capital of the project, the investors will bear the loss. Equity investors therefore bear a higher degree of risk than any other providers of capital. For this reason, equity capital is also referred to as risk capital. However, if a project proves to be highly successful, then the residual value of assets, after all obligations are met, will certainly exceed the initial equity capital of the project. This surplus will accrue entirely to the providers of equity capital in the form of capital gains. Thus, while equity investors bear the highest risk, they also stand to make the biggest gains if a project is successful. In a BOT project, the fixed assets will be transferred to the host government at the end of the concession period, ordinarily at no cost, so the equity investors' return on investment will come only from revenues generated during that period. Thus, the terms of the contracts must compensate these investors fairly for being the biggest risk takers in the project.

## Debt capital

In contrast to equity capital, a project's senior debt has the highest ranking of all capital. Senior debt has first claim over all the assets of a project and must be repaid first, according to a predetermined schedule. Only after the claims of senior debt are satisfied can the claims of others be considered. As such, senior debt bears the lowest risk of all capital. Correspondingly, the returns to senior debt are usually limited to just the interest payments on the loans, irrespective of how successful the project may be, that is, lower risk is balanced by lower returns.

All things being equal, equity investors would prefer a debt-equity ratio as high as possible, while creditors would prefer a debt-equity ratio as low as possible. A higher debt-equity ratio reduces the exposure of equity investors, while increasing the potential returns to their capital, while a lower ratio increases the certainty that loans will be repaid and hence lowers the risk to creditors. However, investors' exposure in a BOT project will depend not only on the amount of equity funds they subscribe initially but also on their contractual commitments. In some cases, one reason why project sponsors want to have as high a debt-equity ratio as possible is to retain funds for other potential projects. From the standpoint of a project company, however, the higher the debt-equity ratio, the less sound its financial structure and the more vulnerable it would be to a deterioration in the business environment.

There are no hard and fast rules as to the correct or best debt-equity ratio. This changes from sector to sector and from country to country. Suffice it to say that the higher the risks, the lower should be the debt-equity ratio. But whatever the ratio, care must be taken to ensure that it is prudent in the light of prevailing project and market conditions.

**Financial Structuring**

**9**

According to experience in project financing, only few cases exceed an 80/20 ratio; projects exposed to market risks tend not to exceed 60-65 per cent debt leverage, while power projects with firm take-or-pay arrangements may reach 70-80 per cent debt leverage.

## Mezzanine capital

Mezzanine capital is a more flexible instrument than either pure equity or debt. The key characteristic of mezzanine capital is that it has both debt and equity features and, as such, a risk profile that is somewhere between debt and equity capital. Examples of mezzanine financing are subordinated loans and preference shares. Both have the characteristics of debt, in that regular payments of interest and/or capital are involved. However, payments are subordinated to senior debt and need only be made when project funds are available. When they are not available, mezzanine financing is treated like equity and no payments are made; to that end, mezzanine financing provides projects with an additional equity cushion. However, when funds are available, mezzanine payments take precedence over any distributions to equity capital, such as dividend payments. Thus, while mezzanine financing is subordinated to senior debt, it is still senior to equity capital, and the returns paid to mezzanine capital are designed to reflect this order. For bearing greater risk than senior loans, mezzanine capital will be rewarded with potentially higher returns. This is achieved in one of two ways: higher interest rates than the project's senior loans and/or partial participation in the profits or capital gains of project equity (partial to reflect the fact that it bears less risk than pure equity). Partial participation in capital gains can be achieved by providing holders of subordinated debt or preferred shares with share options, convertible rights or warrants, so that they can subscribe for shares of the project, usually at a nominal price. This mechanism is commonly referred to as an "equity kicker".

For project sponsors, the advantage of mezzanine financing is that it enables projects to be financed with more debt and less equity and yet, if the mezzanine financing is properly structured, not have to bear the full burden of higher debt service in the early years, when the project cash flow is tight. Therefore for the same amount of equity investment, the sponsors are able to retain a higher shareholding interest in the project, which gives them higher returns on their investment if the project succeeds. In this regard, it is worth noting that projects rely on expectations of higher future cash flows to attract mezzanine financing today. Mezzanine financing is also used by equipment suppliers and construction companies to facilitate their participation in the project. Quite often this participation is financed out of their contractual profits. For the project's senior creditors, mezzanine financing improves the creditworthiness of the project by providing an additional equity cushion. Finally, it is a way for the providers of mezzanine financing to enjoy near-equity returns on their investments without taking the full risk of equity capital. Ultimately, however, a project's capital structure, that is, its mix of debt, mezzanine and equity financing, will be dictated by the readiness of investors and creditors to advance their own funds, in view of their perceptions of the risks involved.

## Sources of financing

Debt, equity and mezzanine capital are usually provided by different sources. Where a single source provides more than one type of capital, the different types of capital may be handled by separate departments.

### *Equity capital providers*

In the first instance, equity capital for a project will come from the project sponsors or other investors that have an active interest in the project. This would include governments (to the extent that they wish to participate as investors), contractors, equipment suppliers, purchasers of output (e.g. utility companies that have a vested interest in the project's output) and entrepreneurs. Equity investment by these parties will also substantially reduce, if not preclude, the chances of them losing interest in the project. Additional equity, if needed, would be sought from passive sources, such as institutional investors (e.g. pension funds, insurance companies, mutual funds) and possibly the general public through local or international capital markets. Institutional investors and individual market investors are passive investors in the sense that, unlike project sponsors, they are not normally involved in the promotion and development or the management and operation of the projects in which they invest. Their capital is used to top up the equity requirements of a project (i.e. the shortfall that cannot be met by sponsors).

Several specialist equity funds focusing exclusively on infrastructure investment have emerged in Asia and Latin America. This is in direct response to the massive demand for infrastructure construction and financing in these regions, arising from their higher economic growth rates. Such funds differentiate themselves from other funds and institutional investors in that they tend to be active rather than passive investors. Because they specialize in infrastructure, these funds are generally prepared to take a substantially higher equity interest in projects than the more passive diversified investment funds and institutional inves-

**Financial Structuring**

**9**

tors. They also tend to have management teams that have a specialized knowledge of infrastructure projects and that typically play a more active role in structuring the projects they finance.

### Commercial banks as a source of debt and mezzanine financing

Commercial banks are the most traditional source of debt financing. To a lesser extent, they are also providers of mezzanine capital. However, one key characteristic of commercial banks is worthy of note. The sources of funds of purely commercial banks (as compared to universal banks, which combine the functions of both commercial and merchant banking) are primarily short- to medium-term floating rate deposits. To avoid problems of interest rate and term mismatch, most commercial bank loans are primarily short- to medium-term floating rate credits (normally three- to five-year terms and rarely longer than seven years). Long-term credits in excess of seven to eight years account for a fairly small percentage of a bank's asset portfolio, while equity investments are negligible to non-existent, either by choice or as a consequence of regulatory restrictions or concerns about lender liability.

For this reason, the activities of commercial banks are focused primarily on earning a margin between the interest rate they receive on loans and the interest rate they pay on deposits, with little or no motivation to earn capital gains from equity investments. Their operations essentially revolve around the creditworthiness of their borrowers and the security of their loans. Much stress is put on prudential lending and actions aimed at ensuring loan repayment. If the creditworthiness of borrowers or the mortgage provided on loans is less than satisfactory, commercial banks will seek assurances from more creditworthy third parties, such as guarantees from parent companies, governments or quasi-government agencies.

In this sense, commercial banks are on the whole focused on shorter term and less risky credits and are not particularly well suited to financing infrastructure projects, which are generally long-term. For these reasons, sponsors are increasingly looking to sources other than commercial banks to meet their long-term funding needs and using commercial banks primarily to meet their shorter term funding needs, such as working capital and construction financing; once construction is completed, the latter is replaced by longer term or permanent financing.

An attractive feature of commercial bank credits is their flexibility. Commercial banks are generally more willing (than institutional investors, for instance) to tailor loan structures that meet the specific needs of clients. Also, in the event of default, rather than simply forcing borrowers into bankruptcy, commercial banks are prepared to work with them to consider ways in which their operations and repayment schedules might be restructured, so that operations can continue and the loans eventually be repaid. As a consequence, notwithstanding the short-term nature of commercial bank credits, they continue to play an important role in project financing and at any one time will still account for a large portion of the senior loans of a project.

In appraising a project, commercial banks carefully consider a number of interrelated issues:

- Commitment to the project of the sponsors and other major participants, in terms of investment and personnel. As already indicated, financing institutions will want as much as possible to link the returns accruing to the project sponsors with the long-term success of the project.

- The achievability of the project's budgetary, completion and technical targets, as any slippage will have an adverse effect on the economic viability of the project.

- The experience and capabilities of project management in implementing this type of project, as they will be crucial in ensuring that the project's time, budgetary and technical targets are met, if they are indeed realistic.

- The reliability of the assumptions on which the input supplies and demand projections are based, as this will determine the degree of confidence in the project's cost and revenue targets.

- The strength of government support to help the project succeed, its understanding of the private sector's profit motives and its attitudes towards risk sharing.

- Commitment at the highest levels of government will substantially increase the confidence of the financing institutions that the government will do its best to ensure the project obtains all necessary approvals and is successfully implemented.

While they are prepared to be more flexible, commercial banks will nevertheless want to retain the integrity of their security. To do so, they will usually impose stricter and more comprehensive covenants (restrictions) on borrowers than would bond investors. These covenants, contained in the project credit agreement specifying the debt financing and loan security structure, give commercial banks a substantial degree of influence over the implementation of the project. Some of the more common covenants are as follows:

- The project must be operated in accordance with good practice.

- It must obtain and maintain appropriate permits, approvals and consents.

- It must comply with project contracts, budgets and plans, which may not normally be materially changed without the lender's written consent. This mechanism allows the lenders to retain a substantial degree of control and involvement in all stages of the project.

- Appropriate insurance policies must be arranged for.

- The borrower must undertake not to pledge any assets of the company to third parties other than as specifically contemplated by the credit agreement ("negative pledge" clause).

- Lenders' consent is required for all capital expenditures and other investments, unless they are specifically set forth in project budgets that have already been approved by the lenders.

- Dividend payments are restricted if the company is in default on its loan agreements.

- Dividend payment levels are linked to financial ratios.

- Dividends must be repaid to the project company when certain events happen, such as payment defaults, failure to meet required financial ratios or failure to maintain required reserve accounts ("call back" provision).

- The project company may be required to create a cash reserve to cover unknown contingencies.

- Lenders may require that the reserve be put in place before the project starts operation, or that it be built up from earnings after the commencement of operations but before any payment of dividends.

- The project's equity funds must be drawn down before loan funds are drawn down.

- Taking on other debt may be restricted. This limits hire purchase, leasing, borrowing and guarantees and inhibits future funding without the lenders' consent to finance additional works or variations. Other debt may be permitted in some cases, if it is subordinated in a way that strips the subordinated creditor of all its rights, so that senior creditors may act almost as if there were no junior creditor, or as if the junior creditor's capital was quasi-equity, i.e. mezzanine financing.

A key area in which lenders want to exercise control is control of the project in default. Lenders require rights to step into the shoes of the defaulting or insolvent parties and manage the project. The key aim of default clauses is to provide the project with an early warning system in case of emerging difficulties and to allow lenders to halt further drawdowns, refuse release of distributions to promoters/sponsors and refuse release of completion or other guarantees.

### Export credit agencies as a source of debt financing

An important source of long-term credit is export credit agencies (ECAs). As lenders, ECAs have the same concerns and requirements as commercial banks and would also be signatories to the credit agreement. However, there is one important difference: ECAs are usually State-owned, and their primary objective is the promotion of their country's exports. As the terms offered by ECAs are usually substantially more generous than those of commercial banks and may be subsidized, export credits are much sought after and highly suited to the financing of long-term infrastructure projects. The main drawbacks are that they are usually tied to the purchase of equipment from the ECA's country and usually require government guarantees. Meanwhile, some ECAs, such as the Export-Import Bank of the United States and the Export-Import Bank of Japan, recognizing that developing countries are shifting away from sovereign borrowing and that project finance for infrastructure development is gaining importance, have established financing lines on a limited recourse basis.

### Bilateral and multilateral aid agencies as a source of debt, equity and mezzanine financing

In addition to the preceding sources of capital, many developing countries can also access financing from bilateral and multilateral agencies, such as that provided by the United States Agency for International Development (USAID), the Canadian International Development Agency (CIDA), the Overseas Development Administration of the United Kingdom (ODA), the World Bank, the Asian Development Bank (ADB) and the European Bank for Reconstruction and Development (EBRD). A list of such agencies is contained in a UNIDO document from 1983.[8]

Although it is obviously not an up-to-date list, it should still prove useful. Funds from these agencies are provided for very long terms (up to 20 years or more), but most provide the funding exclusively to governments, or with government guarantees only, especially where subsidized and grant funds are concerned. In the case of bilateral agencies, funds may also be tied to the purchase of goods and services from the country providing the funds.

To promote growth of the private sector, some agencies also provide debt, equity and mezzanine financing for private sector projects, including involvement in BOT projects. Such agencies include the International Finance Corporation (IFC) of the World Bank Group, the Private Sector Department of ADB, the Merchant Banking Department of EBRD, the Commonwealth Development Corporation of the United Kingdom and the Overseas Private Investment Corporation of the United States. While funding for the private sector is usually provided on commercial rather than subsidized terms, it is also usually provided on an untied basis and for longer terms than commercial sources of funds.

### Institutional investors as a source of debt, equity and mezzanine financing

Institutional investors are non-bank financial institutions such as insurance companies, pension funds and investment funds. Institutional investors distinguish themselves from commercial banks in that they mobilize long-term contractual savings (i.e. monthly contributions to life assurance policies and pension plans are normally made over many years and cannot be withdrawn freely) as opposed to short-term deposits. By virtue of the long-term nature of their funds, many institutional investors are able to provide long-term debt (10 years or more), mezzanine and pure equity financing. Institutional investors are therefore an important source of long-term funds for large infrastructure projects.

As providers of long-term capital and, more particularly, equity and mezzanine financing, institutional investors are prepared to look more at the long-term prospects of a project than merely at its short-term repayment capabilities. In this respect, the risk-reward profiles are markedly different from those of commercial banks. Nevertheless, institutional investors are different from project sponsors in that they are not normally involved in the promotion and development or the management and operation of the projects in which they invest, and they are therefore not

---

[8] *Financial Resources for Industrial Projects in Developing Countries*, Industrial Investment and Financing Series, vols. I-IV (PI/61/Rev.2).

normally prepared to bear the development and construction risks of a project. To attract institutional or individual investors from the world's major financial centres for equity investment in the infrastructure projects of developing countries, a number of equity funds have been established. These infrastructure equity funds allow investors to mitigate risks by investing long-term capital in a diversified portfolio of infrastructure companies and projects in developing countries and to seek higher returns than they could hope for with comparable investments in industrialized countries. Some funds can provide a mix of financing, such as equity, subordinated debt, completion guarantees and bridge loans to cover the construction period.

### Role of national and regional development banks

As indicated in chapter 8, there is a difference between the financial appraisal and the economic appraisal of BOT projects. The former looks at the financial viability of projects from the standpoint of project sponsors, investors and commercial lenders, while the latter looks at the economic viability of projects from the standpoint of national costs and benefits and the best use of a country's resources. It is conceivable, therefore, that a project that is economically viable is not financially viable and vice versa. Examples of such divergence are infrastructure projects that are critical to the economic development of a region but which governments decide to implement on a non-tariff basis or for which they decide to charge user fees that do not fully cover operational costs. In such cases, the economic benefits of the projects would be high but private sector interest in the projects would be limited, as there would be no prospects of earning commercial rates of return on their investments.

To bridge the gap between economic and financial viability, public sector intervention and support are called for. The establishment in the late 1940s of national and regional development banks, or development finance institutions (DFIs), was in part an attempt to bridge this gap. However, the view in the 1950s and 1960s was that since one could not always rely on the private sector to implement projects beneficial to the national interest, it was necessary for the State to step in and fill the gap. In this context, DFIs were seen as necessary substitutes for the private sector, where economic and financial divergence existed. Events in the 1980s and 1990s, however, have altered this perception substantially. Today, the view tends to be that the private sector is more efficient than the public sector in implementing and operating projects. Thus, rather than substituting for the private sector, DFIs should create an environment that would be conducive to the private sector's participation. In situations where projects are clearly in the national interest but are not financially feasible, DFIs might provide performance guarantees, subordinated loans, low-interest loans and equity capital to meet funding gaps. Through such intervention, the return on private sector investments could be enhanced and private capital mobilized. However, to ensure that benefits are maximized, subsidies and support would be designed to preserve the private sector's incentive to perform and to ensure that the threat of penalty for non-performance is not removed.

### Capital markets

The need for long-term capital to finance infrastructure projects in developing countries is enormous. As indicated above, institutional investors are an important source of long-term capital. Outside the project finance area, institutional investors also invest heavily in the public securities markets (international capital markets) by way of investment in marketable debt and equity securities. Inasmuch as BOT schemes are typically one-off projects, for which special-purpose companies are established, capital for these schemes is substantially limited to the more conventional sources of project finance, such as direct investors, commercial bank credits and export credits. It is much more difficult to obtain investment-grade credit ratings for special-purpose companies with no operating records. This in turn makes it more difficult for them to issue marketable securities and to tap the world's largest sources of long-term capital. Nevertheless, independent power producers in the United States and even in some developing countries are tapping the capital markets directly by issuing bonds. The key to accessing financing from the capital markets has been the sponsors' ability to bring together reputable and extremely creditworthy project participants through all phases of the project cycle and hence to construct strong and highly rated security packages.

### Maximizing the benefits from bilateral, multilateral and export credit agency funds

Bilateral sources of financing, including export credits, are normally the most attractive funds available to a BOT project in terms of lower interest and longer loan periods. However, such funds are generally available only to promote the exports of the countries providing the funding. This means that the use of bilateral funds may result in the purchase of equipment and technology that is not necessarily the most appropriate for the borrower. Moreover, the lower cost of the funds may be offset by higher prices for the equipment and technology.

Notwithstanding the limitations of bilateral financing, its benefits can still be maximized if the increasingly competitive forces of global markets are carefully exploited. If a sector is of particular interest to the international community (power and telecommunications are good examples), then it may be possible to promote keen competition among equipment suppliers from different countries and thereby obtain the most favourable financing conditions. For instance, an invitation to bid for the supply of equipment could require bidders to arrange financing without sovereign guarantees. If equipment suppliers are sufficiently attracted by the project, they could be motivated to provide their own corporate guarantees in place of sovereign guarantees. Such corporate guarantees may be acceptable to ECAs and bilateral agencies in the place of government guarantees. By carefully sequencing the choice of equipment and financing arrangements, it may be possible to transfer some credit risks from the borrower country to the equipment suppliers, while ensuring that the prices paid for equipment and services remain competitive. Indeed, if the project is well structured, with a good security package, it may even be possible to attract export credits on a limited or non-recourse basis. The provision of export credits with corporate guarantees or on a limited or non-recourse basis is still very rare, but their emergence in recent years is extremely significant and points to the possible direction of future developments. Nevertheless, it remains true that whenever a party to a BOT project is asked to bear risks that it cannot fully control, an additional cost will normally be imposed to compensate for undertaking those risks.

As for multilateral financing, some fairly strict rules apply. Apart from financial viability, projects are also required to meet certain minimum social cost-benefit standards.[9] For this reason, it generally takes longer to process multilateral loans than private sector loans. To the extent that multilateral agencies see themselves as playing a catalytic role, they will also set limits on the maximum percentage of total project cost they will finance and use their own participation in the project to mobilize additional funds from third parties. There are three ways in which the impact of multilateral agencies can be maximized and the mobilization of third party funds facilitated:

- In supporting a project, multilateral agencies are in effect putting their own reputation, or stamp of approval, behind the project. This may be sufficient to attract additional private sector financing for

---

9 For a discussion of social cost-benefit analysis see two UNIDO publications, *Guidelines for Project Evaluation* (United Nations publication, Sales No. 72.II.B.11) and *Guide to Practical Project Appraisal: Social Benefit-Cost Analysis in Developing Countries* (United Nations publication, Sales No. 78.II.B.3), and two books by I.M.D. Little and J. A. Mirrlees, *Social Benefit-Cost Analysis* (1986) and *Project Appraisal and Planning for Developing Countries* (London, Heineman Educational Books, 1974)

the project. The multilateral agency that has probably been the most successful in using its own participation to mobilize third party funds for private sector projects has been the IFC. Apart from encouraging the inflow of additional equity capital, it has also devised a syndicated loan structure to attract more debt financing from commercial banks. This is done by a two-part syndicated loan: an A loan for IFC's own account and a B loan for the account of commercial banks participating in the syndicate. IFC does not guarantee any of the lenders in the syndicate but puts itself forward as the lender of record for both the A and B loans. This reduces both the chances of the loans being rescheduled and the cost of funds.

- Where multilateral financing is not available or not used, multilateral agencies can still facilitate the flow of capital into emerging markets by providing political risk insurance. In April 1988, MIGA was established as a member of the World Bank Group, with the primary purpose of enhancing "the flow to developing countries of capital and technology for productive purposes under conditions consistent with their development needs, policies and objectives, on the basis of fair and stable standards for the treatment of foreign investment". MIGA achieves this by providing insurance coverage for the following:

  - Currency transfer, to protect against the inability of investors and lenders to convert and transfer local currency into foreign exchange.
  - Expropriation, to protect against direct or indirect acts by host governments that reduce or eliminates ownership of, control over, or rights to insured investments.
  - War and civil disturbance, to protect against damage to, destruction of, or disappearance of tangible assets, including that arising from politically motivated acts of sabotage and terrorism.
  - Breach of contract, to ensure enforcement of arbitration awards and judicial sentences for damages arising from the breach of contracts by host governments.

The above coverage encourages foreign investment by increasing a foreign investor's confidence that its rights are protected. Such insurance may possibly also be used to enhance the credit rating of a project, often above that of the host country. Such credit enhancements would facilitate a project's access to the international capital markets, since many institutional investors are restricted, by regulation, from investing in the debt securities of companies with low credit ratings.

- A third approach, thus far used only for projects funded by the public sector, is co-financing. Under this arrangement, multilateral agencies provide limited guarantees to private sector lenders to attract longer term funds. For example, while 5-year loans may be readily available from commercial banks, a project may require 10-year loans. To attract longer term funds, a multilateral agency might offer commercial banks a repayment guarantee for the last two years of a loan (i.e. years 9 and 10). This may then be sufficient to induce 10-year loans, with the commercial banks taking on the additional risk for years 6-8.

### Maximizing local currency funding

The use of foreign exchange funds to finance infrastructure projects results in exchange risk exposure for infrastructure projects, in that most of them generate little or no foreign exchange revenues. The mobilization of local currency funding is, therefore, an important aspect of BOT financing. However, this may be difficult in some developing countries. If capital, on attractive terms and for the required amounts and in the desired currencies, is to be mobilized, new mechanisms and structures need to be found. To date, the financial markets of developing countries have been characterized by the dominance of commercial banks, a narrow choice of savings instruments and interest rate distortion in the credit markets.

As a first step, new financial instruments need to be introduced and more flexible financial policies adopted to promote the development of both the bond and equity markets. To this end, careful use of existing infrastructure facilities can play an important catalytic role. For instance, financially sound utilities, such as power companies, can be restructured as corporate entities that would be suitable for listing on local securities exchanges and that would issue debt and equity securities. Owing to the relatively steady and predictable income stream of public utilities, bonds issued by such entities are considered to be high in quality and low in risk and are much sought after by institutional investors. The issue of these bonds raises long-term capital for public utility investments, and their proliferation would deepen the domestic bond market and introduce tools for the effective implementation of monetary and interest policies (e.g. through open market operations).

The transformation of public utilities into corporations and their listing on securities exchanges would allow them to move beyond issuing straightforward bonds. Restructured utility companies should be able to issue mezzanine capital instruments, such as low-interest bonds with warrants, convertible bonds, income bonds and other sophisticated financial instruments. The equity element compensates investors for the low interest rates. The low interest rates on these instruments reduce the front-end pressure on project cash flows. As a utility company establishes a track record, its international credibility is enhanced. This will enable it to gradually access international capital markets, including the raising of equity capital through the issue of new shares by the repackaged utilities. Indeed, as BOT schemes come to the end of their operating periods, instead of merely being transferred back to the government, it may be more beneficial to governments, the private sector and the general public for them to be listed and sold off, either partially or in full. Increasing the supply of securities in the domestic market further promotes the development of that market and also increases the efficiency of savings mobilization.

# ▪ Financial structuring techniques

The challenge of financial structuring is to establish the appropriate mix of debt, equity and mezzanine financing for a project that, while optimizing the use of financial resources, also ensures a sound financial structure for the project.

## Components of project costs

In deciding on the type of capital and sources of financing to be used, it is important to first identify the main components of project costs, including financing costs, so that the needs and risk characteristics of each can be matched by the appropriate funding. The main components of project costs are normally as follows:

- *Pre-investment costs.* These are the costs incurred by project sponsors in developing the project concept and preliminary project design.

- *Bidding and procurement-related costs.* A BOT concession can be awarded through either competitive bidding or direct negotiation with sponsors. In both cases, the government agency responsible for awarding the concession has to carry out an outline study of the project to collect information needed for the bidding documents and to prepare themselves for negotiations with the sponsors. The bidders and sponsors also have to undertake extensive design and analysis work to prepare their bids and to have meaningful negotiations with the government.

- *Project development costs.* On the basis of the preliminary project design, the project sponsors have to further develop and refine the BOT scheme during the bidding and post-concession award period.

- *Construction costs.* This is the main component of expenditure in any project. It includes the construction of the entire BOT facility, including the purchase and installation of equipment.

- *Operating costs.* These are the costs involved in operating the BOT facility upon completion of construction.

- *Termination costs.* At termination, costs may or may not be involved. If the project agreement requires the BOT scheme to be transferred in sound physical and financial condition, then any shortfall needs to be made good by the project company prior to the transfer. If the transfer is on an as-is basis (see case-study 4, the Navotas I Power Station, in the annex to chapter 8), any investments required to make good the facility will be for the account of the agency taking over the facility. A third possibility is that the transfer may involve a cash payment by the government agency taking over control of the BOT scheme.

## Sequencing the financial package

Having identified the components of project costs as described above, appropriate financing for each can then be arranged, in the following typical sequence:

- *Pre-investment and project development cost.* As initiators of a BOT scheme, or winners of a competitive bid, the pre-investment as well as the project development costs is borne by the project sponsors. Until such time as the project is constructed and operational, the pre-investment and project development activities are non-productive and may never generate a return. As such, they are funded by risk capital from the project sponsors and counted as a part of their equity contribution to the project.

- *Bidding and procurement related costs.* During bidding and procurement, each of the parties takes care of its own costs. The govern-

Financial Structuring

9

ment bears the costs of the outline study and preparation of bid documentation, while the sponsors bear the costs of preparing their bids. The government may fund its costs as part of normal government expenditures, while sponsors finance their expenditures with risk capital, which would again count towards their equity contribution. Sometimes arrangements are made for the costs of bids to be partially borne by the government or the winning bidder.

- *Construction costs.* At the start of construction, the project company should be established, with all the necessary debt, equity and mezzanine financing already finalized. The funds would be drawn down in the following sequence:

    □ As a first step, the equity funds of the sponsors are drawn down.

    □ Commercial bank loans are drawn down next, although in some of the more creditworthy developing countries, debt and equity are sometimes drawn down *pro rata*. In highly developed economies, the drawdown of debt financing may even precede the drawdown of equity.

    □ Simultaneous with the above two drawdowns, bilateral and ECA funds would be drawn down, as required, to pay for the purchase of tied equipment and services.

    □ Project risks are considered to be highest during the construction phase, when expenditures are highest and before project revenues begin. Traditionally, institutional investors have been reluctant to undertake construction risks, so that during construction, the project company will have to rely on equity financing from the sponsors and funds from commercial banks, bilateral agencies and ECAs. This is true unless guarantees are provided, either by the host government or the sponsors, to persuade institutional investors to advance their funds. Such guarantees may also be requested for commercial bank or ECA financing during construction.

    □ By the end of construction and start of operations, when project risks are substantially reduced, long-term debt, equity and mezzanine financing from institutional investors is drawn down to refinance or take out the short-term debt of the commercial banks and to provide the project with long-term or permanent financing.

- *Operating costs.* Once up and running, the BOT facility will require working capital for its operations. For this purpose, internal funds of the company may be supplemented by short-term loans from commercial banks.

The sequencing of the financial package is illustrated in table 4.

## ■ Summary comments

In arranging limited or non-recourse financing for BOT schemes, it is evident that the actions and responses of the government, sponsors, contractors, operators and suppliers must all take into consideration the perceptions and concerns of the financing institutions as they will determine the shape and form of security required and the financing available to the project. The views of the financial institutions will also determine the mix of debt, equity and mezzanine capital to be used. The creditworthiness and financeability of BOT schemes will depend critically on a set of consistent and interrelated agreements between the project parties that adequately address the aims of the sponsors and the perceptions and concerns of the financing institutions.

While the main aim of governments, as far as BOT schemes are concerned, is to attract private capital to meet infrastructure investment needs and to off-load risks and the burden of financing, they must take care to do so in a way that, while providing a sufficiently attractive return to private investors, will also protect the national interest. Similarly, they must neither expect the private sector to bear unreasonable risks nor allow them to abuse monopoly situations that may arise in BOT schemes. Projects should be structured so that the risks and benefits of the government and the private sector are properly balanced and the project becomes a win-win undertaking for both sides.

The key is to focus on those attributes and characteristics of BOT schemes that are needed to attract sponsors and lenders, while designing a regulatory framework that allows government sufficient, but not excessive, control and ensures that private sector behaviour is not detrimental to the national interest. For sponsors, these attributes and characteristics may be summarized as follows:

- A clear set of rules and regulations that govern BOT schemes: what is permitted and what is not; what will be regulated and what will not. To ensure transparency, a number of countries have passed legislation specifically to regulate BOT schemes.

**Financial Structuring**

**9**

## Table 4. Sequencing of the BOT financial package

| Activity | Type & Source of Financing |
|---|---|
| Pre-investment and development costs | Risk capital from project sponsors |
| Bidding and procurement | Risk capital from project sponsors Possible support from government |
| Financial structuring and development of security package | Equity capital from project sponsors |
| Agreements with institutional and other investors | Equity capital from institutional and other investors |
| Agreements with equipment suppliers | Long-term Loans from export credit agencies for equipment purchase |
| Agreements with prime contractor and subcontractors on cost of construction | Short-term loans from commercial banks to finance construction |
| Financing reestructuring as completion of construction approaches | Long-term Loans from non-bank financial institutions and specialist investment funds |
| Financial closing Start of construction | Drawdown of equity and loan funds |
| Operation | Working capital from the project company and short-term loans from commercial banks |

- An appropriate sharing of risks by the public and private sectors.

- Rules and regulations that permit an adequate rate of return for the risks that project sponsors are asked to assume, i.e. an appropriate balance between risk and reward.

For lenders, they are as follows:

- Satisfactory coverage of all costs incurred up to project completion and the achievement of stipulated performance without further recourse to the lenders.

- Sufficient recourse to creditworthy parties if the project is not completed, is abandoned or never achieves the stipulated performance levels.

- Project revenue source that is reliable and creditworthy, with pricing features that assure coverage of debt service and operating costs.

- Reliable system for ensuring that project revenues are available and allocated in a timely manner to service debt and that such revenues will be in the currency of the debt service, or easily converted into such currency, at an exchange rate that will not make the project unviable.

Designing a security package to mobilize financing for a project is an iterative process. This work, usually undertaken by a financial adviser (e.g. a bank or investment banking firm), is based on the adviser's understanding of the regulatory framework, what the sponsors wish to achieve (in terms of cost, return on investment, degree of recourse etc.) and what is acceptable to the financial community (in terms of risks, security, rates of return etc.). As the structure is developed, a dialogue is established with the financial community, so the acceptability of different structures to that community can be tested. The structure is then adjusted in the light of responses from the financial community and the process repeated until a security package acceptable to both sponsors and the financial community is found.

A typical security package is shown in figure VII. It illustrates the contractual arrangements involved, the interrelationships between the various project parties and the flow of funds into the project. While the structure will vary from project to project, the basic principles and elements underlying the structure are similar for most BOT schemes.

Finally, it is important to note that the set-up cost of BOT schemes can be quite high. First, BOT schemes are a fairly recent phenomenon, at

**Financial Structuring**

**9**

least in developing countries, so many of the parties involved are unfamiliar with what is required to implement them successfully. There is, therefore, substantial caution on all sides. Secondly, the contractual arrangements involved in BOT schemes can be fairly complex, and the process of contract drafting and negotiation with governments, public sector corporations, creditors, contractors and raw materials suppliers can be time-consuming and costly. Thus, before participating in BOT schemes, sponsors must be prepared to commit substantial financial and managerial resources to initial project definition, bid preparation and contract negotiation. They must also look at BOT schemes as businesses that have to be managed over the long term rather than merely as a means to win more construction contracts and increase equipment sales.

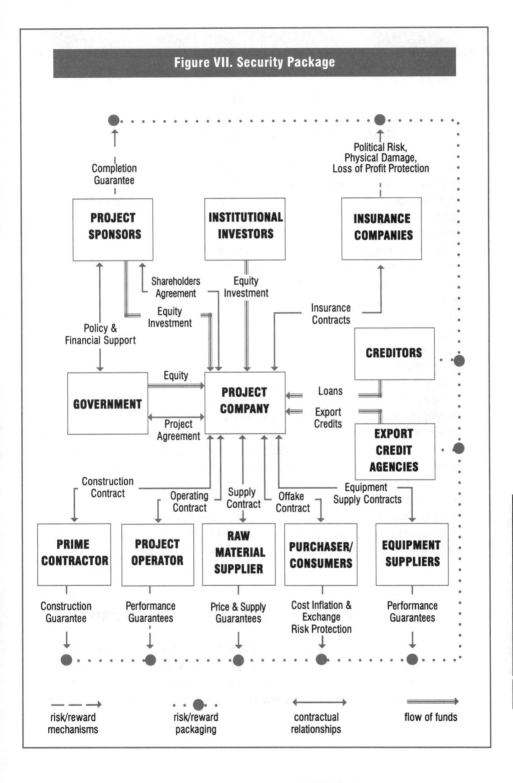

# Figure VII. Security Package

**PROJECT SPONSORS**

**INSTITUTIONAL INVESTORS**

**INSURANCE COMPANIES**

Completion Guarantee

Political Risk, Physical Damage, Loss of Profit Protection

Shareholders Agreement

Equity Investment

Equity Investment

Insurance Contracts

Policy & Financial Support

**CREDITORS**

**GOVERNMENT**

Equity

**PROJECT COMPANY**

Loans

Project Agreement

Export Credits

**EXPORT CREDIT AGENCIES**

Construction Contract

Operating Contract

Supply Contract

Offake Contract

Equipment Supply Contracts

**PRIME CONTRACTOR**

**PROJECT OPERATOR**

**RAW MATERIAL SUPPLIER**

**PURCHASER/ CONSUMERS**

**EQUIPMENT SUPPLIERS**

Construction Guarantee

Performance Guarantees

Price & Supply Guarantees

Cost Inflation & Exchange Risk Protection

Performance Guarantees

- - - → risk/reward mechanisms

···●··· risk/reward packaging

←→ contractual relationships

⇒ flow of funds

**Financial Structuring**

**9**

# TWO CASE-STUDIES

## CASE-STUDY 1: TATE'S CAIRN TUNNEL, HONG KONG

The financing for the Tate's Cairn Tunnel Company (TCTC) comprised shareholder equity of HK$ 600 million and a term loan facility of HK$ 1.55 billion provided by a consortium of banks, arranged by the Bank of Tokyo, the China Development Finance Company (Hong Kong) and the Fuji Bank. In implementing the project, shareholders' equity was drawn down first to fund the initial 15 months of construction work, with the term loan facility being utilized to complete the project and to cover the operating expenses during the initial years of operation. Income is generated through tolls, which are payable according to vehicle type (in all, there are nine individual vehicle classifications), on an ascending scale, from HK$ 4 for private cars to HK$ 8 for two-axle heavy goods vehicles, with an additional HK$ 5 being payable for each additional axle. Subsequent toll increases during the 30-year franchise for the project are subject to government approval.

TCTC expects to receive modest periodic increases in income during the franchise period, with royalty payments to the Government being levied at 2.5 per cent of gross operating receipts for the first five years of operation, rising to 5 per cent after that. It is expected that tunnel operating costs will be between HK$ 55 million and HK$ 60 million per year, the majority of which is for salaries and vehicle expenses.

Repayment of the term loan facility is to be achieved within 12.5 years from the date the tunnel is first opened to the general public. It is expected that dividends will be paid to the shareholders within seven years, depending on certain events. Growth forecasts prepared by TCTC based on low-, medium- and high-growth scenarios all show dividends payable within seven years of opening. Attached to the facility provided by the banks are a number of terms and conditions requiring the borrower, TCTC, to provide guarantees against such items as construction cost and time overruns. Since the project was completed well within both criteria, the financial undertakings of TCTC have been discharged with remarkable ease.

## CASE-STUDY 2: CHANNEL TUNNEL, FRANCE-UNITED KINGDOM

One of the largest, most visible and contentious BOT schemes to be implemented in recent years is the Channel Tunnel between France and the United Kingdom. Following the signing of a treaty between France and the United Kingdom on 14 February 1986, four major agreements were set up within the contractual framework. The financial structure of the project has a number of salient features.

### The concession contract

The contract is between Eurotunnel, the project concessionaire, and the Governments of France and the United Kingdom. It gives the concessionaire the right to construct, own and operate the project for 55 years.

### The railway usage contract

The railway usage contract was signed on 29 July 1987, the date of ratification of the concession, between Eurotunnel and the national railways of France and the United Kingdom. It covers the terms agreed with the national railways of France and the United Kingdom for the operation of conventional trains through the tunnel. The railway usage contract allows the use of up to half the tunnel capacity.

### The construction contract

The contract for a BOT project is generally awarded on a fixed price, lump-sum, turnkey basis. This was not the case with the Channel Tunnel. Instead, the construction contract between Eurotunnel and Transmanche Link, the contractors, contained three separately priced pieces of work: a lump sum for the British and French terminals and the fixed equipment in the tunnels; a target price covering the tunneling work itself; and a provisional sum with respect to the rolling stock, with the lump sum part of the contract accounting for only about 40 per cent of the total contract price. For BOT projects in general, however, the larger the share accounted for by fixed price in the construction contract, the greater the comfort of the banks.
To begin with, proposals for the Channel Tunnel were submitted by a consortium of 10 contractors and 5 banks. This consortium later split up, with the banks forming the nucleus of the banking syndicate for the project. The contractors, meanwhile, formed a group called Transmanche Link and negotiated the construction contract with Eurotunnel. The construction contract covers all design, engineering and construction work. It is in many ways a performance-related contract, since at the time of its negotiation only an outline design was available.

### The credit agreement

The fourth major contract is the credit agreement, which was entered into between Eurotunnel and a syndicate of 215 banks on 4 November 1987. The core group of these banks had been present when the original project proposal was submitted in October 1985. An underwriting group of some 50 banks negotiated the credit agreement before syndication. The agreement allows for an 18-year loan life and is linked to the concession contract, the railways usage contract and the construction contract. It places a number of duties on the borrower associated with these other contracts. Most of the negotiation for the credit agreement took place during 1986 and the first half of 1987, in parallel with the equity funding programme for the project. Funding for project work, up to the end of 1986, was provided by the original group of banks and contractors, by way of cash contributions and the secondment of personnel to the project. These contributions were capitalized as the first tranche of equity (equity 1). Towards the end of 1986, a second tranche of some £200 million in equity was injected through private placement (equity 2). This was sufficient to fund the work up to the next stage, which was the main equity placement, in November 1987 (equity 3). The equity 2 tranche of £200 million was a substantial sum, which provided time for agreements to be negotiated and legislation to be passed. The main construction work was also initiated during this time. For instance, at Sangatte, on the French side, an enormous shaft about 57 m wide and 55 m deep was sunk even before the main tranche of funds was raised.

The equity funding programme and arrangement of credit facilities had to be carefully coordinated. Equity 1 was committed by the original promoters and enabled a small group of banks to provisionally commit themselves before signing the concession contract. Between equity 1 and equity 2, the loan underwriting group was formed and the main elements of the credit agreement began to emerge. This was finalized in mid-1987, and loan syndication took place before the raising of equity 3. The first drawdown of the loan occured on 2 November 1988.

# THE CONTRACT PACKAGE

# ■ Introduction

A BOT project involves a number of important contractual arrangements among the participants. A brief description of the main contracts follows, more or less in the chronological order in which they are usually established.

The first in importance, although not necessarily in time, is the project (or concession) agreement. As the only truly unique document in the BOT contract package, it will also be discussed separately in chapter 11. The other contracts in a typical BOT package are commonly used in one form or another in all sorts of other contexts throughout the commercial world.

Nevertheless, in a BOT project all the contracts must fit together into an integrated whole. Together, they define the respective rights, obligations and risks of each party. The provisions of the web of interrelated contracts underlying a BOT project must be consistent and complementary. For example, *force majeure*, choice-of-law and dispute resolution clauses should be consistent throughout all contracts to the maximum extent possible. None of the contracts in a BOT project exists in isolation. All are interrelated and must be effectively coordinated.

# ■ Consultant agreements

If the host government has no expertise of its own in the field of BOT arrangements and related matters, it may need to recruit outside consultants to help identify and define the project and put together its request for proposals. In this situation, from the point of view of the host government, the first set of BOT contractual documents will normally be agreements to hire the outside consultancy. Three kinds of expertise will usually be involved:

- Technical expertise in the relevant industrial sector (e.g. power plants, ports, roads, telecommunications).

**10**

**Contract Package**

- Financial consultancy, for knowledge about potential sources of funding, financing structures and instruments, foreign exchange, capital markets, feasibility studies, and various other matters that lenders will require as part of the security package.

- International business legal counsel to help the host government shape the legal framework for the BOT project, draft or review necessary documentation, and help establish the contractual documents with the BOT project sponsors.

The basic issues to be addressed in the consultant agreement are the scope of work, qualifications and experience of the main consultants, type of consultancy contract, pricing and payment provisions and professional liability.

Consultants must be chosen with care. Host governments usually organize a roster of consultants, rating them in terms of their general qualifications and reputation, adequacy for the project and experience in the country or region.

Consultants are usually retained on the basis of a time-based fee for services, which can be hourly, daily or monthly, plus out-of-pocket expenses (these are known as time-based contracts). For some assignments a fixed retainer may be appropriate (known as lump-sum contracts, percentage contracts or cost-plus-fixed-fee contracts). In some cases a success fee may be appropriate.

The host government should establish procedures to review the progress of consultants' work in relation to the agreed-on terms of reference and schedule. It should retain the right to terminate consultants' arrangements if it becomes dissatisfied with the service being rendered or if the services are no longer needed.

Host governments should be aware that technical assistance and capacity building are available from bilateral and multilateral agencies, including UNIDO. Such assistance could be funded through loans, grants or trust-fund agreements.

# ■ Preliminary consortium agreement

From the point of view of the initial sponsors of a BOT project, the first important contract will be the one they agree among themselves, usually referred to as a preliminary consortium agreement or a joint venture agreement. Typically, the initial sponsors will enter into such an agreement in order to respond to a government request for proposals or to propose a BOT project that has not been solicited.

The agreement among the sponsors will provide for an initial sharing of the substantial costs required to do feasibility studies, to hire outside advisers, to prepare tenders and to do other preliminary development work. This preliminary agreement will commit the parties to various undertakings, in principle, subject to the negotiation of more definitive agreements. One critical commitment, of course, is to make specified amounts of equity investments in the project company when formed. The parties may also agree at this stage to provide additional support in the form of stand-by equity or stand-by subordinated loans, if these should be eventually required as part of the financing package.

A preliminary consortium agreement will also indicate the parts of the project that some members of the consortium intend to provide (e.g. construction, supply of major equipment, operation and maintenance). However, the agreement should provide that the project company will be free to negotiate with other providers if the consortium member is unable to provide the services or goods in question on an arm's-length basis, at competitive market prices.

The agreement should also provide a mechanism whereby those with a majority economic interest in the consortium can drop one or more of the participants in certain circumstances (for instance, if the construction price offered by the construction contractor member of the consortium is clearly uncompetitive). The extent to which, and the circumstances in which, the costs of a member dropped from the consortium are to be reimbursed by the other members should be spelt out, as should whether, and on what terms, a member may drop out voluntarily. As noted earlier, if confidential proprietary information is to be shared among the participants, then either the preliminary consortium agreement or an ancillary agreement should contain appropriate contractual provisions to protect the confidentiality of the information.

**10**

**Contract Package**

# ▪ Project company agreements

By the time the project company is formed, the final consortium often includes other parties in addition to the initial sponsors. In a BOT scheme, the project company at that stage may include a number of active and passive sponsors, such as contractors, equipment and material suppliers, a host government agency or utility, operators, portfolio investors and institutional equity investors. The contractual agreements among the final consortium members will expand the preliminary consortium agreement and will establish long-term binding commitments among the parties. Many of these commitments will be included in the formal organization documents of the project company itself (charter, by-laws, company statutes, partnership agreement etc.). Others may be set forth in separate agreements among the consortium members (e.g. a shareholder's agreement).

The precise juridical form of the project company will depend on the company laws and on the tax laws and foreign investment laws of the host country and the home countries of the various sponsors.

Public limited liability companies, private limited liability companies, partnerships of various kinds (normally with special-purpose, limited-liability companies as partners) and joint venture companies with either corporate or partnership characteristics have all been used in the BOT context. A limited liability company is often the preferred vehicle. The organizational documents will contain binding commitments for the equity contributions and stand-by support required of each participant and will provide for board representation, voting control and transferability or non-transferability of shareholdings, admission of additional equity investors, withdrawal of investors and a number of other matters.

# ▪ The project (or concession) agreement

The project agreement is central to a BOT project. It is normally preceded, however, and to some extent determined by the provisions set forth in the government's request for proposals, in the sponsor consortium's bid and in the award that the host government might issue to the winning bidder.

The project agreement will set forth the rights and obligations of the host government and the project company (see chapter 11). The obligations might include the ones described next.

# Host government

The host government will typically do the following:

- Authorize the project company to be engaged in the project for the period of the concession.

- Provide the land, easements, air rights etc. required for project or promise to exercise power of eminent domain if required.

- Provide, whenever necessary, access roads and utilities for project (to the degree not included in project company obligations).

- Agree not to authorize competing projects in case such projects would undo the economic projections on which project feasibility is based.

- Set forth the amount and method of payment for the project (if it is contract-based) or determine the amount and method of charging the public (if market-based). In the case of contract-based revenues, there may be a separate off-take contract (it may be with a different government agency) covering the sale of the project's output and the amounts and method of payment.

- Provide for inflation adjustment, foreign exchange convertibility and exchange rate protection to the degree necessary.

# Project company

The project company will typically do the following:

- Design, develop, finance, construct, complete, test, commission, operate and maintain the project according to specific design and performance criteria.

- Protect the environment through appropriate use of pollution control equipment and environmentally sound construction and operation techniques.

- Provide periodic reports to the supervising government agency and give it access to the project for inspection purposes.

**10**

**Contract Package**

- Pay liquidated damages to the government for delay or failure to complete the project or to meet expected performance. The project company may seek in return a bonus payment for early completion or better-than-projected performance.

- Provide insurance coverage for the project, particularly third party liability.

- Provide training and employment for local employees and sub-contractors with a view to maximizing technology transfer and capability building.

- Include specified amounts or types of local content in the project (e.g. manpower, engineering and other services, equipment, raw materials) to promote the local economy.

- Transfer the project in good working order to the host government at the transfer date.

# ▪ Off-take agreement

For a BOT project to be "bankable" it must have at its heart a sufficiently certain revenue stream. The project agreement may itself spell out the terms under which the BOT project company is expected to earn its revenues. In some cases, for example in a power plant project, the revenue stream will be embodied in a long-term power off-take contract or power purchase agreement with the potential consumer of the power to be generated (for example, a government-owned power distribution company). Each sector, each country and indeed each project will have its own pricing formula for an off-take contract, but some parameters will be fairly constant.

Normally the government will guarantee a minimum payment, usually in the form of a capacity fee, payable on a take-or-pay basis, that is, payable for a certain amount of capacity, as long as the project company demonstrates that the plant can operate at that minimum capacity, whether or not the government actually takes the electricity. The lenders to the project will want to make sure that this minimum take-or-pay payment is sufficient to keep the project going (i.e. capable of operating at the target minimum capacity) and to service the project debt. If it is not, they normally insist on other forms of credit support to cover any shortfalls.

A power off-take contract would also normally provide for an energy fee on a different basis, for power actually generated and sold. The pricing formula here normally takes account of the variable or marginal costs that the project company has to bear to generate electricity, with a small profit factor. The combined capacity fee and energy fee should be designed to do three things: to assure the lenders that sufficient revenues will be available to cover project debt service; to assure the equity investors that, if they build and operate the project as planned, they will recover their investment and earn a reasonable return to compensate them for the equity risk they are taking, which should be based on expectations as to revenues that are agreed between the host government and the investors; and to afford a reasonable sharing of the benefits between the investors and the host government if the project is more successful (for instance, if it is able to generate and sell more power or to do so more efficiently) than had been expected.

Careful attention to these details in the project agreement and in the implementing off-take contract can avoid a situation in which a project company is able to earn unreasonable windfall profits. If such contingencies are not properly foreseen and dealt with in the off-take contract (and elsewhere), the equity investors could end up earning excessive returns, meaning that the host government will end up paying more than it needed to for the project.

An off-take contract is appropriate for any project providing goods or services that can be delivered on a long-term basis to an identified purchaser (power, water, telecommunications and even, in some cases, toll transportation facilities). An example of the latter is the Channel Tunnel, where long-term user agreements were established with the national railroads of France and the United Kingdom.

In other cases, such as a toll road or metro rail system with market-based revenues, the appropriate government agency will commit itself to the level of tolls or fares that may be charged and the monopoly conferred by the concession. Issues such as variable rates of return based on actual levels of traffic or passenger usage will need to be addressed by both the project company and the government to assure a reasonable rate of return commensurate with the risks undertaken, to guard against unreasonable windfall profits and to provide a fair sharing of benefits.

# ■ Construction agreement

Lenders are prepared to look primarily to the revenue stream of the BOT facility once it is operating. But what of the period before start-up? What is their security? How do lenders analyse what is known as the completion risk? Here, they look primarily at the construction agreement.

Most BOT proposals and projects are done on the basis of a lump sum or a fixed-price turnkey construction contract. Lenders will look primarily to the project company for cost, schedule and completion guarantees during the construction period. The project company, in turn, will try to reallocate as much of this risk as possible to the construction contractor or, where appropriate, into the insurance market.

The construction agreement for a BOT project will be discussed in chapter 12. Experience in negotiating construction contracts shows that it is critical to focus on risk allocation in as flexible and realistic a way as possible. All parties want to minimize their completion and performance risks. Yet risks cannot be eliminated, and they all have a cost associated with them. "Someone" must accept (or share) every element of risk. The challenge is to diversify the risks and to allocate each risk to the party best able to manage it. Risk allocation and management should be analysed together.

Cases in which a contractor offers to bear virtually unlimited risks must be viewed with skepticism. The host government must carefully assess the contractor's ability to undertake this risk as it can prove entirely illusory.

# ■ Equipment supply contracts

If the project requires substantial heavy equipment in addition to the construction itself, the project company, either directly or indirectly through the construction contractor, will negotiate with various equipment suppliers for the supply of such equipment. A power plant, for example, will need boilers, turbines, generators and other large pieces of electrical equipment. An urban transit system will need engines, passenger vehicles and track. Each type of equipment will be the subject of contracts separate from the construction contract.

Equipment supply contracts will vary little from those entered into in a traditional infrastructure project. For this reason, they are not discussed further in the *Guidelines*.

# Operation and maintenance contract

In many BOT projects, the project is not operated and maintained by the project company itself but is contracted out to a firm experienced in the operation and maintenance of the particular type of facility. The firm that takes responsibility for this may be one of the equity participants in the project company. The operation and maintenance (O&M) contract will define parameters for operating efficiency. It usually includes penalties for failure to meet these base case efficiency levels and bonuses for exceeding them. Maintenance standards are specified as well. Host governments should require the project company to include in the O&M agreement provisions that promote the employment and training of local citizens and the transfer of technology.

As noted earlier, it will be essential to insure that the rights and obligations of the parties to the construction, equipment and O&M agreements are defined in a manner that is consistent and complementary. Disputes, for example, should be handled in a single forum under an agreed-on law. Ordinarily, these disputes can only be resolved equitably by having all interested parties present to state their position at one time in one place. The important thing is for the project to be able to move forward.

The operation and maintenance of BOT projects will be discussed in chapter 13.


# ■ Insurance contracts

A BOT project requires extensive insurance coverage, including casualty, third-party liability and, often, business interruption insurance. The international insurance market has developed several innovative forms of insurance specifically designed for BOT projects. It will be up to the host government, and to a certain extent the lenders, to decide whether the cost of such insurance is justified (it will, of course, be added to the total cost of the project and eventually paid, directly or indirectly, by the host government or local consumers). It may be more rational in many cases for the host government to provide a stand-by loan commitment to cover the same risks. In any event, insurance professionals must be consulted because increasingly sophisticated and creative coverage is becoming available as experience with BOT projects accumulates.

# ▪ Financing contracts

The financial "engineering" of a BOT project can either be relatively straightforward or exceedingly complex. The degree of complexity will depend on the difficulty of financing the project, the nature of the risks involved, the sophistication of the capital markets in the country in which the project will be located, the degree of equity commitment the sponsors are prepared to make, the degree of support being provided by the host government, the availability of hedging instruments for foreign exchange risks and many other factors (see chapter 9).

In the typical BOT project, a syndicate of commercial banks provides the basic construction loan and may provide the permanent financing. The two loans may be contained in a single loan facility at the outset or may be structured as separate financing involving different lenders. The financing at each stage may involve several different levels of senior and subordinated debt. Since there are fewer risks to the lender once construction is completed and the operational phase begins, it is not unusual to see different lenders willing to participate in the permanent financing and thus to have, for instance, funds raised by long-term notes issued to insurance companies, pension funds and the like used to repay all or part of the initial construction loan when construction is over and operation begins.

Normally, there will also be commitments for stand-by loans or additional stand-by equity, which are sometimes backed by letters of credit or bank guarantees obtained at the sponsors' expense, to cover cost overruns or delays during construction or revenue shortfalls during operation. The sponsors will in turn seek to have these eventualities covered by liquidated damages in the construction and O&M contracts. The contractual provisions to pay liquidated damages are normally backed by performance bonds. Insurance might also be used to cover these eventualities.

In host countries where strong capital markets or institutional investors exist, part of the financing can come from notes or debentures offered to local investors. Some BOT projects have included either direct loans from the local government for part of the project cost or stand-by commitments to make subordinated loans in, for instance, the event of *force majeure*, where no other project participant is willing to cover the risk.

There is no absolute rule as to how much of the project costs will be covered by debt financing and how much by equity. On the equity side, the original equity of the project sponsors will already have been defined in the agreements relating to the formation of the project company. Some BOT projects, however, have contemplated additional equity being raised from outside investors, either at financial closing or as part of the permanent financing at completion of construction. At the latter point, a successful BOT project begins to resemble a public utility and can therefore be made attractive to investors as a stable, relatively safe investment. Particularly where the local capital markets are sophisticated and large enough, a BOT project may well contemplate raising additional equity during the operational phase. If such equity is an essential part of the financing package, there should be a commitment from an underwriter to place the equity.

## ■ Security package

The lenders to a BOT project will normally require fairly elaborate security arrangements.

Firstly, project revenues are usually paid not to the project company but into one or more escrow accounts, maintained by an escrow agent. The escrow agent is often one of the banks that are acting as lenders to the project. It is always independent of the project company. Payments are made from the escrow accounts according to stipulated priorities. The lenders normally insist that a special debt reserve escrow account be established and maintained sufficient to pay debt service for a minimum period (six months or longer) before any distributions can be made to equity investors.

Secondly, the benefits of the various contracts entered into by the project company (for example, the turnkey construction contract, performance bonds, supplier warranties and insurance proceeds) as well as the other assets of the company will normally be assigned to a trustee for the benefit of the lenders.

Thirdly, the rights and obligations of the various lenders among themselves will be spelt out in an intercreditor agreement.

Fourthly, lenders will normally insist on the right to take over the project from the original sponsors and investors in the case of failure to meet a defined financial and technical benchmark, well before the bankruptcy stage, and to bring in new contractors, suppliers or operators to complete or operate the project.

Fifthly, numerous policies insuring against a variety of risks (for example, political, fire and other casualty, *force majeure*, delayed completion and liability) will be secured.

Finally, commercial lenders, export credit agencies and multilateral finance agencies may request measures of government support to

**10**

**Contract Package**

protect the lenders against any substantial general or country risk over which the project sponsors have little or no control and that could impact the project's viability or cause it to fail.

In chapters 11-13, the key features of the project, construction and O&M agreements are presented.

# THE PROJECT AGREEMENT

# ▪ Main features and functions

Contracts known as "project agreements", "concession agreements" or "implementation agreements" have become the main legal instrument for the arrangement of BOT projects. The provisions of these contracts (in the following subsumed under the term "project agreement") will vary depending on the type of infrastructure facility and the legal and economic conditions of each country. The main features and functions of project agreements are, however, similar irrespective of the type of facility and the country concerned. The three most important functions are discussed below.

Firstly, the project agreement is the basic contract between the host government (or a government entity) and the project company authorizing the project company to construct and operate the project, usually for a specific period of time, and establishing the parameters of the concession. It stipulates the tariffs and terms of payment under various conditions and defines the performance standards to be met by the project company in the construction, operation and maintenance of the project in question. The project agreement is the document that identifies the risks associated with the project and allocates them between the government and the project company. It specifies the support to be provided by the government, the supervision mechanism required by the government and the actions to be taken if certain eventualities occur during the life of the project. Finally, the project agreement stipulates the terms of the transfer of the project at the end of the concession period.

Secondly, the participation of third parties in BOT arrangements is closely coupled with the content of the project agreement. Legally, the project agreement is a contract between the government and the project company. Yet, because the performance of third parties such as financiers, constructors, suppliers, purchasers and O&M companies and the spread of risks between the various actors is essential for the implementation of any BOT project, their concerns will have to be met in the project agreement as well. First and foremost, the project agreement has to provide for the financial, commercial and security terms needed to make the project capable of being financed (bankable).

Thirdly, the project agreement is used as the tool for coordinating and integrating the various financial, construction and operation contracts constituting the contract package required for a BOT project (see chapter 10). In other words, it is used as the centre of the complex web of contracts, usually of a transnational character, that is needed for the packaging of BOT infrastructure arrangements and that defines the particular BOT project.

# ■ The legal nature of a project agreement

As already indicated, the majority of countries applying the BOT scheme to infrastructure projects have used the project agreement as the main legal instrument for the complex BOT arrangements. Some countries, however, owing to their legal and administrative traditions, have granted BOT projects by an administrative act known as a concession authorization or by an authorization license. The authorization may be brief, referring to a mandatory concession legislation, or may be as detailed as a project agreement, depending on the legal and administrative system of the country concerned.

In any event, the difference between the legal nature of a project agreement and the legal nature of an authorization should be clearly perceived. Where the contract form is used, the government is acting in a commercial capacity such that general contract law and commercial law are applicable to the BOT arrangement. By contrast, according to most legal systems an authorization or license is characterized as an administrative act governed by the administrative law of the country.

This difference between a project agreement and an administrative authorization may have a number of practical consequences. For example, in general an administrative authorization or a license is revocable or can be amended by the government at will without the consent of the project company; by contrast, a project agreement, as a contract, typically will only be alterable if so provided for in the agreement or by common consent of the parties. The enforcement by the project company of an administrative act may also be more uncertain than the enforcement of a contract, depending on the administrative system and legal tradition of the host country. These are significant issues in terms of the bankability of a BOT infrastructure project. It is further assumed that the contract is a more flexible legal instrument than an administrative act for coordinating the complex and transnational structure of most BOT arrangements.

For such reasons, the project agreement with its legal nature of a contract is preferred as the key legal document for BOT arrangements worldwide.

# ■ Negotiation and negotiability

It is usually assumed that the provisions of a project agreement are negotiable contract terms and that most project agreements accordingly are the end products of a negotiation process between the government and the project company. Such assumptions, however, are in need of some qualification.

As discussed in chapter 6, national and international laws and regulations normally require the use of competitive bidding as the procurement method in order to achieve efficiency, fairness and transparency in the procurement process. Within the competitive bidding approach, the scope for negotiating the terms of the project agreement may be very limited. Usually, the government drafts the conditions and terms of the project agreement to be entered into with the successful bidder. The draft of the project agreement, supplied to the prospective bidders as part of the bidding documents, constitutes the basis for tender preparation, the evaluation of the bids and the risk analysis. The government usually makes it clear in the instructions to bidders that a responsive bid must conform with the draft of the project agreement. Unless this is done, each bid may be submitted on different contractual terms, which will make it difficult for the government to compare and evaluate the bids.

Prior to tender and during the evaluation stage, clarification of contract terms may be requested. The bidders may also be entitled to submit firm, alternative bids. But no negotiations will take place at those stages. Indeed, negotiation with bidders during the tendering proceedings, including negotiation of contract terms, is prohibited by most international bidding rules, as discussed in chapter 6.

There have been exceptions to the strict exclusion of negotiation of contract terms within the competitive bidding method. Some national bidding regulations permit negotiation of non-substantial contract terms during the evaluation process. Such negotiations, however, have usually been limited to understandings and reservations made by the bidders in their bids.

In any event, the use of the competitive bidding method for BOT infrastructure projects severely limits the possibility of negotiating the terms and conditions of a project agreement. Where competition among the bidders is tough or if a government insists on avoiding delays in reaching the project agreement, the contract terms prepared by the government are not subject to real negotiations unless the government, in the bidding documents, has clearly allowed certain terms to be discussed.

Where applicable law or international rules do not require a competitive bidding procedure or the government chooses not to adopt such a procedure, the government may conclude the project agreement by a negotiation approach. Even in this situation, it is not correct to say that the terms and conditions of the project agreement are negotiable contract items in the widest sense of this expression.

For one thing, the parties must take into account the different types of relevant mandatory laws and regulations in the host country, usually of a technical, administrative, fiscal or other public nature, such as infrastructure sector laws (electricity sector laws or communication sector laws) and laws relating to environmental protection, safety standards or foreign exchange. The parties must also take into account mandatory rules in other countries if those rules are relevant to the performance of the project. Thus, the law of the country of the suppliers of technology may regulate the contract terms upon which technology can be transferred under a project agreement.

Furthermore, when negotiating and drafting a project agreement, the parties may find it advisable to examine and to apply provisions of previously concluded and implemented agreements in order, for example, to facilitate the financing of the BOT project in question. These are all issues which in practice limit the negotiability of the terms and conditions of a project agreement within a negotiation approach.

Generally speaking, it may be to the advantage of most BOT projects to limit the scope for negotiation of the terms and conditions of project agreements. The experience in regard to negotiation of project agreements has clearly shown that negotiations may lead to long delays in reaching the agreement and therefore add to the project cost, both in real terms and in terms of lost opportunity.

# ▪ The diversity of project agreements

Project agreements are diversified with regard to their content, their structure and the wording of the provisions. They range from huge, complex contracts, tailor-made for a particular infrastructure project (for example, the expressway agreements in Thailand, the power contracts proposed for Pakistan and a great variety of transnational agreements influenced by multinational financial agreements) to straightforward and to some extent standardized contracts for each infrastructure sector, as in China's BOT programme.

Nor have the project agreements been static. Although the BOT concept is a relatively new approach to the financing and operation of infrastructure projects, the project agreements have changed somewhat in accordance with new experiences, the involvement of new infrastructure sectors and the legal traditions and market positions of the countries adopting BOT schemes.

On the whole, however, there is less variety in the content of project agreements than might be expected. While the project agreements in use today may differ considerably from earlier ones in structure and in the drafting technique applied to the contract provisions, they contain largely the same categories of provisions.

Some project agreements, in particular in Asia and in South America, appear to have been strongly influenced in regard to structure and drafting technique by the Anglo-American legal tradition. This means that the contracts are very detailed and comprehensive and sometimes structured in a way that may be difficult to follow. This style may be due less to legal tradition than to an attempt to cover the many regulatory needs that are expected to be raised during the long concession period and to supplement national legal frameworks that are considered to be less-than-adequate for supporting BOT arrangements. As pointed out in chapter 4, the comprehensiveness of any project agreement will to a large extent depend on the legal framework of the country in question. If the framework is conducive to BOT projects, the drafting of a project agreement will be relatively straightforward. In countries with legal systems that are less supportive of or less transparent to the BOT approach, the project agreements must try to be more-or-less self-sufficient.

## ■ Some guidelines for structuring and drafting project agreements

### Addressees for the project agreement

For the reasons stated above, project agreements are usually drafted by the government or a government entity. Before drawing up a project agreement, the government may find it useful to identify the main addressees for the agreement. Clearly, most project agreements are first and foremost addressed to project managers, financiers of the projects and officials supervising the implementation of the projects—and not to contract lawyers alone. The project agreement accordingly should primarily be drafted as a management tool for these actors to help to bring about the financial, construction and operation management discipline so essential for the success of BOT arrangements. This means that the project agreement should be structured primarily with attention to the performance standards and the projected implementation stages of the BOT project in question, placing the more juridical and usually hypothetical provisions in the background.

Recognizing the project manager, supervising officials and financiers as the main addressees further implies that the drafting technique applied to the contract provisions should be as precise and surveyable as possible. For example, it is advisable to avoid using legal concepts such as "reasonable", "material", "negligent" or "best endeavour" in the financial, construction and operation provisions of a project agreement or long, casuistic enumerations followed by phrases like "including but not limited to...". Short sentences, surveyable sections and a logical reference system will also help to make a project agreement more manageable to the addressees in a BOT project.

## A framework for project agreements

It is not possible to recommend a model for project agreements that would be suitable for all types of BOT projects regardless of the infrastructure facility, the country in question and the legal system. The structure described in this section is only meant to be a framework for the categories of provisions commonly found in project agreements. Part I naturally identifies the parties and defines the basic terms of the BOT concession. Part II, following in chronological order the implementation phases of the project, defines the rights and obligations of the parties from site acquisition, through design, construction, testing, operation and maintenance, to the final transfer at the end of the concession period. Part III comprises what may be termed the general obligations of the parties, that is, provisions applicable to all phases of a BOT project (compliance with law, environmental protection, lenders' security provisions and so forth). Grouping such provisions clearly simplifies the project agreement. Taken together, parts II and III of the agreement may serve as a contractual flow chart for the management and supervision of the projected implementation of a BOT project. Part IV defines and regulates the consequences of changed circumstances, breach of contract and other situations only hypothetically relevant for a BOT arrangement. Depending on the legal traditions of the contracting parties, there may also be chapters on assignment of the project agreement (part V) and some miscellaneous provisions at the end of a project agreement, including provisions on dispute resolution (part VI).

# I. THE BASIC TERMS OF THE CONCESSION

## 1. The parties, recitals and definitions

A project agreement normally begins by identifying the parties to the agreement and the capacity in which they are contracting. Certain recitals or "whereas" provisions typically follow. They provide background and context for the later substantive sections of the agreement. These two initial sections are usually followed by a Definition of Terms. It is advisable to coordinate the Definition of Terms with the use of those terms in the context of the contract provisions. Theoretical definitions or definitions transferred from previous contracts may cause problems of interpretation and clarity.

## 2. Granting the concession

The fundamental rights and obligations both of the government and of the project company should be described early in a project agreement. They are the main rules of the agreement and provide a clear-cut background for the understanding and interpretation of the exception provisions found elsewhere in the agreement.

## 3. Conditions precedent

Often, a number of events must take place before a project agreement can become effective. These "conditions precedent" are frequently listed after the provision granting the concession. They may include the following:

- There is evidence that both parties are properly organized.
- There is evidence that both parties are authorized to contract.
- Necessary permits and licenses have been obtained.
- Financing is in place.
- All other conditions necessary to start construction have been properly satisfied or waived.

It is often the case that the effective date of the project agreement (which determines, among other things, the commencement of the concession period) begins when the parties certify that all conditions precedent have been satisfied or may be deemed to have been satisfied.

## II. IMPLEMENTATION OF THE PROJECT

### 1. Construction of project facilities

This comprehensive section will normally include—as a minimum—the following provisions:

▫ *Land acquisition and use*. This provision regulates

- Acquisition of the project site and the necessary right-of-way.
- Allocation of the cost for the acquisition.
- Project company's rights to own or use (lease) the land.
- Conditions of the site.
- Clearance of the site.

Normally the government is in the better position to acquire or expropriate the site in the public interest at a fair price, which would be beneficial from both the cost and time standpoints. Whether the project company should own or lease the land required for the project may be of some importance for the lenders' security arrangements (mortgage arrangements).

▫ *Design*. The project agreement will define the following:

- Design and specification criteria to be followed by the project company when preparing the design for the project.
- The parties' rights to review and approve the design and design criteria.
- Procedures for review, change and approval of designs.
- Responsibility for deficiencies in the design of the project.

The design drawings consist of those incorporated in the government's tender documents, the more detailed design drawings submitted with the project company's winning bid and, ultimately, whatever additional drawings are necessary to complete the project. While the government will reserve the right to review and approve the design drawings, the project company will remain solely responsible for their quality and contents. Approval by the government does not relieve the project company of its responsibility for the design of the project.

▫ *Construction*. The project agreement should place full responsibility for construction cost, schedule and completion with the project company. It should define the time for the commencement of the construction, the construction milestones and the quality of the construction work, including what documents, laws, regulations and standards are to be followed. Specific provisions should be drafted to cover such subjects as the following:

- Obtainment of approvals and licenses required for the performance of the construction work.
- Selection and approval of construction contractors and subcontractors.
- Supply of equipment and materials.

- Definition of the quality system for quality assurance.
- Content and timing of construction progress reports.
- Government rights to access for inspection and testing.
- Clearance of the site on completion of construction work.

For projects as large and complex as most infrastructure projects, unforeseen construction issues may arise during the performance of the work. It may therefore be a good idea to provide in the project agreement for design changes to meet the evolving requirements of the construction process. Further, it should be accepted that in case of a dispute the parties must continue to perform their work pending later settlement of the dispute. Compliance with the construction schedule is essential to any BOT arrangement. A provision on continuation of performance pending dispute resolution may therefore be added to this section of the project agreement.

▫ *Testing and acceptance of construction.* Provisions on test procedures and acceptance of construction work and deliveries of goods are part of most larger industrial contracts. Such provisions will set forth the procedures and the programmes for testing the facility to confirm that it meets its design and other standards stipulated in the project agreement and applicable laws and regulations. Such provisions should specify the following:

- Notice of testing.
- Joint inspections and tests.
- Issue of certificate of completion.
- Deemed certificate of completion.
- Responsibility of the parties.

It is internationally recognized practice that the testing of construction work and the issuance of a certification of completion does not relieve the project company of responsibility for defects or delays in the construction work.

If the performance test discloses minor defects that are impractical or unreasonable to require the project company to remedy by repair or re-delivery, the project agreement may provide for the lack of conformity to be remedied by tariff/toll reductions or by a claim for compensation. The amount of tariff/toll reduction over the concession period should, if possible, be calculated by the use of appropriate mathematical formulas.

▫ *Delay in completion.* Penalties for delays in construction work for which the project company is responsible are spelt out in this section of a project agreement. To collect such penalties, the government is entitled to draw upon a performance bond submitted by the project company.

One issue to be addressed is the consequences of delayed completion owing to acts or omissions of the host government in contravention of its obligations under the project agreement. The majority of project agreements appear to provide for extending the concession period to compensate the delay. This solution may not be satisfactory to a project company that has to pay principal and interest under the financing documents as of the agreed completion date. To meet this situation, the government may consider a provision that compensates the project company for the incremental financing costs.

Another issue here is the question whether to offer a bonus to the project company for early completion: there is no clear answer for BOT projects. Motivating the project company in this way would, however, serve to reduce the delay risk for the lenders.

## 2. Operation and maintenance

In some project agreements, the provisions on operation and maintenance of the project facilities (like the provisions on transfer of the project at the end of the concession period) form a separate main part of the project agreement. This is simply a matter of preference. In any case, poor or inefficient operation and maintenance of the project facility can cause the performance of the project and the revenue generated by it to fall below projected levels. It can also cause premature wear and tear on the project facility and its components. The project company can, to some extent, mitigate this risk by entering into a long-term O&M contract with an experienced operator. The provision defining the right of the project company to select a qualified O&M contractor and the government's right to approve the contractor and the O&M contract is therefore essential in this section of a project agreement. In addition, specific provisions should be drafted in the project agreement to cover such operation and maintenance subjects as the following:

- Operation parameters.
- Maintenance and repair standards or targets.
- Schedule and substance of periodical overhauls of the project facility.
-  and monitoring.
- Toll/tariff formulas and adjustment of the formulas.
- Toll/tariff collection system.
- Operation and maintenance bond.
- Project company's failure to maintain and repair and the government's right to carry out maintenance and repair.
- Services to users of the project facility.

To attain high operation and maintenance standards and sustain a high quality of service to the users, it is advisable to set performance standards or output targets rather than to demand particular operation, maintenance and service programmes or methods in a project agreement. The government may also consider payment mechanisms that encourage improvements in the quality of service.

## 3. Financial management

The way in which expenses and revenues are to be incurred, recorded and disbursed should be precisely specified in a project agreement. For example, in a toll road BOT project, such provisions may include the following:

- The toll structure.
- Toll collection.
- Method of toll adjustment.
- Currency protection for a variety of currency risks, including convertibility, availability of foreign exchange, devaluation and repatriation.
- Consent to escrow account.
- Financial statements.
- Accounting.
- Government's rights in the event of project company's default under the financing documents.

The pricing structure in a BOT project should not only reflect the risk transferred to the project company. It should also, as far as possible, provide an incentive for the project company to operate the project well.

## 4. Transfer

A check-list for transfer issues to be considered when drafting this section in a project agreement is provided in chapter 14, which deals with the transfer of the project at the end of the concession period.

## III. GENERAL OBLIGATIONS THROUGHOUT THE CONCESSION PERIOD

The provisions in a project agreement that must be observed during all phases of the implementation of a BOT project may be organized in three sections: first, the general obligations of the government; second, the general obligations of the project company; and third, the general obligations common to the government and the project company. This organization of general obligations is followed, for example, by the United Nations Convention on Contracts for the International Sale of Goods.

## 1. General obligations of the government

The general obligations of the government should include essential provisions on the protection of the project company against the consequences of changes in the laws and regulations of the host country that would adversely and materially affect the project company. The risk of changes in laws and regulations, inherent in any long-term contract, is of particular concern to lenders to a BOT project.

Another important general provision may define the government's ongoing obligation to assist the project company in obtaining and sustaining permits and approvals and to otherwise streamline the bureaucratic process associated with the project's implementation.

The general obligations of the government may further include provisions on the following:

- Import and export permissions.
- Tax and duty incentives.
- Safety and security protection.
- Employment permits.
- Access to public utilities.
- Performance guarantees for public sector entities that are parties to the construction and operation of the project.
- Protection from competition.

The latter issue will have to be settled case-by-case. The main point is to balance the project company's need to protect the expected revenue flow from the project with the need to meet future demands and changes.

## 2. General obligations of the project company

The most essential general obligation of the project company is that it must comply with the laws and regulations of the host country during implementation of the project.

Another important project company obligation during design, construction and operation of the project has to do with environmental protection. Normally the project company and its subcontractors are required to take all reasonable steps to ensure that the environment is protected throughout the project. Obligations to curtail harmful environmental impacts should be identified and spelt out in the project agreement. Compliance with non-material changes in environmental laws and regulations during the concession period may be included in the project company's environmental obligations.

Other ongoing obligations of the project company may include the following:

- Compliance with safety standards.
- Obtainment and renewal of approvals and permits.
- Use of competitive national constructors, services and goods.
- Protection of labour rights.
- Employment and training of national personnel.
- Technology transfer.

- Project company's responsibility for subcontractors and their employees.
- Project insurance to be obtained.

If the project in question is to be connected to existing infrastructure, as is the case with roads, power plants or railroads, the project agreement may require that the project company minimize disruption to users during construction and maintenance. Afterwards, the maintenance and overhaul routines of all connected facilities must be coordinated.

## 3. Common obligations for the government and the project company

Some obligations or commitments are common for the parties. For example, the *force majeure* provision defines in which unforeseen and unavoidable events either party is entitled to suspend its obligations under the project agreement. Other provisions on common obligations may cover the following:

- Rights to project documents, including ownership of design and drawings.
- Confidentiality as to information and documents obtained.
- Obligations to cooperate.
- Warranty against improper payment.

## IV. BREACH OF CONTRACT AND OTHER FAILURES TO PERFORM

Strict adherence to contract terms relating to the performance of obligations is particularly important in BOT arrangements, as a failure by one party to adhere to the contract terms might have serious financial consequences for the other party and for the lenders. Infrastructure projects usually involve vast sums of money at every stage of project implementation; moreover, the non- or limited recourse nature of financing for BOT projects makes the investors particularly vulnerable to defects, delays or other failures to build and operate the project. It is therefore advisable to prepare and agree upon precise stipulations in the project agreement defining the obligations to be performed and the consequences of a failure to perform those obligations.

This part of the project agreement should deal with some of the remedies that may be available under the contract to the government or the project company if the other party fails to perform its obligations under the project agreement or under the law applicable to the project agreement. It should be noted that usually a project agreement entitles the relevant lenders, upon the occurence of a default under the financing documents, to exercise the rights (and obligation) of the project company under the project agreement. Most project agreements also require provisions to be included in the financing documents to the effect that the government shall be given the opportunity to cure a default by the project company.

# 1. Contract termination

The project agreement should provide for termination when the government or the project company is in substantial breach of the contract or where the contract cannot be performed for a substantial period for reasons of *force majeure*. Provisions on lump sum payments to be made to the project company in case of termination of the contract are usually found together with the provisions giving the right to terminate the contract or in an appendix to the project agreement. The level of payment will depend on the reason for the termination, that is different sums to be paid for termination due to breach of contract by the government, by *force majeure* or by the project company. Upon payment of the compensation, the project facilities are returned (transferred) to the government, in principle in accordance with the transfer provisions of the project agreement. The termination section of a project agreement should thus cover the following:

- The government's right to terminate the project agreement.
- The project company's right to terminate the project agreement.
- Termination notice.
- Rights and obligations of the parties upon termination.
- Compensation payments.
- Notice to lenders.
- Rights of lenders.

Certain host countries may insist on reserving for themselves the right to take over (buy out) the project company's assets at any time after the construction of the project. The terms for the government's takeover of the project and thus the termination of the project agreement may be specified in a buy-out provision in the project agreement. The payment to be made to the project company in case of buy-out may be stipulated to the same amount as that payable on a termination for breach of contract by the government.

# 2. Liability for breach of contract

Provisions on liability for breach of contract usually supplement compensation by the liquidated damages specified in the delay and penalty clauses of the project agreement, in the sense that they compensate for losses caused by failures not specifically covered by liquidated damages and penalty clauses. A contract section on liability for breach of contract may include provisions on the following:

- Terms and conditions for compensation.
- Exemptions from the obligation to pay compensation.
- Benefits gained from failure to perform.
- Duty to mitigate the loss.
- Currency of damages.

It may be decided to exclude, mutually, liability for consequential damages in cases where the party in breach of contract has not been guilty of gross misconduct.

### 3. Liability for personal injury and damage to the property of third persons

The construction and operation of infrastructure projects may result in personal injury to employees or users of the project facilities and other third parties or in damage to their property. The legal issues surrounding damages to be paid to third persons are to a large extent based on the law of the host country and not on the contract. The government and the project company may, however, wish to provide for an internal and final allocation of such liability risks between them in the project agreement. Such liability provisions may specify the following:

- Terms of hold harmless or cross-indemnity arrangements.
- Liability for environmental damage.
- Mutual notification of liability claims.
- Exemption from liability for consequential damages to the other party.

The parties may also wish to provide for liability insurance coverage against such risks, transferring the ultimate responsibility for the injuries and damages to the insurance company.

## V. ASSIGNMENTS AND PUBLIC SECTOR CHANGES

A project agreement should ensure that a party cannot assign the contract or any essential part of it without consent from the other party. Project companies and their financiers may be concerned that the public entity with which they are dealing could be privatized, restructured or dissolved or that it might undergo some other major change of status during the concession period. In that case the project company may wish to include adequate assignment provisions in the project agreement and assurances from the government that a new or surviving entity will become fully liable—and will be able—to perform the contracting entity's obligations.

## VI. MISCELLANEOUS PROVISIONS

Depending on the legal tradition of the contracting parties, there may be some additional provisions in a project agreement covering such issues as interpretation of the project agreement, resolution of disputes and procedural matters. International lenders to a BOT project in developing countries usually expect the project agreement to be governed by the law of a neutral jurisdiction and for disputes to be settled by international arbitration. These issues are likely to cause some difficulties in international commercial contracts.

# VII. APPENDICES

Finally, it is customary to add appendices to the project agreement covering issues that normally require detailed regulation and specification. The following appendices are found in many project agreements:

- Project description and specification.
- Necessary licenses, permits and approvals.
- Description of land and rights of way for the project.
- Preliminary design criteria.
- Procedures for the government to approve the project company's proposal for design changes.
- Procedures for the government to request design changes and additional work.
- Environmental impact assessment and environmental performance reporting system.
- Quality system.
- Programme and procedures for testing.
- Project operation parameters.
- Operation and maintenance criteria.
- Tariff/toll rates and tariff/toll revision formula.
- Specifications for the tariff/toll collection system.
- Training programme.
- List of initial shareholders and percentage interests.
- Insurance.
- List of pre-approved contracts.
- Rights and obligations of the parties upon termination.
- Form of bonds (guarantees).
- Overseeing and monitoring rights of the government.
- Form of legal opinion of counsel for the project company.
- Form of legal opinion of counsel for the government.

There is often a provision that if the content of the main body of the project agreement conflicts with that of the appendices, then the main body prevails. Such a provision should not, however, be used in a BOT project agreement, where the technical specifications, financial instruments or legal matters may have been set out in more detail in the appendices than in the main body of the agreement, making the appendices equally important.

# ■ Standardized agreements

## Need for standardized agreements

The case-by-case approach to preparing complicated project agreements tends to add substantially to project costs because of the time needed to draw up the agreements, the difficulties in managing them and the uncertainty they involve. Unfortunately, it appears that the early BOT project agreements, which were very country-specific and protective of the investors, greatly influenced later project agreements and discouraged fresh approaches to contract drafting that could be applied to different situations and that would respond more satisfactorily to specific needs.

One way forward would be to standardize the project agreements as far as possible, at least at the country and/or the sectoral level, and to modernize them to reflect later BOT experience.

## Arguments against standardization examined

Reservations have been expressed about standard conditions for project agreements. It is argued that the BOT market is so unique and the applicable laws in the host countries so varied that standardized contracts have no place there. Instead, tailor-made project agreements with detailed and specific conditions related to each BOT project are required. Another argument against standardized agreements is that it might be difficult to identify common contract provisions because each contracting party, as well as the financiers of the project, has its own contract culture and will want to have the project agreement drafted and structured in the form it is used to.

To some extent, these arguments are valid. Obviously, the content and comprehensiveness of a project agreement depends on the applicable legal framework of the country in question. This does not, however, prevent the development and application of national standardized agreements. Nor can it be disputed that the specific conditions of a project agreement must be adjusted to the characteristics of each infrastructure sector: that is why countries that use standardized project agreements have developed them for each main infrastructure sector.

Otherwise it is somewhat difficult to accept the argument that BOT projects are so unique that standardized agreements cannot be used. In other commercial areas involving large-scale projects, large investments and high risk, standardized contracts have been used for a long time.[10] The current use worldwide of these standard contracts is evidence of their practicability and their balanced conditions.

Nor is the argument for tailor-made project agreements supported by the analysis in this chapter. As indicated above, the underlying similarities of the project agreements in use appear to be far more striking than their differences. It is also debatable whether the differences in culture among financing institutions should prevent the application of standardized project agreements. On the contrary, financing institutions normally welcome standardized documentation.

In short, the BOT approach is hardly so unique as to make the use of standardized contracts less practical here than elsewhere.

## Advantages

The development and application of standardized project agreements, preferably for each infrastructure sector, might become a cornerstone in a country's BOT strategy. This has been the case, for example, in China, where the authorities have developed a standardized project agreement for each infrastructure sector where the BOT approach is to be used. The potential advantages of standardized project agreements include the following:

- Experience shows that the costs of BOT projects and the time needed to prepare and develop them may be reduced considerably by using standardized project agreements and other standardized project documents.

- The comparison and evaluation of bids is greatly facilitated if the bids are based on the same well-known contractual terms.

- Standardized project agreements may facilitate the financing of BOT projects since the financiers will be familiar with the content of the agreements.

- The nation-wide use of standardized project agreements allows the government to plan, control, monitor and supervise private sector infrastructure projects.

---

[10] For example, the General Conditions for Supply and Erections of Plants and Machinery for Import and Export (prepared under the auspices of the United Nations Economic Commission for Europe) and the conditions of contract for works of civil engineering construction and for electrical and mechanical works (prepared by the Fédération internationale d'ingénieurs-conseils).

- The application of standardized project agreements keeps private companies with ample resources and experience from exploiting their advantage when negotiating with national or local authorities.

- Subcontracting and the negotiating of other project-related contracts, including the construction contracts and the credit agreements, are greatly facilitated by the use of standardized project agreements.

- Standardized project agreements are usually more carefully prepared, resulting in a higher contract quality than case-by-case project agreements, which are often drafted under time constraints.

The use of standardized project agreements does not, of course, preclude adding special conditions to a project agreement if they are needed. Indeed, since they are likely to stand out from the familiar standardized provisions, the special conditions would more easily attract the attention they deserve.

## Drafting considerations

The basic framework described in the preceding section and the categories of contract issues identified may help with the drafting of standardized project agreements. Two other considerations should also be taken into account when drafting standardized project agreements. Firstly, the provisions should be likely to gain the approval of financial institutions. In other words, the standardized project agreements should be bankable. The bankability of a BOT infrastructure project depends, of course, on a number of factors that cannot be regulated in standardized agreements, such as tariff issues, the rate of return, the project's technical feasibility and the offer of incentives. However, certain provisions—those on legal changes and other political risks, on foreign exchange and currency issues, and on land rights, *force majeure*, lenders' security—are clearly of interest to prospective lenders to BOT infrastructure projects.

Secondly, the standardized project agreement should be drafted so as to make the obligations balanced and mutual. Some of the project agreements in use in developing countries may unnecessarily tilt in favour of the project companies, even taking into account poor credit ratings and/or market situations. On the other hand, a standardized contract that tilts decidedly towards the government may discourage serious sponsors. In the end, neither situation can be satisfactory to either party. Even if imbalanced agreements are signed, they will not be conducive to the atmosphere of trust and cooperation that is essential to good contract performance.

International institutions with broad knowledge and experience in the BOT approach, including UNIDO, can help government authorities to draft standardized project agreements.

# THE CONSTRUCTION AGREEMENT

Construction

**12**

# ■ Introduction

The format and terms of a BOT construction agreement are similar to those of conventional agreements for the construction of industrial or infrastructure facilities. The BOT contractor faces the same commitments and risks as the contractor for a conventional project. In a BOT scheme, however, the relationship of the construction agreement to the complex framework of other contracts, in particular the project agreement, and the different interests of the participants may vary considerably from the relationship in more conventional schemes.

The construction agreement is one of the principal contracts that puts the project company, the equity investors and lenders, and the host government at risk. They will all be concerned that it provides adequately for timely and within-budget construction, as well as for a facility whose performance meets the agreed standard of performance. The sponsors need to be assured that delays and cost overruns are strictly controlled and that the risk of their occurrence is borne by the construction contractor.

Any material breach by the contractor could render invalid the pre-investment feasibility studies and projections used to confirm the viability of the project. Because the financing is structured on a limited or non-recourse project finance basis, lenders to a BOT project take a greater interest in the construction agreement than lenders to a conventional project. They will be concerned that cost and time overruns could jeopardize the servicing of the debt and the availability of revenues to cover contingencies.

Although the construction risk is normally allocated to the project company and in turn to the construction contractor, the host government also has an interest in how that risk is managed. There may well be political and other consequences of delay in the construction of an infrastructure project. The host government will try to prevent any circumstances (cost overruns or technical defects) that would place completion and/or operation of the project at risk and perhaps require it to offer financial and other unexpected support to the project company.

The construction agreement is one of many important contractual arrangements among the participants in a BOT project, and it must be drafted so as to be consistent and harmonized with those other arrangements.[11]

# ■ Contracting options

## Types

The BOT construction agreement usually takes the form of a turnkey contract, which gives the contractor responsibility for completeness and functionality. There are three principal alternatives for pricing turnkey contracts:

- Lump sum (fixed price).

- Cost plus (reimbursable cost plus fees).

- Measured unit price.

- Combinations of these.

The most common and favoured strategy in BOT projects is the fixed-price turnkey contract.

### Lump sum (fixed price)

The contract form with the maximum certainty for the project company and lenders is the lump-sum, or fixed-price, turnkey contract. It places primary responsibility upon the contractor to properly and accurately price the works, including the risks and contingencies inherent to all contracts. The contractor agrees to perform the entire contract scope of work for a fixed price established at the time the contract is entered into, which is final and binding and not subject to escalation or adjustment of any kind other than those specifically provided for in the construction

---

[11] A comprehensive treatment of the contractual issues that may have to be dealt with in a construction agreement is contained in the UNCITRAL Legal Guide on Drawing Up International Contracts for the Construction of Industrial Works (United Nations publication, Sales No. E.87.V.10).

agreement or eventual change orders. The requirement to commit to a price at an early stage when it is difficult to calculate a reliable estimate of construction costs exposes the contractor to a much wider spectrum of risks than in the other contracting approaches, discussed below.

Lump-sum turnkey contracts are frequently used in situations that require competitive bidding, complete design and specifications prior to commencement of the work and firm budgeting and financing.

Another feature of lump-sum turnkey contracts is the incentive to build within a certain time. Since the project company can earn revenue only once the facility is commissioned, most construction agreements give contractors time bonuses for early completion but also call for liquidated damages to be imposed if the work is not completed by the agreed date.

Such incentives can mean that less time is required for construction. For example, in the Tate's Cairn Tunnel project in Hong Kong, the contractor used imaginative construction methods that allowed it to open several excavation faces and to complete construction three months ahead of an already tight schedule. Early completion of construction can also increase investor confidence and enhance the project's public image.

Use of the lump-sum contract method does, however, somewhat limit the ability of the project company to strictly control the project. If the project company attempts to dictate the way in which the contractor carries out the work, whether through instructions or change orders, the contractor may have to be paid an additional fee or given more time in which to complete construction.

Several variants of the lump-sum (fixed-price) strategy have been used. Hopewell Holdings of Hong Kong undertook to build the coal-fired power station at Shajiao, China, under a fixed-price turnkey contract establishing one-source responsibility. It then negotiated a turnkey contract with a consortium of equipment suppliers and contractors for a fixed price, fixed schedule and mutually agreed quality terms. The project companies for both the Sydney Harbour Tunnel and the Dartford River Crossing (United Kingdom) entered similar arrangements.

Depending on the complexity of the works, different contracting strategies may be combined. One example is the Channel Tunnel construction contract, where the project sponsors company, Eurotunnel, assumed the construction risks and arranged a stand-by facility for cost overruns. Approximately half the inshore construction work-the terminals in the United Kingdom and France and the fixed equipment in the tunnels-was under a fixed price contract, while the tunnelling works were on a target cost basis and the rolling stock was contracted under a provisional sum.

### Cost plus

Cost-plus turnkey contracts are usually the form of contract most preferred by contractors as they involve the least risks. The contractor performs the specified work and is paid his costs, plus an additional amount for profit. A number of variations of the cost-plus contract exist:

- Cost plus a fixed-sum fee, in which the contractor is reimbursed for the cost of its work and paid a fixed sum as its profit or fee.

- Cost plus a percentage of the cost, in which the contractor receives a sum to cover the cost of its work as well as a reasonable percentage of that cost as its fee. This type of contract is said to provide the least incentive for the contractor to reduce costs, since higher costs result in a larger fee.

- Cost plus incentive fee, in which the contractor is reimbursed for the costs of its work and the fee is a percentage of the difference between actual costs and target costs if there is a saving.

A cost-plus approach is normally undesirable in a BOT project because it requires fixing the cost of the whole project at the outset in order to address financing, rate of return and other critical issues.

### Measured unit price

This type of contract requires the contractor to perform the work in exchange for a fee established by measuring the entire contract work at scheduled prices. Like cost-plus agreements, this approach also has drawbacks in the context of BOT projects.

## Conflict of interests

The BOT method of financing creates certain potential conflicts of interest between the project's participants. This is particularly true in the case of the contractor and the supplier of equipment.

In some BOT projects the contractor and major equipment supplier are investors in the project company. In such cases the investment is made with the intention of directly winning the construction contract or the equipment supply contract. The contractor and the equipment supplier will thus wish to avoid competitive bidding and will instead want to negotiate a risk-free contract, taking their profit from the construction contract. Non-competition and risk-free terms are not in the interest of the host government, the lenders or the sponsors.

On the other hand, as investors in the project company, the contractors are interested in ensuring that the project is completed on time and within budget and that it operates at or above the defined performance level, so they will therefore want quality equipment.

It is essential that such conflicts are recognized and risks allocated at an early stage in the negotiations between the project participants.

## Contract terms

While the project company may propose a particular contracting strategy, it is often the requirements of the lenders and the host government that dictate the project procurement strategy and the minimum terms in the contract.

### *Lender requirements*

Lenders usually require that the construction of the project is procured on a lump sum (fixed-price) turnkey basis. They want to ensure that the construction contractor is committed to a defined scope of work, to a firm price for the construction works and to a stipulated time in which to carry out those works. Appropriate warranty and liquidated damage provisions will be required as an incentive to complete on time or earlier. To ensure that the contractor is not prevented or hindered from completing on time and within budget, lenders also seek to limit the project company from changing the scope of works. In this connection, the role of any project management organization appointed to oversee the work must be clearly defined. The circumstances in which the contractors may claim relief for *force majeure* should also be limited, clearly defined and coordinated with the project agreement.

Lenders usually require that contractors bear project risks for completion and performance. In addition to penalty provisions for late completion, they will also seek penalty clauses linked to the operational performance of the facility. The interests of the lenders usually coincide with those of the host government and sponsors in so far as all these parties would like to encourage more than just base-line performance.

Bonds and guarantees will also be sought by the lenders. Examples of such requirements include performance bonds, retention bonds and, where the contractor is a subsidiary of another organization, guarantees from a parent company or ultimate holding company. In addition, lenders will wish to confirm that the contractor has a proven track record of competency and experience in all areas relevant to the project, as well as the financial ability to carry out and complete the works.

### Host government requirements

Initially, the host government will wish to see that its BOT strategy framework and its procurement rules and standards for the construction works have been fully complied with. Of particular interest will be the extent of involvement by local companies and services in the construction phase, as a BOT scheme is one way to transfer technology and build capabilities.

The host government shares the sponsors' interest in having the construction completed within specifications, budget and time. The failure to do so will ultimately reflect badly on the government, with both financial and political consequences.

Since its overall requirements to be followed by the construction works and contractors are defined in the project agreement, the host government will want the construction agreement to be in complete harmony with the project agreement.

# ▪ Key contractual issues

## Timing

Keeping to the planned schedule is of particular importance in BOT projects, as the commencement of the commercial operation gives the project company the revenue needed to service the debt and earn the expected return for the equity investors. The timing must be realistic. While some additional time for contingency should be written into the project planning to allow for delays outside the parties' control, a careful and independent review of the construction schedule is essential.

For a BOT project, as for any complex construction project, the discipline of scheduling is at the heart of budgetary control. An achievable schedule should be presented by the contractor, demonstrating the order in which he proposes to carry out the works. Construction work should be scheduled, monitored and revised to minimize or eliminate the impact of any delays.

Incentives for the contractor to complete on time can take the form of a bonus for early completion and a penalty for late completion. Liquidated damages provisions should reflect the loss likely to be suffered by the project company in the event of a delay. They should cover at least the net debt service and other fixed costs for which the project company is liable.

Other options to penalize delay include acceleration provisions. If the delay falls within the contractor's sphere of responsibility, then the costs of accelerating should be borne by the contractor. A formula for calculating the costs of acceleration, where the delay is outside both parties' control, should also be provided.

## Quality

A quality assurance procedure should be described in the construction agreement. The standard of quality expected should be clearly defined and the design parameters set out in a functional specification. Such a standard is often related to a particular industry code or norm. It should include relevant health, safety and environmental considerations. Use of materials that comply with the specifications and that are of a certain standard should be required.

Provisions should also address the situation where workmanship and/ or materials fail to meet the required standard or quality. The sponsor will want a procedure to identify and remedy defects as soon as practicable and at no additional cost to the project.

## Performance

It is crucial that a BOT facility functions properly and that certain performance parameters, including quality and quantity of products and level of output or off-take, are attained. Since failure of the facility to perform at the projected level means the loss of revenue to the project company and threatens its ability to pay interest, loans and equity returns, operational and performance guarantees are usually requested from contractors. Such guarantees are often supplemented by availability guarantees, which specify the duration of a plant's operation.

## Pricing and payment

The construction agreement should clearly define the scope of works and the liability parameters. Costs of risk management the contractor will be responsible for are added to the costs of construction.

Construction works are usually paid in instalments. Terms-of-payment clauses are important to ensure that the contractor is not overpaid through stage payments. The payments should be linked to the value of work that has been carried out. A specified percentage of each instalment payment or retainer amount is usually withheld in an escrow account pending successful completion and testing of the facility. If the contractor is behind schedule, the contract mechanism should permit withholding money until it catches up. There should be a procedure for certifying the progress and the value of work carried out before payment is made.

## Subcontracting

Works may be subcontracted for a number of reasons, including the need for a particular expertise in certain aspects of the construction work or the lower cost of local contractors. The right to subcontract should normally be subject to the approval of the host government and the project company. Similarly, the procurement of major items of equipment by subcontractors should be monitored by and subject to the approval of the project company and, depending on the project, the host government. Provisions covering the liability of the contractor for the failure of its subcontractors or suppliers are important as there will often be no direct contractual link between such third parties and the project company.

Host governments should encourage subcontracting as much as possible in the country, provided that local companies are competitive and reliable. The project agreement will usually define the overall requirements for subcontracting.

## Availability of spare parts

A general obligation should be placed on the construction contractor to procure sufficient spare parts for the project. It should require the contractor to compile an inventory of spare parts that need to be maintained.

Just as they encourage local subcontracting, host governments may encourage the acquisition of spare parts locally. The project agreement and the construction agreement have to be harmonized so as to carefully allocate the responsibility for spare parts between the contractor and the O&M operator.

## Claims by the contractor

If the contractor undertakes to construct a facility on a lump-sum basis, it assumes the pricing risk of not having taken into account all that is necessary to carry out the work. In a turnkey project, this includes risks connected with underestimating the work involved after the detailed design has been finalized.

However, claims for additional payment and/or for extensions to the time for completion have to be met by the project company to the extent that it, or others for whom it is responsible, change the scope of the work from that for which the contractor tendered. The right of the project company to change orders or to instruct the contractor to execute the work in a particular way should be carefully defined in the construction agreement.

The project agreement should dictate the limited circumstances in which the project may be changed and by whom. Host governments should pay strict attention to such provisions. Issuing instructions to change the works can materially add to the cost of the project.

Given the limited equity of the project company and the restrictions on the drawdown of funds, the project agreement may arrange for the availability of contingency funds, normally in a stand-by or reserve facility. Nevertheless, the project agreement and financing agreements are likely to apply very stringent conditions on the circumstances in which such funds can be drawn.

The construction agreement should provide for a mechanism to deal with any type of claim by the contractor. Procedures and deadlines for notification of a claim must be spelt out. Such a contractual mechanism should provide for the deferred settlement of claims arising during construction, preserving the rights of the contractor but allowing the project to continue to completion.

# ▪ Security

In many jurisdictions, physical assets that are firmly attached to land belong to the owner of that land, often the host government in infrastructure projects. If the project fails, the assets therefore revert to the government and the right to build and operate the project is revoked. Thus, the conventional form of security available to lenders is valueless in most BOT projects. In such cases, other more appropriate clauses or guarantees must be provided. The construction contractor should be obliged by project sponsors and lenders to procure a variety of bonds to secure his performance.

Generally speaking, a bond is an undertaking to make payment or offer some form of assurance in the event of defaults or circumstances affecting the schedule, construction or quality of the facility. Bonds can be issued by banks or surety companies in the form of a bond, guarantee or stand-by letter of credit. In BOT projects, bonds will usually constitute payment obligation in favour of the project company. Five types of bond are used:

- Bid (or tender) bond, which compensates the project company with a certain proportion of the contract price if the winning bidder decides not to proceed.

- Performance bond, which should ensure that if the contractor defaults the bondsman procures completion by another contractor at no additional cost to the project company.

- Retention bond, which may be issued in lieu of withholding a percentage of each instalment payment to the contractor. It may be called in the event the contractor fails to remedy defective work or materials.

- Advance payment bond, which is recommended as security against, for example, the non-delivery of equipment or the insolvency of the contractor in cases where the contractor has been paid, in advance of carrying out any work, to purchase equipment that is to be manufactured but installed at a later date.

- Maintenance bond, which aims at securing the project company against defects that could incur during the start-up or maintenance period, as specified in the construction agreement.

The bonding and guarantee situation under the BOT contractual framework is complex. It may take one of the following forms:

- Unconditional on demand or first demand, executed without proof of default, i.e. no conditions are attached to invoking the security.

- Conditional, commonly executed if there is proof of the requisite fault. Failure to meet any of the conditions will mean the bond is forfeited.

- Documentary, executed on demand but the demand includes a means of certifying the grounds for calling the bond. In general, such bonds are issued as undertakings to pay upon presentation of specified documents.

An undertaking from the parent or ultimate holding company of the contractor should be required if the contractor either is, or is employing, a subsidiary company of a larger organization. Also, there should be a joint and several liability provision if the contracting organization is a joint venture or consortium. This will permit redress against all or any of the members of the consortium in the event of calling the bond. Finally, the bond should be of long enough duration to cover all liabilities of the contractor, and any amendment or variation to the construction agreement should not serve to waive or reduce liability under the bond.

# OPERATION AND MAINTENANCE CONTRACT

O & M

13

# ▪ Introduction

Once the construction of the BOT project is complete, the facility is ready
to be put to its intended use. Whether it is a toll road or a power plant,
someone will have to carry out and oversee its day-to-day operation and
maintenance. Most sponsors retain an experienced company to do this
if they do not have the expertise to do it themselves. Accordingly, the
choice of the operator and the elaboration of the terms and conditions of
the operation and maintenance (O&M) contract will be key factors in the
success of a BOT project.

The O&M contract is the agreement that defines the duties and responsibilities of the project company and the operator with regard to
day-to-day operation of the facility. A typical O&M contract addresses
the following issues:

- Scope of the operator's services.

- Project company's responsibilities.

- Warranties and guarantees.

- Compensation.

- Access to books and records.

- Insurance.

- Liability and indemnification.

- Defaults and remedies.

- Term and termination.

- Dispute resolution.

- Choice of law.

O & M

13

The interests of the sponsors, host government and lender will be affected by this contract, and it will generally be executed only after those entities have approved the provisions regarding each of the issues important to them.

It is critical that the O&M contract provisions be consistent with and complementary to the provisions of the other BOT project contracts. For example, differences among dispute resolution procedures in the various contracts can breed chaos when problems arise and parties to different contracts blame one another, only to discover there is not a single forum where the disputes can be resolved.

# ▪ Choosing an operator

Selection of the right operator is the single most important decision that bears on the successful operation of a BOT project. The operator should not be a generalist but should have the skills and experience needed to operate the project successfully. As it is usually advisable to choose an operator that has a vested interest in the project's success, the operator is very often an investor in the project company. This ownership interest provides an added financial incentive for the operator to perform its services in an exemplary fashion and gives the operator a fiduciary responsibility that would otherwise be lacking.

# ▪ Operation and maintenance risk allocation

There are various financial and other risks that inevitably arise throughout every project (these were discussed in detail in chapter 8). One of the purposes of the project contracts is to apportion those risks among the various participants so that each party knows who is responsible in every situation that might arise during operation. The O&M contract allocates certain risks to the operator and others to the project company. Insurable risks are transferred to insurance companies. The task, of course, is to determine who bears what risks.

The project, and the relative strengths and knowledge of the participants, largely determine which party is able and willing to bear a given risk at the lowest cost. For example, it is more than likely for the project company rather than the operator to take the risk of the facility being destroyed by a natural disaster. Even though the risk will most likely be placed with an insurance company, the project company built the facility in the first place and is in a better position to understand what would be involved in rebuilding it. On the other hand, the operator may have more knowledge about the supply of materials needed to operate the facility and may be in a better position to evaluate the risk of not being able to perform if those supplies are interrupted. Risk allocation is usually the most difficult and the most important subject of the negotiations between the project company and the operator when drafting the O&M contract.

Once risks are allocated, the parties will seek insurance for some of them. All insurance policies should name the operator, the project company, the host government and the lenders as insured parties. The policies should contain language requiring the insurance company to notify all additional insureds at least 30 days before cancellation of the policy for any reason. The O&M contract should also contain waivers of subrogation to protect the interests of the various parties and to ensure that the risk is clearly on the insurance company that assumed it.[12]

The party bearing the risk often bears the burden of indemnifying the other party for losses that are the indemnitor's responsibility. The O&M contract should precisely set forth the terms of such indemnification obligation, including, for example, the degree to which consequential damages or defence costs are to be covered. This obligation is part of the web of contractual rights and responsibilities underlying all BOT contracts. There are circumstances where the project company might have to indemnify the O&M operator. For example, if the project company takes steps that make the O&M operator's costs higher or that prevent it from earning certain performance bonuses, indemnification may become an issue.

In short, risk management is an important aspect of the O&M contract, and the parties must ensure that all operation risks are allocated fairly and clearly.

---

[12] In some projects, the parties may consider *force majeure* insurance. This is specialized insurance that guards against the risks of some natural disasters, strikes or other eventualities that are excluded from standard liability insurance policies. The value of this insurance may or may not be equal to the damage or defence cost, and careful consideration should be given to the needs of the project before deciding to purchase or forgo this coverage.

# ▪ Operation of the facility

## Consistency of operation commitments

The O&M contract must carefully set forth how the project is to be managed. Within the framework of the underlying concession and the financing agreements, the project company will have assumed certain obligations regarding the facility's operation and maintenance. Accordingly, great care must be taken to ensure that all the operation responsibilities undertaken by the project company are either transferred to the operator (usually the favoured approach) or, in special circumstances, deliberately left outside the O&M contract, with adequate provision in other parts of the overall project plan for their accomplishment.

## Competing interests of the parties; performance guarantees

The host government and the lenders must approve the O&M contract before it can be implemented, and they will want to be assured that their concerns are met. The host government is concerned primarily with whether or not the project will operate as planned (for example, whether it will provide the power that the country needs or whether the road will carry traffic efficiently). The host government will also be concerned that the project should comply with all laws, including environmental and safety laws. Although the project may be exempt from some legal requirements by virtue of the project agreement, it would be unusual for any significant legal requirements to be waived.

The lenders are concerned primarily with whether or not project revenues will be sufficient to repay their investment with interest. The sponsors, in addition, want to assure themselves that the project revenue will be sufficient to provide a reasonable rate of return. To satisfy themselves of this, the sponsors and lenders want a minimum performance level set in the O&M contract. Performance specifications could take the form of a minimum operating capacity or minimum output of electrical power (which the host government would probably have to guarantee to purchase on a take-or-pay basis) if the project is a power plant or a maximum percentage of lost revenue from missed or uncollected tolls in a toll road project.

The project company, operator, host government and lenders must agree on any performance guarantee, based on the financial needs of the project and the feasibility studies. Once all this information is compiled, the financial models will dictate the minimum acceptable level of performance from the lenders' perspective. The project company, which is expecting a reasonable return on its equity, will want a higher level of performance. The operator, on the other hand, will naturally want to provide only the most minimal performance guarantees. Eventually, the parties will have to agree on a realistic performance guarantee based on the underlying realities of the project and reach an acceptable compromise to their conflicting interests.

## Operator's acceptance of the facility

After completion of construction and initial start-up and testing, the operator should be required to inspect and accept the facility as meeting the required performance guarantees of the construction contractor and should also have the responsibility for obtaining and managing any warranty work as a result of defective construction or equipment. It is usually in the best interest of the project to have the operator involved from the outset. However, the operator's representatives must be present during start-up and testing as well as during the punch-list phase of the project. The operator is going to have to use the facility to perform specified functions, and it is in the best position to determine if the facility has been completed in a manner that will allow it to do so.

## Substantive operational concerns

Three major concerns for the operation of the facility are (a) the supply of fuel, utilities and other materials, (b) the demand for the product or service and (c) the delivery of the product or service. For example, for a coal-fired power plant, the operator will need a steady supply of coal to feed into the furnaces to produce the power, a market for the power and a network of transmission lines for distribution. The loss of any one of these components would render the project incapable of performing its intended function. Although it may be advisable to require the operator to keep enough coal on hand to avoid shutdowns due to supply delays, the operator cannot be responsible for keeping the railroads, the shipping companies and the mines that supply the coal operating smoothly. The operator, on the other hand, must remain knowledgeable about developments in the supply and transportation sectors so as to anticipate and minimize disruptions caused by problems in either sector. It will most likely not be responsible for maintaining demand within the power grid or for the grid itself. These responsibilities will rest with unrelated third parties or the host government, or they will be waived in the case of *force majeure* events. Often, demand will in effect be guaranteed by the host government's purchase agreement.

For a toll road, supply is of less concern than demand and delivery. The key demand question for a road is, Who is responsible for attracting users? The operator might be responsible for marketing, but unless its compensation is tied to increased use, it would not have as much incentive as the project company to perform this function. With respect to delivery, the toll road operator will be responsible for keeping the road in good repair and collecting tolls.

## ■ Maintenance of the facility

The O&M contract will detail the operator's responsibilities for the equipment installed at the facility. Scheduled or preventive maintenance, as well as minor repair work, is likely to be entirely the operator's responsibility.

If the project company will purchase equipment that requires vendor maintenance agreements, these should be negotiated in consultation with the operator and then assigned to the operator. Such an assignment will keep the project company out of potential disputes between the operator and the vendor and will preserve the integrity of the O&M structure whereby the project company can look to the operator alone to handle such problems. If, instead, a vendor under contract to the project company is made responsible for the proper functioning of equipment, a problem can arise if the performance guarantees cannot be obtained because of defaults by the vendor. From the perspective of the project company, it is imperative that the operator should have as much responsibility as possible for the proper technical operation of the facility.

The structure of the O&M contract with regard to (a) responsibility for equipment failure or replacement and (b) capital improvements (such as upgrades to take advantage of new technology) must be carefully negotiated. If the operator is to take the risk and responsibility for those outlays, it will expect more compensation than if they stay with the project company. For example, in a toll road project, it may well be that installation of an automatic vehicle identification system is an attractive investment for the project company because it will streamline access to the road and increase the number of users. The operator would, however, have little incentive to make such an investment from its own funds unless its fee were to increase as traffic usage increased.

The operator will have the duty to keep the road in good repair, because its useful life will normally be much longer than the term of the O&M contract. The maintenance standards to be applied throughout the project life must be carefully defined. It may be that existing standards set forth in the country's infrastructure (e.g. highways) statutes can simply be incorporated by reference. Alternatively, there may be reference to well-recognized industry standards. But in all cases, the O&M contract must define clear maintenance standards against which to measure the O&M contractor's performance.

The issues of maintenance and capital improvements are critical to the condition of the facility at the end of the concession period. For a toll road, periodic maintenance as called for in the relevant existing statutes may be all that is needed. By contrast, as the turbines and generators of a power plant reach the end of their useful life, the typical O&M contract would be drawing to a close. It may be better in this situation to have the host government upgrade the facility after transfer, or to infuse the project with fresh capital and carry forward with a new O&M contract. The operator's obligation to the project company under the O&M contract, and the project company's obligation to the host government under the project agreement, must be carefully coordinated with respect to capital improvements, refurbishment and upgrades that go beyond normal maintenance.

Two other aspects of maintaining the facility deserve brief mention. First, it will be the operator's duty to keep appropriate business records and logs and to generate reports for the project company, host government and lenders. Secondly, the O&M contract should grant the project company the right to inspect the facility and its business records, and it should extend this right to the representatives of the lenders and the host government. In particular, the host government will want to periodically inspect the project to ensure that it is being operated and maintained in accordance with the applicable laws and regulation. The project company should exercise its right of inspection frequently enough to ensure compliance with all applicable agreements and legal and other requirements.

Because it is important that the operator be responsible for performing the O&M obligations that the project company has undertaken in the project agreement (except to the degree that adequate provision has been made elsewhere for the project company to perform such obligations), it is advisable for the O&M contract to refer to the other project documents that set forth the O&M obligations of the project company and for those agreements to be attached to the O&M contract. The operator should then agree to be bound to the project company to the same extent the project company is bound. This will reduce the chance that the obligations of the project company are construed as broader than those transferred to the operator in the O&M contract.

# ▪ Technology and training

It is important to deal with technology issues in the O&M contract. These issues include the ownership of proprietary data, protection of trade secrets and restrictions on transferring technology. For many projects, computer software programs will need to be created to run the equipment that automates the facility. The host government will want to retain the right to use that software after the concession expires and the operator will want to retain the right to the software so that it may either modify it for use on other projects or sell it to other companies. Both interests can be accommodated by granting the host government a non-exclusive licence to use and modify the software. If the host government wants to modify the software, however, it will need access to the source code. Typically, the source code will be kept by an escrow agent and the rights of the government or the project company to the source code will be heavily negotiated. This access, as well as access to other trade secrets of the operator and any secrets of the government, project company or lenders, should be protected by appropriate licence agreements and confidentiality agreements.

Because as much local labour should be utilized as possible consistent with meeting the facility's needs, the operator should be required by the O&M contract to train the local workforce to operate the facility. The scope of such a mandate can vary widely, depending on the complexity of the facility and the needs of the host government.

# ▪ Compensation

There are various options available to compensate the operator for its services. They include fixed price, cost plus a fee and performance-based compensation.

In a fixed-price contract, the operator will receive a flat fee for providing its services. While this option represents the lowest risk alternative to the project company, it is usually appropriate only where both scope and magnitude of the service to be rendered can be predicted with some accuracy and are unlikely to fluctuate.

A more common arrangement is a cost-plus-a-fee contract. Here, the fee is either a fixed percentage, a percentage tied to performance or a combination thereof. The cost portion could include all the consumables necessary for the operation and maintenance of the facility, as well as the costs of any third party contracts being administered or entered into by the operator, and the cost of the operator's employees. The exact fee percentages necessary to compensate the operator adequately will vary from project to project. In some instances, as with a coal-fired power plant in a country in which the government already owns extensive coal reserves that will be made available to the plant free of charge, the cost of the O&M contract would be much lower than if coal were purchased at market prices. Of course, the work necessary to operate the facility would be the same.

The fee can also be tied to specified criteria to create a performance-based incentive for the operator to provide the best available service. Fee increases for superior performance can be coupled with liquidated damages for poor performance. These arrangements are particularly useful when the operator is an equity investor in the project company with a significant stake in the success of the project.

However the compensation is structured, it is important both that the operator should be given an opportunity to make a reasonable profit and that the contractual language should protect the host government from having to pay windfall profits for operation and maintenance of the project.

# ■ Financial records and budgets

Careful financial records must be kept of the income and expense for the operation and maintenance of the project. The operating budget must be prepared and approved at least annually; it should show all major categories of expenses and that the projected revenue will be sufficient to cover the necessary outlays. Often, the lenders require that project receipts be placed into an escrow account, to be disbursed only in accordance with specified terms. This arrangement prevents the equity partners of the project company from being paid out prematurely and assures that funds are available to cover all project expenses. The operator must be required to comply with the provisions of the project documents concerning the collection and disbursement of funds and should be required to make its detailed records, books and accounts available for review, audit and copying by the project company and the lenders.

# ▪ Disputes

There is one overriding goal that should be sought in any O&M contract dispute resolution procedure: the ability to resolve the dispute quickly, without disrupting the operation of the project. Various decisions made in the O&M contract can affect this goal. First, the parties should decide which law will govern the dispute. When dealing with the many entities involved in a BOT project, often from different countries and often doing business in a third country, the choice of law becomes important. All the agreements in a BOT project should be governed by the same law. The law selected will usually be a jurisdiction related to the project or at least well understood by the key participants. The minimum require- ment should be for a jurisdiction with well-developed commercial laws. Secondly, a precise dispute resolution procedure should be set forth. Usually, binding arbitration will be designated after consultation and mediation have been exhausted.[13]

Since most BOT projects are highly specialized facilities, it is usually preferable to set up a hierarchical dispute resolution process of negotia- tion, followed by mediation and, finally, binding arbitration.

Thirdly, all the parties to the BOT project should agree to be made a party to dispute resolution proceedings, thereby precluding the neces- sity for multiple proceedings and ensuring the fastest possible resolu- tion of the problem. Finally, both the operator and the project company should be obligated to perform their respective duties despite the exist- ence of a dispute, in order to prevent the dispute from disrupting the project while the resolution process is under way.

# ▪ Termination

The O&M contract will end either at the expiration of a specified term or upon termination by a party. Its duration and terms should be sufficient to allow all the parties to attain their contractual goals. The project com- pany will always have the right to remove the operator for cause. In some carefully defined circumstances the operator may be removed without

---

[13] Litigation is not a preferred resolution process. Litigation in either the local courts of the host government or those of some other interested jurisdiction requires the participants to educate a judge or a jury on technical issues to a much greater degree than would normally be necessary with industry-knowledgeable mediators or arbitrators.

cause. The mechanism for compensating the operator in these circumstances must be clearly defined. In the case of replacement without cause, the operator typically would be entitled to some sort of payment to compensate it for its unrealized return on its investment in the contract. In a default termination, the operator would only be entitled to payment for work properly performed and would often be subject to either liquidated damages or for any increased cost owing to its faulty operation and maintenance of the facility. The operator will usually not have the right to terminate the agreement without cause but will be able to terminate for a material breach by the project company that is not cured within a reasonable period of time.

The O&M contract must carefully define the events of default and the various remedies, cures and timetables to which the parties must adhere. Although the possibilities for material non-performance by the operator are too numerous to list, they will usually be tied to failure to perform the actions necessary for the safe and reliable operation of the project. The project company will usually have far fewer material obligations, the most important of which will be to compensate the operator and not to interfere with project operations. Depending on the duties of the parties set forth in the O&M contract, however, the project company may have a number of responsibilities material to the successful operation of the project, and the failure to perform any of them could be grounds for default. The O&M contract should provide that written notice and an appropriate opportunity to cure must be given before the opposing party has the right to terminate.

The lenders or the host government may also have the right either to terminate the operator or cause the project company to do so. The mechanics of these provisions should be incorporated into the O&M contract, along with a description of the rights and obligations of the parties after termination. It is imperative that any and all confidentiality agreements, as well as the dispute resolution and indemnity provisions of the agreement, remain in effect after termination. Finally, the effect of termination on any performance bonds, warranties and insurance policies should be detailed.

## ▪ Summary

The O&M contract is a critical part of the BOT process. It should, in principle, be drafted well in advance of its intended use. The operator should be brought in as early in the process as possible, preferably as an equity investor in the project company, and should be consulted on all aspects of design and construction that will affect its ability to operate and maintain the facility. Care must be taken to ensure that the O&M contract is consistent with the other project documents and satisfies all legal requirements. If any obligations are intentionally omitted from the O&M contract, the project company must be sure to provide for their accomplishment, either by itself or by an entity other than the operator.

# TRANSFER OF OWNERSHIP

Transfer

14

# ▪The meaning of transfer

An essential element of a BOT project is that at the end of the concession period, all the project company's rights in the project are transferred to the host government or its designee, normally free of any charge. For the past decade, the build-operate-transfer formula has been the most popular approach to privately financed infrastructure projects in developing countries. One reason is that many countries consider it a matter of national interest, strategy or security that infrastructure should remain under public ownership and control. Many governments have tended to view their resort to the private sector as an exceptional measure, taken only to develop, finance and build infrastructure projects.

The BOT concept permits private sector financing and efficiency to be applied to infrastructure projects, while at the same time allowing the government to retain strategic control over the project and ensuring that the project is transferred back to national authority at the end of the concession period.

The fact that the *Guidelines* focus on BOT projects should, however, not be taken to mean that privately financed infrastructure projects must be done only on a BOT basis. Other variants-particularly build-own-operate (BOO) projects-have also been used. Nor does the transfer of existing BOT projects to the host government necessarily mean that the project must remain in the public sector. On the contrary, once the host country has acquired ownership and control of the project from the original project company, the host government will have a number of alternatives other than owning and operating the project itself. It might, for instance, issue a new concession for the project on new terms. A new concession would cover only operation and maintenance of the project, so it would cost less than the original BOT project and would run for a shorter period.

A self-evident but positive feature of the BOT concept is that host governments will have flexibility and a choice to make at the time of transfer.

# ▪ The end of the concession period

The length of the concession period is a function of the economics of the project. The idea is to give the project company the opportunity to earn enough from the project to accomplish the following:

- Pay interest on the project debt.

- Repay the project debt.

- Repay the equity investment of the project sponsors and any other equity investors.

- Pay a reasonable return (including a reasonable profit) to the equity investors to compensate them for the use of their capital and the risk they will have undertaken.

The period of the concession is normally set to allow the project company to build the project and operate it long enough to accomplish these four goals. It will be limited by certain factors. Normally, it will not be shorter than the duration of the debt financing; it will not be longer than the expected economic life of the project assets and it will also not be longer than the normal time horizon of equity investors, who generally expect to recoup their investment in full, together with a reasonable profit, within 20-30 years. This is because potential profits beyond that period must be so heavily discounted to arrive at their present value that they are generally disregarded. However, the charges or fees to be paid by the public or consumers (e.g. toll road users or power purchasers) must also be taken into consideration when deciding the concession period. A short concession period may result in high charges to the public, which could be politically unacceptable. The optimum concession period will balance these needs.

In the case of *force majeure* or of breach of contract by the authorities that, for instance, causes a delay in the construction, most project agreements provide for an appropriate extension of the concession period as a remedy to the project company.

# ■ The terms of transfer

The project agreement provides in detail the terms of transfer, which may include the following:

- Conditions for and timing of the transfer or, possibly, the renewal of the concession.

- Scope of the transfer.

- Maintenance and monitoring schedule prior to the transfer date.

- Supply of spare parts after the transfer.

- Transfer of insurance and contractor warranties.

- Technology transfer.

- Training of local personnel needed for the further operation of the project.

- Environmental compliance.

- Definition and allocation of transfer costs.

- Warranties.

- Passing the risks.

- Cancellation of contracts and assignments.

- Removal of objects owned by the project company.

- Release of maintenance bonds.

- Transfer procedure.

The BOT project agreement normally provides that at a reasonable time before the transfer date the project company and the host government will get together to work out arrangements for the transfer. It may in some cases set forth in considerable detail the scope of transfer, such as the improvements, buildings, machinery, equipment, fixtures, fittings and spare parts that are to be transferred. In other cases, it may provide that the project will be transferred as is.

The normal solution regarding maintenance has been for the host government to require that the project assets be maintained in good working order during the life of the concession, normal wear and tear excepted, but up to some minimum standard of quality. The host government and the project company stipulate in the project agreement the minimum quality standards that need to be met at the time of transfer. Normally, the project company is not required to replace major pieces of equipment unless such replacement was specifically foreseen in the project budget at the outset.

The project agreement and, possibly, the O&M contract should make clear precisely what standards of maintenance, reliability and performance the project is expected to meet at the time of transfer. Moreover, appropriate monitoring procedures need to be included, usually involving inspection and certification of the project to assure the host government that the contractual standards have been met when the transfer takes place.

As a rule, the project agreement will specify, under the technology transfer provision, that an appropriate number of copies of plans, as-built drawings, blueprints, operating manuals, instructions and computer programs (including licences to use such programs, where appropriate) are to be turned over to the host government at the time of the transfer.

Another increasingly important area of concern is environmental compliance. Just as the project agreement will normally have required the project company to comply with local environmental laws and regulations, it should be clear, either contractually or as a matter of law, that the project company is obligated to transfer the project free from known and undue environmental hazards.

# ▪ Costs of transfer

The costs of transferring the project to the host government at the end of the concession period should be explicitly dealt with in the project agreement. The main costs are the direct and indirect costs associated with the transfer itself, such as the following:

- Transfer or stamp taxes, recording costs and notarial fees.

- Fees for new permits and approvals.

- Employee termination costs.

- Costs of training the government employees who will take over responsibility for operation and maintenance.[14]

- Fees to third party experts for any required inspections or certifications.

- Internal costs and expenses of each party (management time, costs of surveys, inventories, inspections etc.).

- Legal fees that either party may incur in documenting the transfer.

There is no hard and fast rule for the allocation of these costs. One possible solution would be to have the host government, as transferee, pay for the direct additional costs caused by the transfer, such as transfer taxes, notarial fees and new permits; to have the project company pay for employee termination costs, additional training, and required inspections and certifications; and to have each party bear its own internal costs as well as the costs of its legal counsel.

## ■ Warranties upon transfer

A fundamental issue to be resolved in connection with the transfer of ownership is whether the project company will provide any warranties to the host government with respect to the project assets to be transferred. At the very least, the host government should insist that any unexpired warranties that are available to the project company, either by contract or by law, such as the warranties of maintenance contractors or equipment suppliers, be assigned to the host government at the time of transfer. If necessary, the project company's contractors and suppliers should be required to consent to such assignment as part of the original contractual documentation.

Beyond the assignment of third party warranties, the project company may be required to provide a general warranty at the time of transfer that the project assets are in good working condition, have been properly maintained and meet the minimum construction and performance standards required by the project agreement. There are valid

Transfer

**14**

---

[14] Some governments will require training throughout the implementation of the project.

reasons for the government to require such a warranty at the expiry of the concession period. A one-year warranty to repair or replace defects, for example, might discourage the project company from a policy of benign neglect as the transfer date approaches. Another approach is to require a one-year prolongation of the maintenance bond.

# SOME CRITERIA FOR A SUCCESSFUL APPLICATION OF THE BOT CONCEPT

Chapter 15 summarizes the factors that are important to the success of BOT projects in developing countries. The decision whether or not to utilize the BOT concept will depend, of course, on the particular project and the circumstances prevailing in the host country at the time, but host governments, sponsors and lenders will look at the factors that are particularly important for success.[15]

## The project must be financially sound, feasible and affordable

First and foremost, the project must be financially and economically sound. Secondly, it must be feasible from a practical standpoint. Thirdly, the costs of the service or the fees charged must be affordable for the users. Sponsors and host governments must be convinced at the outset that the project will be successful throughout its lifetime. A feasibility study must therefore conclusively demonstrate the financial and economic viability of the project under different scenarios. It must show a stable source of revenue over the projected operating period. The revenue must be sufficient to cover the debt and operating expenses and to provide a fair rate of return for equity investors, as well as to provide a cushion against contingencies and changes. Assumptions used in the feasibility study, including demand estimates, inflation rates and interest rate projections, must be realistic and, where possible, supported by detailed historical or comparative data.

## The country risks must be manageable

A BOT project, like any foreign investment, requires a stable political and economic environment. Even the most practical and financially viable BOT project may not be attractive to sponsors and lenders if the country risks are perceived to be too great. Finance on reasonable terms may be unavailable in countries with a very weak credit standing. The

---

[15] Since discussions of the BOT concept tend to focus on large, complex infrastructure projects, it might be concluded that the BOT concept and the success factors discussed in this chapter have little relevance for small, ordinary infrastructure projects. This is not the case: the BOT concept can be used for a simple road project as well as a for major international transportation network. Indeed, a government should be cautious about selecting a very large scheme as its first BOT project.

**15**

**Success Factors**

legal and economic framework in some countries may not be sufficiently developed to support a BOT construction programme. Political instability, including the risk of expropriation and changes of laws, may frighten off potential private investors. Insurance against political risks and governmental guarantees is not an adequate substitute for a stable and supportive political environment.

## There must be strong government support

Host government support is essential to any BOT project. The private sector's interest in financing such a project will be considerably strengthened if the host government has announced that it wishes to promote public-private partnerships and that it will allow certain infrastructure sectors to be privately implemented under BOT schemes. Since moving public functions into public-private ventures can be difficult politically, the host government's commitment to a BOT policy is critical.

## The project must rank high on the host government's list of infrastructure projects

Sponsors and lenders must be assured that the BOT project under consideration has a high priority in the host government's infrastructure project planning. Some governments may not have enough resources to pursue more than a short list of projects, and sponsors and lenders are not likely to seriously pursue projects that are not on that list. A host government should therefore select a number of BOT projects for active support and announce its commitment to them.

## The legal framework must be stable

An appropriate and stable legal framework that clearly sets forth which government agencies are authorized to develop BOT projects and the laws and regulations that will apply to sponsors and lenders in such areas as foreign investment, corporate law, security legislation, taxation, intellectual property rights etc. is widely recognized as essential for a successful BOT policy. That some developing countries have enacted special legislation to address BOT matters reflects the importance and urgency of this requirement. In effect, the foundation of a BOT project is a web of interrelated contractual arrangements among the host country, sponsors, lenders and suppliers. The enforceability of these contracts is a *sine qua non* for a successful BOT programme.

## The administrative framework must be efficient

Complicated bureaucratic procedures are often cited as a serious obstacle to BOT projects. Seeking approvals from many different ministries and local authorities is very time-consuming and creates uncertainties for foreign sponsors. The host government should therefore offer an efficient administrative process or entity for dealing with the various authorities who grant approvals, permits and licences throughout the construction and operating period. Such approvals, permits and licences must be granted in a fair and objective manner, based on laws and regulations ascertainable at the outset of the project development.

## The bidding procedure must be fair and transparent

The bidding procedure is a very important part of a country's BOT policy. Private sponsors cannot be expected to invest time and resources in the developing of bids if the process for awarding a BOT project is not reasonably orderly, fair and transparent so that the chances for success are predictable. The bid evaluation criteria must be clearly defined and the bids must be evaluated in a public and objective manner.

Although some early BOT projects were awarded after direct negotiations with a chosen sponsor, experience with competitive bidding systems shows that the latter usually lead to terms and conditions more favourable to the national interest. An orderly and transparent bidding procedure should also win public support for private sector participation in infrastructure projects.

## BOT transactions should be structured so as to be concludable within a reasonable time and at a reasonable cost

The private sector will be more interested in BOT infrastructure projects if the host government is able to conclude BOT transactions within a reasonable time and at reasonable cost. Sponsors are reluctant to propose BOT projects if the host government has a history of carrying on long and expensive negotiations that never reach a conclusion. In the past, the long time and high cost of moving from the announcement of a BOT project to its conclusion has been a major drawback and has kept a number of BOT projects from going forward. It is therefore essential that host governments have a consistent and clear procedure to be followed, that they establish standard contracts and other documentation and that they set - and abide by, as far as possible - timetables and milestones for the procurement of BOT projects.

**15**

**Success Factors**

## The sponsors must be experienced and reliable

The technical ability, experience and financial strength of the private sponsors is of paramount importance and must be clearly established. Lenders to a BOT project place great weight on the choice of sponsors and their ability to manage and support a BOT project. A BOT project should therefore not be awarded to the lowest bidder unless that bidder also satisfies the other essential criteria.

## The sponsors must have sufficient financial strength

Attracting sufficient equity is one of the key challenges for all BOT projects. Governments and lenders will require the private sponsors to have a large enough financial interest in the BOT project to make it difficult for them to abandon or neglect the project. BOT projects must be structured so that the sponsors have the capacity to absorb financial risks and the incentives to do everything reasonably possible to make the project a success.

## The construction contractor must have sufficient experience and resources

The lenders will insist that the prime contractor, preferably selected on a competitive basis, has the technical and managerial competence, staffing and financial strength to fulfil its contractual responsibilities. Although ultimate responsibility for the performance of the contractor rests with the sponsor group, the failure of a prime contractor can be a serious setback for any BOT project.

For BOT projects, the lenders will also usually require a fixed-price turnkey construction contract or a similar scheme providing for liquidated damages, a performance bond and construction and equipment warranties.

## The project risks must be allocated rationally among the parties

The rational allocation and management of project risks is another factor critical to a successful BOT project. Simply stated, this means that (a) all major risks are identified, (b) the identified risks are allocated to the parties most able to bear them in terms of cost and control and (c) the allocated risks are managed in a rational way, usually by a combination of contractual arrangements and financial commitments.

It is advisable to address the risk problem at an early stage of BOT development. All too often the private sector is so concerned about reducing its exposure and the host government so concerned about trying to transfer all risks to the private sector that the parties lose sight of how much the project is actually paying for a particular risk allocation. Every transfer of risk has a price associated with it and is only as meaningful as the assets that underwrite it.

## The financial structure must provide the lenders adequate security

The ultimate success or failure of a BOT project revolves around the sponsors' ability to arrange financing. Lenders require that the project will pay off the loans as they become due and that adequate security is provided in case of default.

Various techniques to protect the lenders against non-payment of their loans must therefore be built into a BOT arrangement. Such techniques will normally include safeguards such as a real estate mortgage, completion and equipment guarantees, take-or-pay contracts, stand-by credit arrangements, reserve accounts to cover future debt service, assignments of the benefits of all project contracts, insurance, and a power of attorney or trust arrangements that allow lenders to take over and exercise the rights of the sponsors well in advance of a default under the loan agreements.

## The currency, foreign exchange and inflation issues must be solved

Currency convertibility, foreign exchange and inflation risks can be large stumbling blocks to the success of BOT projects. When investments in a BOT project are in foreign currencies and the income from the project is in local currency, the sponsors and the lenders will have to be satisfied in three areas:

- That foreign currency to cover repayment of the principal and interest on any foreign exchange financing will be available in the host country.

- That the host government will allow project revenues to be converted to the currency of the loans and transferred offshore.

- That the project is protected against losses from exchange rate fluctuation and inflation.

**15**

**Success Factors**

Inflation in the host country will also affect the financial success of a BOT project and the ability of the sponsors to repay the lenders. This risk, too, will have to be managed in the structuring of a BOT project, by indexing or other well-recognized financial techniques.

## The BOT contractual framework must be coordinated and must reflect the basic economics of the project

The contractual framework governing a BOT project is complex. The development and integration of the legal documents and their terms and conditions in accordance with the economics of the project are crucial for success. The drafting of a contract package for a BOT project is a challenge with many pitfalls along the way. That the host government must use qualified legal counsel goes without saying. Normally, the basic terms and conditions of the project agreement should be outlined as early as possible in the BOT process, preferably in the tender documents from the host government.

In all stages and at all contractual levels it is essential to avoid surprise terms in the contracts. If a party feels that the contract terms are unfair there is a danger that it will walk away from the project or at least be uncooperative.

## The public and the private sectors need to cooperate on a win-win basis

One element runs through successful BOT projects: in large part, they were successful as a result of efficient cooperation between the public and private entities. BOT projects that are beneficial to both parties, known as win-win projects, have a much greater likelihood of success. Fair rewards for both parties encourage cooperation and efficiency.

# GLOSSARY[1]

**ADB**: Asian Development Bank.

**AMORTIZATION**: Reduction of loan outstandings, usually in accordance with an agreed repayment schedule.

**(ANNUAL) RATE OF RETURN**: An undiscounted method of investment appraisal that computes the profit or return on an investment, expressed as an average annual percentage of its cost, averaged over the life of the investment.

**APPRAISAL**: Analysis of a proposed investment to determine its merit and acceptability in accordance with established decision criteria. The process of examining the attractiveness of a project, from economic, technical, social, commercial, environmental and other viewpoints, before the investment is made.

**BID BOND**: A bond given on behalf of a party bidding for a contract to ensure that it will enter into and perform the contract if its bid is accepted.

**BONDS**: Financial securities, usually issued by larger firms with a public listing, to borrow long-term finance. Bonds are purchased by long-term institutional investors, such as pension funds. They are risk-averse and will generally only provide funds to blue chip companies, preferring those with a credit rating.

---

[1] The terms in the glossary have been compiled from different sources: World Bank, "World Development Report 1994–Infrastructure for Development" (New York, Oxford University Press, 1994); Gary Bond and Laurence Carter, "Financing private infrastructure projects": emerging trends and experiences", Discussion paper 23, International Finance Corporation, 1994; Clifford Chance, *Project Finance* (London, IFR Books, 1994); J.L. Hanson, *A Dictionary of Economics and Finance* (London, MacDonald &Evans, 1969); Graham Bannock and William Manser, *International Dictionary of Finance* (London, Economist Books/Hamish Hamilton, 1995); Norman D. Moore, *Dictionary of Business, Finance and Investment* (New York, Drake Publishers, 1976); UNIDO, "Glossary of selected terms used in investment project preparation", 1995.

**BUILD, OPERATE AND RENEWAL OF CONCESSION (BOR)**: A contractual arrangement whereby the private sector entity undertakes the construction, including financing, of a given infrastructure facility and the operation and maintenance thereof. The private sector entity operates the facility over a fixed term during which it is allowed to charge users appropriate fees and other charges not exceeding those proposed in its bid and incorporated in the project agreement to enable the private sector entity to recover its investment and operating and maintenance expenses in the project, plus a reasonable return thereon. In the process the private sector entity may transfer technology and provide training to local companies and personnel. At the end of the fixed term, the private sector entity will have the right to request negotiations for renewal of the concession.

**BUILD, OPERATE AND TRANSFER (BOT)**: A contractual arrangement whereby a private sector entity undertakes the construction, including design and financing, of a given infrastructure facility and the operation and maintenance thereof. The private sector entity operates the facility over a fixed term during which it is allowed to charge facility users appropriate fees and other charges not exceeding those proposed in its bid and incorporated in the project agreement to enable the private sector entity to recover its investment and operating and maintenance expenses in the project, plus a reasonable return thereon. At the end of the fixed term the private sector entity transfers the facility to the government agency or to a new private entity selected through public bidding.

**BUILD, OWN-AND OPERATE (BOO)**: A contractual arrangement whereby a private sector entity undertakes the construction, including financing, of a given infrastructure facility and the operation and maintenance thereof. The private sector entity is allowed to recover its total investment, operating and maintenance costs, plus a reasonable return by collecting fees and other charges from facility users. Under this arrangement the private sector entity owns the facility and its assets in perpetuity.

**BUILD, TRANSFER AND LEASE (BTL)**: A contractual arrangement whereby a private sector entity finances and builds an infrastructure facility assuming cost overruns, delays and specified performance risks. Once the facility is tested and commissioned satisfactorily, title is transferred to the implementing government agency. The private sector entity, however, operates the facility on behalf of the agency for a fixed period under a lease arrangement.

**CAPACITY FEES**: The capital recovery fees, fixed operating fees and service fees.

**CASH FLOW**: As used in benefit-cost studies, the net benefit stream anticipated for a project. Net benefits are available for the service of borrowed funds (amortization, interest and other charges), payments of dividends to shareholders and the payment of profit taxes. Care should be taken to avoid confusing this concept with that traditionally employed in financial projection analysis, which defines cash flow (or cash generation) as after-tax income plus depreciation charges.

**COMPLETION GUARANTEE**: A guarantee, usually given by a parent company or sponsor, of performance of the project company's obligations to bring the project to the point of completion.

**COMPLETION**: Satisfaction of the agreed tests for practical completion of a project, usually marking the end of the construction phase and the beginning of the operating phase.

**CONCESSION**: An arrangement whereby a private party leases assets for service provision from a public authority for an extended period and has responsibility for financing specified new fixed investments during the period; the assets revert to the public sector at expiration of the contract.

**CONCESSION AGREEMENT OR PROJECT AGREEMENT**: An agreement between a host government and the project company or sponsors to permit the construction, development and operation of a project and, usually, to have access to public utilities.

**CONDITIONS PRECEDENT**: Documentary and other conditions required to be satisfied before the borrower can request drawdown or other credit facilities to be made available under the terms of a facility agreement.

**CONSTANT PRICES OR REAL PRICE**: Prices that have been adjusted to remove general price inflation.

**CONSTRUCTION CONTRACT**: The agreement or agreements between the project company and the construction contractor for the design, engineering, procurement, construction, completion and testing of a facility.

**CONSTRUCTION CONTRACTOR**: The contractor or contractors hired by the project company to perform the construction work in accordance with the construction contract and the concession agreement and their respective permitted successors and assigns.

**CONSTRUCTION WORK**: The design, engineering, procurement, construction, installation, completion and testing of a facility and equipment.

**CONSUMER**: Purchaser of products for his or her own (or family's use) rather than for industrial or institutional use or for resale.

**CONTRACTING OUT (OR SERVICE CONTRACT)**: An arrangement with the private sector to perform particular operating or maintenance functions for a fixed period and for specified compensation.

**CONTRACTORS**: Parties that construct or operate a project company's assets and sometimes form part of the sponsor group.

**COST-BENEFIT ANALYSIS**: A method of appraising projects that consists of quantifying costs and benefits, expressing them in annual streams over the life of the project and discounting the resulting net annual flows to obtain a present value.

**COSTS**: Costs are incurred to acquire project inputs such as buildings, machines, materials, labour and utilities. Certain outlays, such as the payment of profit taxes, are costs to the project but not to the country. Such outlays are properly treated as transfers of project surplus rather than costs for the purpose of calculating net present value or internal rate of return.

**COVENANT**: An agreement by a party to perform—or refrain from performing—certain acts, breach of which might constitute an event of default.

**CUSTOMERS**: Infrastructure services may be purchased by a single customer (e.g. power supplied by an independent power producer to an electricity utility) or by many users (e.g. toll road).

**DEBT SERVICE**: The payment of scheduled interest, fees, commissions and principal instalments under a loan agreement.

**DFI**: Development finance institution, e.g. national and regional development banks.

**DEPRECIATION**: The anticipated reduction in an asset's value brought about through physical use or gradual obsolescence. Various methods are used: straight line, declining balance, accelerated etc. Depreciation charges do not represent cash outlays and should not be included in financial or economic cash flows.

**DISCOUNT RATE**: The percentage rate at which future cash flows are reduced (discounted).

**DRAWDOWN**: A borrowing made under the terms of a loan facility.

**EBRD**: European Bank for Reconstruction and Development.

**ECA**: Export credit agency.

**ECO**: Extended cofinancing facility of the World Bank.

**(ECONOMIC) RATE OF RETURN (ERR)**: A measure of the return on funds invested in the project. Unlike the financial rate of return, the ERR looks at it from the point of view of the economy as a whole. This necessitates adjustments to the costs and benefits to correct for any distortions caused by, for example, monopoly or price controls, and the elimination from prices of taxes and subsidies, since these are transfer payments rather than resource costs.

**ECONOMIC LIFE**: The period over which the project would generate net gains. It depends basically on the technical or technological life cycle of the main plant items, on the life cycle of the product and of the industry involved, and on the flexibility of a firm in adapting its business activities to changes in the business environment. The economic life of a project can never be longer than its technical life or its legal life; in other words, it must be less than or equal to the shorter of the latter.

**ECONOMIES OF SCALE**: A characteristic of a production technology whereby unit costs decline with increasing output over a large range. Economies of scale are a major source of natural monopoly.

**EIB**: European Investment Bank.

**ENVIRONMENTAL IMPACT ASSESMENT (EIA)**: An analysis to determine wether an action would significantly affect the environment.

**EQUITY**: Long-term capital provided in the form of shares, signifying part ownership of the company. Equity holders receive dividends and capital gains (or losses), based on net profits. Equity holders take risks (dividends are not paid if the company makes losses), but in return share in profits.

**ESCROW ACCOUNTS**: Accounts into which a borrower or other party may be required to direct payment of receivables or other cash and to which conditions apply restricting access to the funds; possibly charged in favour of the lenders.

**EU**: European Union.

**EVALUATION**: Investigation of how a project turned out in comparison with what was expected of it (see *Appraisal*).

**EVENT OF DEFAULT**: An event that under the terms of a loan agreement entitles the lender to cancel the loan facility, accelerate payment of outstandings and enforce security (such as breach of covenant, insolvency or material adverse charge).

**EXCHANGE RATE**: See *Rate of exchange.*

**EXPORT CREDITS**: Credit or guarantee facilities made available to exporters to promote the manufacture of goods or provision of services for export.

**EXPROPRIATION**: The dispossession of assets by the state or a state entity, for example, under a nationalization programme.

**FEASIBILITY STUDY**: Examination of all the important aspects of designing, constructing and operating a project. It provides all the information for appraisal and investment ideas and finally for investment decision-making.

**(FINANCIAL) RATE OF RETURN**: A measure of the financial profitability of a project from the viewpoint of the enterprise undertaking it. It is the discount rate at which the present value of the costs would equal that of the benefits. Put differently, it is the maximum interest rate that the enterprise could pay on the capital invested in the project and still break even.

**FINANCIAL CLOSING**: The execution and delivery of the financing documents as may be required to evidence the consummation of all transactions necessary for obtaining financing for construction work and commissioning of a facility, together with the receipt of such equity commitments and contributions as may be required by the financing documents.

**FINANCING DOCUMENTS**: Loan arrangements, notes, indentures, security agreements, guarantees and any other documentation relating to the financing for the project but does not include documents or agreements relating to the commitment or contribution of equity by investors.

**FIXED COSTS**: Costs that do not vary with changes in the volume of output.

**FORCE MAJEURE**: Risks arising from circumstances, generally outside the control of the parties, which entitle one or other party to refrain from performing its contractual obligations.

**FOREIGN EXCHANGE**: Currencies of other countries. See also *Rate of exchange*.

**FULL RECOURSE**: A (conventional) financing structure where the borrower–and possibly guarantors–undertake to be responsible for repaying the loan in full with interest, regardless of the success or failure of the project.

**GOVERNING LAW**: The system of law to which the terms and conditions of a contract are subject, either expressly or by operation of the rules of conflict of laws.

**GUARANTEE**: Formal pledge that the contract conditions will be carried out; a manufacturer's or seller's undertaking to repair or replace defective products under certain conditions.

**IFC**: International Finance Corporation, the private lending agency of the World Bank.

**INCOME BONDS**: Bonds that have a set interest rate, but the payment of the interest is dependent upon earnings of the corporation.

**INFRASTRUCTURE (ECONOMIC OR SOCIAL)**: Economic infrastructure are the long-lived engineered structures, equipment and facilities and the services they provide that are used in economic production and by households. This infrastructure includes public utilities (power, piped gas, tele-communications, water supply, sanitation and sewerage, solid waste collection and disposal), public works (major dam and canal works for irrigation, and roads), and other transport sectors (railways, urban transport, ports and waterways and airports). The main items of social infrastructure are education and health services, although housing, water and sewerage can also come into this category.

**INTEREST (COMPOUND)**: Interest calculated on the sum of an initial principal or base and accumulated interest.

**INTEREST (DURING CONSTRUCTION)**: Interest charges occurred during project execution and normally capitalized up to the point in time when the plant starts commercial operation. However, neither interest during construction nor interest during operation is included in the internal rate of return calculations (return on investment).

**INTEREST (SIMPLE)**: Interest calculated on an inital principal and base.

**INTERNAL RATE OF RETURN**: See *Economic rate of return*.

**IPP**: Independent power project. Private power project generating electricity for supply to the grid.

**LEASING**: An arrangement whereby a private party (lessee) contracts with a public authority for the right to operate a facility (and the right to a flow of revenues from providing a specific service) for a specified period of time. The facility continues to be owned by the public authority. Unlike in a concession, the lessee does not have responsibility for investments in fixed assets.

**LENDERS**: The lending institutions that are parties to the financing documents and their respective successors and assigns.

**LIMITED RECOURSE**: A financing structure in which the lender is relying to some degree on the project assets and cash flows for repayment and debt service without full guarantees from the project company or its sponsors.

**LINKAGE (EFFECT)**: The effect of a project on investment, prices and output in related industries and trades. Backward linkages (sometimes known as upstream effects) occur in sectors that supply goods and services to the project, while forward linkages (downstream effects) arise in industries that use the output of the project.

**MANAGEMENT CONTRACT**: An arrangement whereby a private contractor assumes responsibility for a full range of operation and maintenance functions, with authority to make day-to-day management decisions. Compensation may be based partially on services rendered (as for service contracts) and partially on performance achieved (as in profit-sharing).

**MEZZANINE FINANCING**: A mix of financing instruments, including equity, subordinated debt, completion guarantees and bridge financing, the balance of which changes as the risk profile of a project changes, i.e. as a project moves beyond construction into operation.

**MIGA**: Multilateral Investment Guarantee Agency.

**MULTIPLIER EFFECT**: The effect of a project on other parts of the economy produced when income generated by the project works its way through the economy, reactivating idle capacity and creating new income and employment to a multiple of the original stimulus.

**NATURAL MONOPOLY**: An economic activity that is most efficiently carried out by a single producer.

**NCPI**: National consumer price index.

**NET PRESENT VALUE (NPV)**: An estimate of cash flows or the value of production to be generated by a project, net of operating costs and expenses, discounted back to the time of determination. It is a common decision rule in project appraisal, resulting from summing the discounted difference between costs and benefits for each year of the project's life. NPV is an absolute measure of project merit.

**NOMINAL PRICES OR CURRENT PRICES**: Prices that have not been adjusted/deflated to eliminate general price inflation. A tradition in economics is to specify "constant" prices if that is intended; otherwise, the inference is that current prices are intended.

**NON-RECOURSE**: Meaning the same as "limited recourse", sometimes used to indicate that the lender is placing a particularly high degree of reliance on the project.

**OFF-TAKE AGREEMENT**: A long-term agreement to purchase minimum amounts of the product of the project at an agreed price; often entered into by one of the project sponsors on a take-or-pay basis.

**OPERATION AND MAINTENANCE (O&M) CONTRACT**: The agreement or agreements between the project company and the O&M contractor for the management, operation, maintenance and repair of a facility.

**OPERATION AND MAINTENANCE (O&M) CONTRACTOR**: The independent contractor or contractors hired by the project company to manage, operate, maintain and repair a facility in accordance with the O&M contract and the concession agreement and its permitted successors and assigns.

**OPPORTUNITY COST**: Value lost by using something in one application rather than another. The opportunity cost of employing a worker in a project is the loss of net output that a worker would have produced elsewhere. The opportunity cost of using good farmland for suburban housing is the net value of the crops foregone. The opportunity cost of investing in one project is the return that could be obtained from another project. The concept of opportunity cost is the cornerstone of benefit-cost analysis.

**PATENT**: The sole right to make or sell a product or to use a process invented by the person granted the patent. Patents are issued by governments.

**PERFORMANCE BOND**: A bond or guarantee given by a bank in favour of a project company on behalf of a contractor or supplier of a specified percentage of the value of the relevant contract, for example, construction contract or supply agreement.

**POWER PLANT**: The specific power station, together with all equipment, fuel storage and related facilities, protective devices, transformers, switchgear, fixtures and the interconnection facilities and substation (but excluding the transmission line and other facilities and equipment owned or operated by the authority), all to be developed, designed, engineered, financed, constructed, equipped, insured, completed, tested, commissioned, operated and maintained in accordance with the concession agreement.

**POWER PURCHASE AGREEMENT (PPA)**: Contractual agreement to purchase power from an IPP.

**PROJECT**: The development, design, engineering, financing, construction, equipping, insuring, completion, testing, commissioning and operation of a facility.

**PRESENT VALUE (PRESENT WORTH)**: The value today of a future payment, or stream of future payments, by discounting at a specified interest rate. A total present worth (or value) refers to the sum of a discounted stream of costs, benefits or net cash flows. A net present value (NPV) most often refers to a discounted method of investment appraisal that calculates the net value or net benefit of a project when all costs and benefits have been discounted to the present. Expressed in absolute terms, the NPV may be negative or positive, but for the project to be acceptable, the NPV must be either zero or positive.

**PROFIT**: Financial profit is the difference between financial revenues and costs. Economic profit is the surplus of benefits over costs when economic prices are used, after deducting the opportunity costs of capital.

**PROJECT FINANCE**: A financing modality where the lender looks to the project's cash flows to repay the debt and to the project's assets for security. It is also known as structured financing because it requires structuring the debt and equity such that the project's cash flows are adequate to service the debt.

**PUNCH-LIST**: A comprehensive list of items to be completed or corrected by the contractor when the works have been substantially completed; it is work outstanding when the takeover certificate is issued.

**PURCHASING POWER**: The capacity to purchase possessed by an individual buyer, a group of buyers or the aggregate of the buyers in an area or market.

**QUALITY ASSURANCE PROGRAMME**: The programme of quality assurance for the design, construction, testing, operation, maintenance and repair of a facility.

**RATE OF EXCHANGE (EXCHANGE RATE)**: The price, or the indication of the price, at which one can sell or buy, with one's own domestic currency, a unit of foreign currency.

**RAW MATERIALS**: The basic materials used in the production of goods in a manufacturing process.

**REAL VALUES**: Normally, costs and prices that are not adjusted for expected inflation (constant prices as compared to expected cash prices). Sometimes refers to economic values rather than financial costs and prices (resource costs rather than financial values).

**REAL PRICES**: See *Constant prices*.

**REHABILITATE, OPERATE AND TRANSFER (ROT)**: A contractual arrangement whereby an existing infrastructure facility is turned over to a private sector entity to refurbish, operate and maintain for a fixed period, at the expiry of which the facility is turned over to the government agency or to a new private entity selected through public bidding.

**REHABILITATE, OWN AND OPERATE (ROO)**: A contractual arrangement whereby an existing infrastructure facility is turned over to a private sector entity to refurbish, operate and maintain with no time limitation imposed on ownership. As long as the private sector entity is not in violation of its project agreement, it can continue to operate the facility in perpetuity.

**RISK MANAGEMENT**: The identification and acceptance or off-setting of the risks threatening the profitability or existence of an organization.

**SECURITY**: Protection; assurance; indemnification. The term is usually applied to an obligation, pledge, mortgage, deposit, lien etc. given by a debtor in order to assure the payment or peformance of its debt, by furnishing the creditor with a resource to be used in case of failure in the principal obligation. A pledge of financial or physical property to be surrendered in the event of failure to repay a loan.

**SENSITIVITY ANALYSIS**: An integral part of cost-benefit analysis that tests the effect on the rate of return or net present value of possible changes in outcomes, on both optimistic and pessimistic assumptions.

**SPECIAL-PURPOSE COMPANY**: A company established for a particular purpose, for example, to achieve off-balance sheet or advantageous tax treatment or to isolate the parent's other assets from the creditors of the company.

**SERVICE**: In economic science, a useful function fulfilled by a person or organization, for the benefits of which buyers are prepared to pay a price.

**SHADOW PRICE**: The opportunity cost of a good or service; also accounting price.

**SOVEREIGN**: A national government in its role, for example, as a lender or borrower.

**SOVEREIGN LOAN**: A bank loan to a government, usually of a developing country.

**SPONSORS (OR OWNERS) OF THE PROJECT COMPANY**: Providers of equity and the driving force behind a project.

**SUBORDINATED DEBT (ALSO KNOWN AS QUASI-EQUITY OR MEZZANINE FINANCING)**: Unsecured finance that is senior to equity capital but junior to senior debt. Subordinated debt contains a schedule for the payment of interest and principal but may also allow participation in the upside potential of an equity position.

**SUBORDINATED LOAN**: A loan made on terms whereby the lender agrees that some or all payment obligations will rank behind certain other unsecured indebtedness of the borrower.

**SWAP**: The exchanging of one debt, currency or interest rate for another.

**SWITCHING VALUE**: The value an element of a project would have to reach as a result of a change in an unfavourable direction before the project no longer meets the minimum level of acceptability as indicated by one of the measures of project worth.

**SYNDICATED LOAN**: A loan made available by a group of banks in predefined proportions under the same credit facility.

**TAKE-OR-PAY CONTRACT**: An agreement between a purchaser and a seller whereby the purchaser agrees to pay specified amounts periodically in return for products or services even if there is no delivery of the products or performance of the services.

**TENDER**: Offering of a service in response to advertisement (same as a bid).

**TURNKEY CONTRACT**: A contract for the construction of a project and installation of all facilities, providing for the project to be handed over at the point where it is ready for immediate operation.

**USEFUL LIFE**: In accounting and taxation, the period of time for which an asset is capable of being used for the production of income.

# Index

profit sharing 117

project
  company 3, 10, 41, 62, 83, 87,
    89, 110, 124, 134, 148, 154,
    155, 160, 163, 179, 200, 207, 211,
    212, 213, 216, 217, 223, 224,
    225, 234,  245, 248, 259, 264,
    267, 268, 273, 274, 277
  development 10, 19, 25, 59, 71, 94,
    124, 163, 197, 283
  development cost 163, 197
  economics 11
  finance 3, 4, 12, 166, 189, 192,
    245, 295
  identification 19, 21, 104, 130, 133
  implementation 17, 19, 25, 123, 130
  risk 15, 36, 70, 105, 144, 154,
    156, 158, 160, 163, 179, 198,
    249, 284
  sponsor 3, 10, 41, 54, 70, 71, 78,
    154, 156, 163, 167, 179, 180,
    183, 184, 185, 190, 200, 201, 210,
    219, 247, 274
  transfer 27

property rights 52, 87, 147, 282

proposal
  unsolicited- 124

provision
  assignment- 237
  buy-out- 67, 236
  categories of- 228
  confidentiality- 87
  liability- 237

public
  private partnerships 282
  support 283

punch-list phase 263, 295

purchaser 181, 185, 223, 274, 203, 215

## Q

quality
  assurance 85, 116, 231, 251, 296
  standard 76, 90, 276
  system 231, 238

## R

rail network 32

rate of return 3, 4, 12, 15, 70,
    134, 139, 158, 162, 167, 201,
    215, 241, 248, 262, 290
  internal- 134

recourse
  limited - basis 4, 5, 6, 189, 293
  non - basis 180, 193, 294
  non - financing 4, 199

repair work 264

research and development 36, 75, 77, 88

revenue
  flow 65, 148, 234
  market-based- 8, 157, 215
  sharing arrangement 113
  stream 3, 4, 5, 8, 13, 21, 47, 63,
    181, 214, 216

risk
  allocation
    15, 70, 105, 121, 151, 153, 155,
    160, 216, 257, 260, 261, 285
  analysis 225
  associated-infrastructure- 157
  completion- 155, 156, 160, 163, 216
  construction- 14, 163, 191, 198,
    245, 247
  country commercial- 155, 160
  country legal- 155
  country- 154, 220, 281
  credit- 193
  demand- 155, 157, 160
  development- 155, 156, 160
  force majeure- 66, 70, 155, 158, 160
  general- 70, 154, 156, 158

identification 15, 42, 151, 153, 154, 155, 163
inflation- 15, 155, 285
infrastructure- 157
interest rate 155, 165
management 70, 53, 159, 160, 166, 251, 261, 296
management- 155, 158,
market- 14, 158, 184
operating- 155, 157, 160, 164
political 102
political- 67, 146, 149, 154, 155, 160, 162, 166, 194
project- 12, 15, 36, 70, 105, 144, 154, 156, 158, 160, 163, 179, 198, 249, 284
specific project- 154, 156, 158
supply- 155, 158, 164
technical- 155, 157

risk-reward
balance 147
profile 165, 166, 190
provision 70

# S

security
arrangement 47, 48, 219, 230
exchange 195
marketable- 192
package 15, 47, 117, 180, 192, 200, 203, 207, 210, 219

senior debt 65, 183, 184

sensitivity analysis 131, 138, 296

shadow price 135, 138, 140, 297

Shajiao B Power Station 172

spare parts 86, 165, 252, 275

special-purpose companies 192, 296

sponsor consortium 11, 212

standard
safety- 141, 226, 234, 287

subcontracting 81, 241, 252

subcontractor 76, 82, 164, 200, 214, 230, 234, 252

subsidy support 65

supplier 9, 11, 24, 25, 75, 77, 81, 117, 158, 163, 185, 200, 203, 212, 216, 219, 223, 247, 277, 282
domestic- 81, 90
equipment- 11, 62, 75, 117, 163, 164, 184, 193, 200, 216, 247, 277

Sydney Harbour Tunnel 62, 64, 67, 247

# T

tariff adjustment 63

tariff/toll
collection system 238
revision formula 238

tax
concession 60
regimes 49, 60

technological innovation 77, 88

technology
foreign- 33, 75

technology transfer (or transfer of technology)
4, 6, 7, 12, 22, 25, 26, 27, 51, 73, 75, 76, 77, 78, 80, 81, 82, 85, 88, 101, 117, 136, 214, 234, 275

tender
document 22, 23, 78, 79, 90, 94, 103, 107, 112, 114, 116, 144, 146, 230, 286
form 116
invitation-to - document 23
limited - system 23

# W

# UNIDO GENERAL STUDIES SERIES

## The following publications are available in this series:

| Title | Symbol | Price (US$) |
|---|---|---|
| Planning and Programming the Introduction of CAD/CAM Systems<br>A reference guide for developing countries | ID/SER.O/1 | 25.00 |
| Value Analysis in the Furniture Industry | ID/SER.O/2 | 7.00 |
| Production Management for Small- and Medium-Scale Furniture Manufacturers<br>A manual for developing countries | ID/SER.O/3 | 10.00 |
| Documentation and Information Systems for Furniture and Joinery Plants<br>A manual for developing countries | ID/SER.O/4 | 20.00 |
| Low-cost Prefabricated Wooden Houses<br>A manual for developing countries | ID/SER.O/5 | 6.00 |
| Timber Construction for Developing Countries<br>Introduction to wood and timber engineering | ID/SER.O/6 | 20.00 |
| Timber Construction for Developing Countries<br>Structural timber and related products | ID/SER.O/7 | 25.00 |
| Timber Construction for Developing Countries<br>Durability and fire resistance | ID/SER.O/8 | 20.00 |
| Timber Construction for Developing Countries<br>Strength characteristics and design | ID/SER.O/9 | 25.00 |
| Timber Construction for Developing Countries<br>Applications and examples | ID/SER.O/10 | 20.00 |
| Technical Criteria for the Selection of Woodworking Machines | ID/SER.O/11 | 25.00 |
| Issues in the Commercialization of Biotechnology | ID/SER.O/13 | 45.00 |
| Software Industry<br>Current trends and implications for developing countries | ID/SER.O/14 | 25.00 |
| Maintenance Management Manual<br>With special reference to developing countries | ID/SER.O/15 | 35.00 |
| Manual for Small Industrial Businesses<br>Project design and appraisal | ID/SER.O/16 | 25.00 |
| Policies for Competition and Competitiveness<br>Case-study of industry in Turkey | ID/SER.O/17 | 35.00 |
| Manual on Technology Transfer Negotiations | ID/SER.O/18 | 80.00 |
| From Waste to Profits<br>Experiences, Guidelines, Film | ID/SER.O/19 | 75.00 |
| Acceptable Quality Standards in the Leather and Footwear Industry | ID/SER.O/20 | 30.00 |
| Information Sources on the Leather, Footwear and Leather Products Industry | ID/SER.O/21 | 56.00 |
| Guidelines for Infrastructure Development through Build-Operate-Transfer (BOT) Projects | ID/SER.O/22 | 65.00 |

## Forthcoming titles include:

Design and Manufacture of Bamboo and Rattan Furniture   ID/SER.O/12

*Please add US$ 2.50 per copy to cover postage and packing. Allow 4-6 weeks for delivery.*